MOTHERS

OF

SPARTA

MOTHERS

OF

SPARTA

A MEMOIR IN PIECES

DAWN DAVIES

FLATIRON
BOOKS
NEW YORK

MOTHERS OF SPARTA. Copyright © 2018 by Dawn Davies. All rights reserved.
Printed in the United States of America. For information, address Flatiron
Books, 175 Fifth Avenue, New York, N.Y. 10010.

www.flatironbooks.com

Designed by Omar Chapa

Library of Congress Cataloging-in-Publication Data

Names: Davies, Dawn (Dawn S.), author.
Title: Mothers of Sparta : a memoir in pieces / Dawn Davies.
Other titles: Memoir in pieces
Description: First edition. | New York : Flatiron Books, 2018.
Identifiers: LCCN 2017041747| ISBN 9781250133700 (hardcover) | ISBN
    9781250133717 (ebook)
Subjects: LCSH: Davies, Dawn (Dawn S.) | Davies, Dawn (Dawn S.).—Family. |
    Mothers of autistic children—United States—Biography. | Sjogren's
    syndrome—Patients—Biography. | Women authors, American—21st
    century—Biography.
Classification: LCC PS3604.A9532 .Z65 2018 | DDC 818/.603 [B] —dc23
LC record available at https://lccn.loc.gov/2017041747

Our books may be purchased in bulk for promotional, educational, or business
use. Please contact your local bookseller or the Macmillan Corporate and Pre-
mium Sales Department at 1-800-221-7945, extension 5442, or by email at
MacmillanSpecialMarkets@macmillan.com.

First Edition: January 2018

10   9   8   7   6   5   4   3   2   1

With love and gratitude to Dann B. Davies

CONTENTS

NIGHT SWIM   1

THREE PLACES   5

KEEPING THE FAITH   20

GAMES I PLAY   43

PIE   57

FEAR OF FALLING   69

FIELD MANUAL—DIVORCE AND   79
    REMARRIAGE: SUBURBAN OPS

MEN I WOULD HAVE SLEPT WITH   103

KICKING THE SNAKES   118

TWO VIEWS OF A SECRET   135

FOSTER DOG   150

SOCCER MOM   163

THE DRESS   173

KING OF THE WORLD   196

MOTHERS OF SPARTA   217

FOUR ANIMALS   245

ACKNOWLEDGMENTS   261

PUBLICATION CREDITS AND AWARDS FOR THIS MANUSCRIPT

"Three Places." Published as "Don't Like It Too Much." *River Styx,* July 2014.

"Three Places." Published as "Don't Like It Too Much." *Best American Essays* "Notable Essay," 2015. Edited by Ariel Levy.

"Keeping the Faith." *Chautauqua,* June 2016.

"Games I Play." Published as "Sheep to the Cyclops." *Ninth Letter,* Spring 2015.

"Games I Play." Nominated for a Pushcart Award, 2015.

"Pie." *Fourth Genre* (with second companion craft essay, "Secrecy, Privacy and Creative Nonfiction"), August 2015.

"Pie." Nominated for a Pushcart Award, 2015.

"Fear of Falling." *HerStories Anthology,* Summer 2015.

"Kicking the Snakes." *New Plains Review,* Summer 2015.

"Two Views of a Secret." *Saw Palm,* February 2015.

"King of the World." *The Missouri Review,* Winter 2016.

"King of the World." *Best American Essays* "Notable Essay," 2016. Edited by Jonathan Franzen.

"Mothers of Sparta." Finalist in the SLS Disquiet Competition, 2015.

"Mothers of Sparta." Won the 2016 Arts & Letters Susan Atefat Prize in Creative Nonfiction.

"Four Animals." *Blood and Thunder: Musings on the Art of Medicine,* Fall 2015.

NIGHT SWIM

It is a moonless night, dark and rare, and the heat is oppressive, the kind of heat where a deep breath leaves you unsatisfied, suspicious that there was nothing life-giving at all in what you've inhaled, and you are left air-hungry, wet at the pits, forehead greasy with sweat, wishing for the night to be over, for your daughters to exhaust their energy, to cool their dense, hot centers enough to sleep for one more night in this summer that seems to stretch into your future like a planetary ring full of debris, circling forever around something it can't escape. It is thickly hot and you hate it.

You sit beside the pool in a plastic chair, dipping the soles of your feet in the water that is the temperature of spit, fanning your face with your own damp hand, which doesn't help. Back in the yard, your corked-up dog cannot contain his glee and shrieks several times into the sky, warding off something no one can see, and your daughters burst like rays from the cool of the house, drop their towels on the deck, and leap to cannonball into the pool, one like the other, although you can discern subtleties in their silhouettes, how the one crooks her elbow a certain way, how the other curves her back like so, how their hair billows from their heads in differently weighted undulations.

They whoop and cry out into the night, like whistling rockets, arms flailing until they disappear underwater, the force of the waves spreading to the walls of the pool and back.

The water swells over the edge of the brick coping and spreads darkly at your bare feet like a shadow. A bloom of chlorine hits your nose before your daughters erupt to the surface, shouting, shiny diamonds of light reflecting off the lace of wet on their brown arms and necks and faces. They glow, not like reflections of suns and stars, but like stars themselves. The light coming off them is their own.

"My God," you say, without meaning to. They turn and you are startled to see a dusking of their future faces, their grown-up faces, faces that will be shaped by struggle and pain and loss, expressions that will take up residence once they taste the dirt that life feeds them, the profiles that will be theirs once they have given birth. Changed faces. Grown faces, soft, umbral curves replaced by shadows and lines and angles. You lock eyes briefly and they are gone, ignis fatuus, and your little girls are there again.

"Jesus, Mary, and Joseph," you blurt out.

"What?" they say.

"Nothing," you say. "Don't move." And you step inside to get the camera. You can't control any of this, but you will try to capture it, this light, this heat of them, their dual stars Castor and Pollux disappearing, shape-shifting again until they are babies in your arms, then they are women, then they are children enjoying a night swim. You begin taking photographs in the dark.

One of them pushes up out of the pool, the weight of the water pulling her curls down her back in shy, reluctant tendrils as she plucks the bathing suit elastic out of her butt crack and walks away without looking back at you, her tiny scapulae protruding like wings before she turns and smiles, but the smile is not for you, it is nothing but a by-product of her joy, the untethered joy she is still young enough to feel, the joy that comes from leaping off the edge of something into another thing that will catch her, soften the blow, cool her body, temper the flame of youth and the disconnect with future things.

And she sprints and leaps into the sky, untethers from the force field that holds her to you, and she is twenty-one, flying a midnight plane to France to meet her French boyfriend, a man you have not yet met, and she no longer feels the need to call you and tell you where she will be and what time she will be home, because her home is no longer your home and she has entered another orbit. For the rest of your days you won't know exactly where she is on the map, and you won't know what she is thinking, and her shattering smile, and the fake disdain and subtle wrinkling of her nose will be for someone else, and you can only hope you taught her well.

She twists in the air and lands back in the pool, bobbing in the fractal-lit water, laughing and saying, "Did you see me, Mom? Did you see me jump?" Her sister claps and shouts, slaps the water with the heels of her hands, then climbs out of the pool for her own turn.

"Watch *me*, Mom!" she says, and launches herself into the air like a comet, her angular momentum vector glowing in visible lines, and she is grasping lovelorn rescue dogs like clouds, pulling them toward her heart, teaching them to be good, and just when she begins to love them, letting them go to a home she has chosen, this daughter who heals and is healed by Sirius the dog star, this heart of your heart, this woman with the easy laugh, who rotates midair and looks straight at you, and in her fall back to Earth you see the weight in her eyes, the practical shrug of her shoulder, the opening of the hand, the letting go. The woman becomes a child again.

They both come up from underwater, heaving in big breaths, and they bump heads and swim toward you for comfort. You rub their temples and kiss the bumps away, and when they shrug you off, one swims toward a broken engagement, a broken heart, a discarded gown, tear-swept eyes, situational depression, and the other to an ER gurney, fevers, chronic pain, Lyme disease, and you see, in a turn of their thin shoulders, that you will not be able to fix anything in their lives, that there will be no Band-Aid or mother's embrace for what they will one day endure. There is so little to control in life.

"Put your faces down in the water and then come up slowly. I want to take a picture," you say.

"You're crazy," they say.

"I know. Just do it." And they swim to the edge of the pool and obey. They feel the gravity of the moment, the gravitational pull toward you that they have recently begun to fight. They slide underwater, then emerge, eyes locked on the camera lens, rippled turquoise and sky-colored water pulling them back, the expectation of the future blanking their faces, infinity circling their gaze past yours, and as you click two simple photos, paper fossils that will one day remind you how they once walked the Earth, you realize you have taken everything for granted. Your time with them. Their brief speck of time as children, the soft faces that turn to you as if you are the sun, the fact that time seems to move so slowly when in fact it is whipping past you at one thousand miles per hour and why you haven't flown off into space is beyond your comprehension. They will never stay yours, for they weren't yours to begin with. One day they will leave you, shoot off into the sky, and take their place in a bigger constellation. And it's your job to let it go.

Let it go. Let it go.

It's gone.

THREE PLACES

Here's one: It's the woods behind an affordable, thin-walled town-house complex in northeast Virginia. You can call to mind everything—the thick trees, the rolling hills, the galloping creek that is so large across the widest part that it secretly thinks it might be a river, and it gets cocky like that, prancing around, showing some white water, making you want to strip down to your undershirt and day-of-the-week panties and jump in. You are not allowed to swim in the creek but you do, and you fib to your parents about this, because you know nothing will make you stop, until that one day you are squatting in the water, breathless from the smack of the cold on your skin, and you leap out to avoid a copperhead swimming straight for the center of your chest.

The water is surrounded by high, rocky ledges that crumble when you step on them, and you find silver veins of clay when you dig in just the right places. You climb the ledges and explore the necklace of wet caves with a cautious excitement, because in the depths could be a sleeping colony of bats that might dive straight for your face and suck out all of your blood, or a bear waiting to tear you up, or a hobo who pops out and tries to roast you on a spit. You shiver when you see that the caves are empty, and you clap and make small, shrill chirps in various directions to test out the dark echo. You sit down and feel the absence of warmth and light, and the dripping silence, and dare yourself to stay as long as you can, which is less than two minutes, because your imagination is fruitful, and the thought of bats and bears and hobos makes it feel like something is crawling up your spine and into your brain. You panic and hurl yourself back down the ledges, skidding on your tailbone, grateful that you have cheated death again.

The rocky terrain leads up into a wide field, and beyond that, a flat pine-bottom woods. All of your free time is spent here, running barefoot, scrounging wood for your tree house and damming the creek during dry spells, climbing the rocks, and stalking deer: small, placid, white-tailed things that toy with you. It is your dream to catch one and keep it as a pet.

During the school year, you ride the bus to a public school that allows you to work ahead in the self-governed learning packets that are all the rage. You are clever and you know it, and it sets you apart. Each semester you race through your packets, finishing weeks ahead of the other students, with the singular goal of spending as much time as possible in the reading corner, sprawled out in a beanbag, gobbling up novels and fairy tales. The lunch ladies serve delicious grits with cheese and ham steaks on Wednesdays, so you buy school lunch on this day only, tucking two quarters into the pointed corner seam of your jumper pocket. The teachers tease their hair big and wear polyester dresses, and their thick, nylon-clad thighs rub together when they walk. You adore them. They call you Doll-Baby, or Honey Pot, and treat you like a pet.

Picture your small hand, sliding into an icy, clear stream. You are creeping up on the neck of a crawdaddy, carefully, almost surgically in precision, aiming for the place behind his neck where you know his eyeballs can't register. You nab him before he knows what hit him, leaving behind an empty swirl of mud and decaying leaves in the pocket of brown rocks where he once rested. Your coat sleeve is wet to the elbow and cold, but you hand him, perfect, startled, blue as lapis, to your friend Danielle, who puts him in a mason jar full of creek water. Danielle's crooked front teeth make her look like she belongs on the short school bus, but this is not true. She is clever and bold and reckless and free from the desire to please the grown-ups in her life. Indeed, six weeks before, you became blood sisters, the way ten-year-olds are supposed to, behind the Slocums' aluminum shed, using a needle she goaded you to liberate from your mother's sewing kit that you are never supposed to touch. This is not the first glimpse of the rascal in you, and you know it. First the swimming and the fibbing and now this, but no matter—on this day your love for life causes a tickling in your body that can only be alleviated by tearing across a wide field until your legs and lungs burn.

When the sun starts to shine sideways and your hands are stiff with cold, you head home, exhausted and dirty, your stomach empty and gnarling. You smell the beginning of the fire in your neighbor's fireplace, a crisp, sharp, empty smell that reminds you that you do not want to be alone outside after the sun goes down. There could be bats and bears and hobos, after all. You see the light in your living room window and you think about spaghetti and meatballs and *Charlie's Angels,* and a hot bath and your twin bed with the yellow gingham pillowcase and matching curtains. You burst into the house and stop short because your parents are sitting at the dining room table, waiting for you with a cautious look on their faces. *Dagnabbit,* you think, because you know what's about to happen. You have been through this before, five times, in fact, and had hoped to be done with it.

"We have some exciting news," they start, but you already know by the looks on their faces, the hopeful, falsely confident perk of the eyebrows, the folded hands, exactly what they are going to say. "Daddy got a promotion," your mother starts, but you already know what this means: You are moving again. You should have known. Your happiness should have told you. As soon as you get used to the things in a place, as soon as you find your footing, as soon as you give yourself permission to like it, it is time to go.

"We just got here," you say. "It feels like we just got here."

"Don't worry," they tell you. "You'll love New York. We promise."

You drive until you are two hours from the Canadian border, so far north that you expect to see sled dogs. Your heart is bitter. You feel what hate is like, not the hating of people, per se, but the hating of impotence. The hating that comes when you can't do anything to stop anything from happening. You let this bitterness and hatred take over a part of you, even though Sunday school has taught you about forgiveness and people doing the best they can with what they have.

You do not want to be here. You dislike cold and New York is the coldest place you have ever been. People talk differently and everyone is white. But the house is bigger than your old one in Virginia. You note the wall-to-wall carpeting and the fireplace in the family room, which the real estate agent calls the "den," and the quarter-acre yard. There is also a pine tree that has a natural saddle where you can read a Trixie Belden mystery, and a stone fence that houses an elusive chipmunk, but none of it matters. You are the new girl again.

You develop coping skills for this, thoughtful self-talk that reminds you that you are okay, that this, too, will pass, but these skills do not always help you feel better, so almost unconsciously, you include in your social repertoire protective actions, such as looking deferentially away from people when they speak to you, not raising your hand in class, not sitting in the middle or the back of the school bus, and not volunteering anything out loud, ever, lest they call you a hillbilly in front of the cute Irish boy, Kelly Moynihan, who gives you the sympathetic eyebrow in the lunch line. Your caution has erased most of your public self. In Virginia, you were an eye-batting Southern girl, and now you must become something else. Your confidence has been washed again, in hot water with bluing, and you are now a clean, pale cloth doll. You have yet to figure out what kind of personality you must develop to make people like you in this part of the country. With every move, it becomes more of a puzzle.

This school is different, you discover. Teachers are gruff and harried and unsympathetic and when you complain about it to your mother, she says, "It's just how they are up here," but this does not make you feel better. She misses her friends, too, she says, as if this is supposed to make you feel better, but all you think is *Shut up*, because if it were up to you, you would be watching cartoons with Danielle back in Virginia, and fibbing about swimming in the creek, so don't tell you about wishing things could be the way they were.

One winter day, when it is too cold to go outside for recess, you stand alone at the window, feeling sorry for yourself. You cry just enough for the snot to start flowing in your nose. You press your head against the cold glass and let the snot run down, then sniff it back up just before it drips. You repeat this absentmindedly, making a game out of it, wondering why you have no friends. You notice that there is a yardstick's worth of snow piled on top of the picnic tables in the recess area and there is no sign that it will stop snowing. The sky is a dark, slate gray, the color of the slate in Virginia that you used to break off and skip into the creek. You wonder how you are going to get home. You imagine a buckled pack of sled dogs, heaving their way across the snow-covered playground with you behind them, holding on for dear life.

"Indoor hotball!" Mr. Solenski announces, and you think, *Step aside*. Your heart is pounding because you can *play* this game. You love this game. You are a champion. You take your place, hands out, knees bent, and stand prepared. A girl throws the red rubber ball to a weak, fat boy with big hips, whose knees bend in sideways and touch together, and you know you can take him down, so when the ball comes to you, you whip it at the fat boy and he drops it and is out. You pick off student after student, playing easily, yet humbly, gaining confidence with each out, saying cautiously, "Tough luck," to the players who drop the ball. "Tough luck" in Virginia is an expression of sympathy, but in upstate New York, it is a taunt, and every time you say it, you are rubbing the face of the person who dropped the ball straight into their own ineptitude. You do not know this. You win the game, but the other students show you their backs. They do this for months.

Out of necessity, you turn to solitary pursuits to occupy your time. You look for, but do not find, deer in the short woods, wandering in the pines until you accidentally find yourself in other people's backyards. Housewives and younger children stare at you from their sliding glass doors as if you were a yeti, or a drunken outlander, stumbling out from an underground trench somewhere. Dogs on chains aim their bodies at you, lean in, and bark, so you slip back into the woods and walk home. You start laying cracker traps for the chipmunk in your own yard. You ride your bike for hours, up and down the hills, until it is too cold to ride bikes. You unpack your mother's old record player and spend the winter upstairs in the dormer room, listening to show tunes and fifties doo-wop, picking out sounds on a toy organ. When your parents rent you a clarinet from the local music shop, you lose yourself in learning how to play it, then discover forties Big Band, which only further sets you apart from your peers. The friends come to you the way an iceberg melts.

It happens, but it is slow. In the spring you play jump rope with some younger children up the road, and then football with the neighborhood boys. Eventually, you become one of the gang, playing Capture the Flag and Kick the Can, and Pickle and Horse. There is no denying that this achievement has been a crusade. You begin to like your new friends, but you do so with a caution, a guarding of your heart that is new.

Twenty-three months later, five days after you get an invitation to Kelly Moynihan's birthday party, four nights after your first band recital, you walk home in the dark from your dog-sitting job at a neighbor's house. They have a real piano in their front room, and you spend several hours a day there, learning to play "The Entertainer" and "Good King Wenceslas" by ear, with chords. On your walkway, the snow crunches under your boots, and it is a gritty, crisp sound in the silent air, and you feel a springing of joy, the joy of belonging to a place, the joy of knowing your place. You step inside and take off your coat and boots and as you straighten up, you notice your parents are sitting in the living room that no one ever sits in unless there is company. They are waiting for you. *Dammit,* you think. They lead you over to the dining room table and you all sit down. Their hands are folded. There is a pile of real estate magazines and an envelope of developed photographs in front of you.

"We've got some news," they say, and you stand up from the table and try to leave the room. Your father grabs your arm and sits you back down.

"We're moving to Florida. Look!" They seem excited. They slide over snapshots of palm trees and hibiscus bushes and other spotty, spiny, jagged plants, as if the contrast between what you know and what you see in the photographs will be alluring.

"We can go to Disney World anytime we want," they promise, and you suddenly realize where you learned to fib.

"I'm happy here," you say. "I made the band." The tone of your voice, you realize, is starting to edge toward pleading.

"They have a band down there you can be in." Out come more photos, this time of a Spanish-style ranch house. "It's *South* Florida. It's *subtropical*. There are *lizards* that live on the back patio," they say. "And here. We have a pool. You can swim all winter. You'll love it," they promise, like they promised every other time, but you will *not* love it, you tell yourself. You hate lizards. You like mammals. You have spent the last seven months patiently laying out peanut butter crackers on the stone wall, trying to tame the chipmunk, and he has finally agreed to eat his cracker where you can see him, instead of snatching it and scrambling inside the wall. This is important, painstaking work. You are trying to trap him, even for a day, and months of progress will be lost if you leave. Also, you do not want to swim in the winter; you want to learn to ski, like your parents promised you could when they announced that you were moving to New York. Your head goes down in your arms on the table.

"When do we leave?" you ask, because it is inevitable.

"A couple of weeks."

So, in the middle of Christmas break, you say good-bye to the tree you have grown to love, the one you can read in, the one that has an emergency escape route, the one you climbed up twenty-four feet on the day no one was there to witness it. Your friends promise to write, but you know they won't. You yourself won't get past one or two letters. You never do. You get into the backseat of the car and drive away, refusing to speak to your parents until two hundred miles past the Mason-Dixon.

Picture your first look at Christmas in the subtropics, whatever the "subtropics" are. South Florida is not all it's cracked up to be, you decide in an instant, even if there are theme parks and prehistoric alligators and muscled, rashy surfer boys you know won't look twice at you. The Christmas lights look limp and low-rent on palm trees and green grass, you immediately notice, and the plastic Santas and plastic reindeer and plastic nativity scenes look as if they are trying too hard, as if they, too, wish they were somewhere else. Is that Mother Mary, head bowed, sweating into her own lap? Is that wise man about to faint from heat exhaustion? It is eighty-five degrees outside. Christmas in Florida is a sham. You don't care how many palm trees your parents pointed out on the drive down, you still hate it.

You drive up to the new house, unfold from the car, blinking and rumpled. As soon as you step outside, something terrible and frightening happens to your hair and it springs up into some sort of loose, half-crocked Afro around your ears. You immediately begin to sweat. You are strategically unimpressed during the walk-through, refusing to smile at your corner bedroom, the screened-in pool, and the schools within walking distance. Yes, there's a pool, but the yard is a postage stamp, mined with ants that bite the crap out of you any chance they get. There is a smell you cannot identify that you later learn is mold, something to which you prove to be immediately and highly allergic. You start sneezing. You feel a stinging behind your eyes that has nothing to do with a sneeze. No one must see you cry, so you step out onto the front porch to get away from your parents and the real estate agent, who looks like a prostitute in her short skirt and bare legs—no woman can be taken seriously in business with wrinkled, prickly, vagina-looking armpits flapping around (you do not wear sleeveless shirts to this day, do you, on account of that woman's armpits). You watch as a flock of kids your age ride their bikes past your new house, with fishing poles over their shoulders. They are bronze and sweaty. They stare you down with a look you've seen before, a hostile look that reminds you that you do not belong.

Remember fumbling through a day at an overcrowded middle school that is divided into races like the water from the land and the land from the sky. Black kids are *here,* and the white kids are *here,* and the Hispanic kids are over *there,* and none of the groups is particularly friendly, so you don't know where to stand, and though this is a foreign thought, logic tells you that you should stand with the white kids because they look like you. You have become a cow in a herd of cattle, moving mindlessly through chutes as you try to find your new classes. Your head protrudes like a periscope above the throng of people who babble pointlessly to anyone but you. You wear the Docksider boat shoes your parents paid a fortune for at Christmas and cannot afford to replace because the move was so expensive. These shoes, a teen status symbol in New York State, have landed you the nickname "Cap'n Faggot" by the black kids at school. You have never been around black people whose speech patterns you could not understand and you feel like a foreign exchange student, yet you understand pointing and snickering and "Cap'n Faggot" as well as the next person.

You get caught up in trying to "make your mark" as first chair clarinet in the concert band, because you realize that music is your only skill, and this does nothing except cement your position as one of the school's most forlorn nerds. You also spend considerable political effort trying to erase the nickname the white kids have given you: "The Lady Shaver." The inopportune get-together with the concrete side of the swimming pool the day before your first day at school has left you with large, weeping scrapes across your cheek and upper lip and chin, and you show up on your first day sporting Band-Aids all over your face. The scrapes heal in two weeks, but the name lasts far longer.

At age thirteen, you are six feet tall and one hundred thirty pounds. Something about the combination of puberty and the South Florida dew point permanently alters the structure of your hair and it appears to others that you are wearing a wig from a closed-down clown school. Your wardrobe, which you cannot afford to amend, is pure Northern, and stands out in all the wrong ways, and all of this is accented by the black clarinet case you carry around like the president's nuclear football. You hate school. You hate everything about it and everyone in it. There has been no talk of Disney World.

Within a few months, you hear angry voices and doors slamming in the middle of the night. You wonder if there was an affair, because that's why people divorce in the movies, but you have no proof of anything because no one is talking, either to you or each other, but doors are thin, and your mother cries when she thinks no one is home. Your parents divorce as quickly as a summer storm, engineering a slow family tailspin that will take years to right.

Your mother moves into a small, cheap apartment on the other side of town, and you—your body, your mind, your soul—feel as empty as the house you are left to live in. When you come home from school late, the house is empty, the lights are off, and there is no more promise of meatloaf or casserole in the air, but instead mildew and dust, which have been waiting for the right opportunity to take hold and strangle you. In Florida, the outside is always trying to get in, and dank Florida smells are everywhere you go, stifling and wet and spongy. Pool chlorine and suntan oil, and salty air and fish. Black tar heating on the ribbons of suburban driveways. Gardenia and night jasmine that make you wheeze. It is unbearably hot everywhere you go. Hot like you think hell would be hot. In fact, you begin to suspect that you are in hell. Your head is so chronically stuffy that you begin to lose your balance when you stand up. Once, in desperation, you take a Benadryl before school and this makes you so sluggish that you fall asleep while watching a filmstrip in biology. The room is dark and warm, and you nosedive off the high metal stool and hit your face on the floor. Your lip splits. You are the Lady Shaver again.

You try to find things to keep you occupied. A neighbor gives you an old fishing pole, and you fish the canals. You pull up fish you cannot name and throw them back, until you meet up with an old man sitting on an upturned bucket, fishing with a cane pole. He identifies the fish you both catch, patiently, flatly: crappie, bream, bluegill, sunshine bass. You run into him again. And again. You develop a cautious sort of friendship. One day he hands you a second cane pole.

"Use this if you want to really get 'em."

"Thanks," you say, and you wonder if this is candy and he is going to try to lure you into the back of a van.

"You can keep it. It's a good rig. My son did a lot of fishing with that rig."

"Oh, doesn't he still want it?" you say.

"Naw, he's dead."

"Sorry," you say, though you want to say much more than that. You want to ask when and why, and how he is able to get up in the morning with a child in the ground, but you are afraid to stir the man's sadness, afraid to stir your own, so you say nothing.

You fish in silence together in the afternoons until the mosquitoes come out for blood. One day you look in the mirror and your face is as brown as the native kids who rode their bikes past you that first day. Your hair is nearly as blond as it was when you were a little girl, and sits around your head like a halo.

You start to wander the canals farther from home. You see awkward anhingas air-drying their feathers on rocks and pipes, you sneak up on flocks of ibis honking softly before startling them to take flight, you touch the mossy backs of sunbathing snappers. You are able to recognize the thick, quick taunting flight of the Quaker parakeets, who sit in the trees above you and gossip during the hottest parts of the day. Everything here seems to eat each other. You poke at the edges of the canals, kill the empty hours that fill your day, and if it weren't so unbearably hot and buggy, you might agree to reluctantly appreciate the extraordinary, quiet megacosm of nature that no one seems to notice in this place, this place that is built up between a swamp and an ocean, this place that, if you look underneath the hellhole of sprawled suburbia, is quietly magnificent and slightly savage.

Picture a dark South Florida canal in late spring, just before sunset. You step over a wood barrier, and slip past a tilted, broken chain-link fence, and down to where a large mango tree dips over the waterline. The water is dark and moving with a slight current most people would miss. You pick a mango off the ground, turn it for bug holes, then split it open with your thumbs and eat it standing up, leaning forward to keep the juice from dripping on your shirt. A great blue heron stands at the water's edge, crafty and patient, like a pickpocket waiting for his next mark. A moorhen darts neurotically under a dock, crying mournfully for something you will never identify. She sounds like you feel. You are not the type of person to trespass or steal fruit from other people's trees, yet here you are, on private property, and it is not your first time, either. Your father is out with the same woman you found frying bacon in your kitchen this morning, wearing one of his dress shirts and some smeary mascara and not a lot else. You don't remember her name, but it doesn't much matter. She won't last long. It is your mother's night to see you, but you have lied, as usual, made up an excuse about why you can't go over to her empty apartment that breaks your heart every time you step across the threshold.

The house is thirty yards away and no one can see you. You hear dishes clanking and family noises in the distance, but you tune it out. You face east, sitting under a quiet canopy of leaves, and you wait. The sickly sweet mango buds are nearly overpowering, and a few besotted honeybees are taking advantage of this, swaying onto bud after bud, like bar-hopping drunks. The water pops and there is a ripple, and you look hard beneath the surface of the coppery, cloudy depth that is visible only when the sun hits it at a certain angle. It is just a mullet popping up to bite a skeeter, or perhaps rid its gills of itchy parasites. You freeze and wait, until the non-movement causes a tickling in your body that makes you want to scream. Then you see it, an elusive, almost misleading footprint in the water, and they are there. They glide up to the edge of the canal and float, fat and weightless. You slide onto your stomach and hang over the seawall.

Picture your hand, larger now, a little veiny, slowly sliding into the warm, brackish water, silently in the direction of the last of the sun's rays. Gnats dive-bomb your eyes. You pull your hand up slowly, hover it above the surface of the water, which feels warmer still, and you wait. The manatee's face rises up out of the water, an inch, two inches, and meets you halfway, brushing your hand with its baby whiskers. There is nothing to catch, nothing to trap, nothing to conquer, and as you tenderly cup your hand around the baby's face, its mother surfaces, too. She looks at you with a tiny brown eye, then rolls over, trusting, placid, and lets you touch her child. They stay for a few moments, then slowly back down into the deeper water, and are gone. You watch them swim away, wishing for more, feeling an emptiness, but not an unbearable one. This is something, you think. It's not enough right now, but maybe it could be. You admit to yourself, cautiously, that you might like it, thinking, *Be careful. Don't like it too much.*

The sun goes down. You walk home in the dark, kicking a can down the middle of the road, thinking of manatees, thinking of odd birds, and of startled fish, imagining your parents meeting you at the door, asking you to sit down at the dining room table.

KEEPING THE FAITH

Once, when I was twenty, I went on a date with a man I met at the Army Navy store in Cambridge, Massachusetts. He was someone I would not have gone out with under ordinary circumstances, but it was an unusual time in my life, and I was in no position to be picky. It was mid-spring and I had, almost opposite to natural Northern law, lost a few pounds over the winter, and I was looking for some new clothes. Grunge was in at the time, and the Army Navy was a good place to get the kind of cargo pants that we would cut off at the knees, flannel shirts we would rip the sleeves off of, fat-soled Dr. Martens boots, and anarchy T-shirts that we wore as if we were the only generation to rend our garments and rebel against the establishment. I wasn't five minutes into flipping through a rack of spring fatigues when I felt someone looking at me. I turned around and saw a tall guy with an Afro and a Jimi Hendrix mustache taking me in from behind a bin of wool socks on clearance. I squinted my eyes at him and moved away. When he followed me I went to find the manager, and then discovered that he was the manager. His name was Kami, and he said he would like to take me out on a date. I said I wasn't interested, but somewhere in the course of a short conversation, I sort of told him my name and the restaurant where I worked. I still don't know why.

I left without buying anything and thought that was the end of it until he showed up at my job on a Friday night and found me holding a tray of drinks high above my head, my sweat making darker blue bursts of oxford under my armpits as I tried to press through the bar full of unfulfilled yuppies. He stood a head and a half above the crowd and I couldn't miss him. He shouted that it was good to see me, and I told him I was on the clock. His eyes blazed at me again and this time I noticed that they were hazel. He asked me out one more time, hollering his words over the flock of patrons, and when someone said, "Aw, come on, tell him yes," I said yes and everyone applauded. I wasn't exactly pressured into it, but I now know why women who shouldn't say yes end up doing so during public marriage proposals. I scrawled my number on a cocktail napkin and told him to go home, but here's the truth: His efforts had moved me. I was nearly desperate for something (or someone) to come into my life and make me feel better.

Sometimes people think people will do that for them.

I had moved from my home state of Florida to Massachusetts after dropping out of college at nineteen. I am not sure what made me think that college was holding me back from my dreams, but I knew I wanted to experience new things, like most young people do, and I wanted to get out of Florida. New England looked beautiful in photographs, so I packed up and went.

Boston didn't disappoint. It was the exact opposite of the South that I knew: extremely expensive, painfully cold, even in April, and bulging with fast-moving and fast-talking people who pushed through sheets of sleet and mounds of dirty slush on their way to what looked like very important work. I felt an immediate entrepreneurial urge and wanted to be part of this productive, collective energy.

I wanted to start a cheesecake-on-a-stick business, or a T-shirt business with all the great philosophical ideas on them, such as "Beauty" and "Truth" and "Justice" and "Fate." I also planned to become a well-known painter. They say the human brain doesn't mature until twenty-five or twenty-six and there's your proof.

I spent weeks greeting strangers on the street with a smile and a "Hey" or a "Good morning" like we did down South, and they would look at me and clutch their bags a little closer. I wouldn't fit in with that pace or the place, but I didn't know it then.

I found three "artists" looking for a fourth person to share a four-thousand-square-foot commercial loft space next to a fortune cookie factory. I forked over my savings for the deposit and first and last months' rent, and claimed a thousand of those feet as my own. Then I landed a job as a waitress at an upscale Italian restaurant. I got myself a library card for my days off, whereby I immediately checked out one book on how to start a small business and eight novels, which shows you where my sensibilities really lay. I worked nights and read books and painted during the days. Occasionally, I would bake a cheesecake and slice it up and impale the wedges with popsicle sticks.

A week into the new job, a young Brazilian cook called Wagner caught my attention. He was fun, goofy, lived in the moment, and had a twinkle in his eye that made me think there was something special under the surface. When a waiter did something good, like picking up an order on time, or fetching him something from the fridge, Wagner would point his knife at the waiter and start an exchange that went like this:

Wagner: Hey? You know what?
Waiter: What?
Wagner: You okay!

Waiter (suspiciously): Yeah, thanks.

Wagner: No, you not listening. *You* . . . okay.

Waiter (brightening): Thanks.

Wagner: No. Really. You *okay*.

Waiter (big smile): Yeah? Thanks!

Wagner: What you doing hanging around here, bastard! Get out on the floor, you!

Wagner and I had little in common, including language, but we started dating anyway. Wagner was not particularly deep or intellectual, so in a way I was kind of marking time. This was mostly because Wagner was extremely handsome and I was still a child. Wagner liked ribs and sauce and beer and slapstick comedy. He liked picking a boiled lobster clean while sitting by the heat of a bonfire. He liked action movies, especially those starring Clint Eastwood. He abruptly switched to Portuguese when he was doing a bad job explaining things in English, then he got mad when the American he was talking to didn't understand his Portuguese either. He cooked me breaded chicken livers and a cake that looked like it was made of cream cheese, but when I cut into it, I found it was made of meat and peas, and the icing formed from mashed potatoes. Wagner liked to drive fast in the dark, and he peed on me once at the outdoor shower at Salisbury Beach when I bent over to clean the sand off my feet, which made him laugh for a long time. He had an extravagant laugh.

I almost went to Brazil with him the following Christmas to meet his family, but before we bought our tickets, he got nervous. He decided I was too tall for his family to handle, and our height difference would embarrass him in front of his competitively masculine brothers. Don't ask. It's both appalling and true. I was a lot taller than Wagner. I was that tall girl who would, every once in a while, suspend my lack of faith and order something from a tall girl catalog and wait nervously until the package arrived in the mail. Then when I ripped it open with a measure of hope, it would always be short—mournfully short, hillbilly short, even though it came from a tall girl store. But it is what it is. Some guys mind. Some don't. Some like it.

Wagner went home without me for Christmas and rode his motorcycle up and down a mountain at high speed until he drove himself into an unmarked construction hole at two in the morning. He died alone in the dirt. To me, his death was abstract—a midnight phone call from my sobbing restaurant manager, a largely one-sided conversation that beat me to a pulp in about two minutes. I never saw his body. I never went to a funeral. I didn't know if his family knew about me, so I didn't contact them.

Things didn't feel right at the restaurant after that. I missed Wagner's cheerful goodness in the kitchen, so I quit and got a job at a seafood joint in the Back Bay, serving lobster and clam chowder to tourists. I wasn't well. My mind was starting to buckle, and I began to twist Wagner's death, which was a freak accident, into a suspicion that I would soon die too—abruptly, or protractedly, but always tragically. If it happened to Wagner, it could happen to me, I thought. It was a cold winter and I wanted to go home where the sun knew how to shine, but I was broke.

I kept my feelings to myself, showed up to work, and no one, including me, knew that I was drifting down into the compass-free land of depression. I didn't share my troubles, mostly because I didn't know how to talk about how my days were spent slogging through puddles of fear, and how I closed each night with a bout of midnight hypochondriacal genius, with thoughts of pancreatic cancer and brain tumors and lymphoma cutting loose in my head like naughty whack-a-moles I could never seem to plug. I didn't understand that I was grieving; I just thought I was weak. I was poised, locked in amber, struggling to step over a dangerous, stalagmite-filled pot-hole, straddling that place between childhood, where things existed because I was told they did, and adulthood, where I was facing a crippling lack of meaning and purpose.

Once you know you will never see someone again, nostalgia for what could have been makes you love them more. I had loved Wagner, I think, and we were left unfinished. I walked the streets we used to walk, rode the T alone to the places we used to go. More than a few times, I walked past his old apartment late at night, wonder-ing who was in there turning the lights on and off, living carelessly, lightly, in the space he once took up. Once when I had a bad day, he had grabbed my shoulders, shaken me hard, and said, "Keep the faith, you. God not gonna mess up, never," with such force that it rattled my teeth and took my breath away. Then he hugged me. I also remembered making fun of him because he couldn't say "Clint East-wood" with his heavy Brazilian accent. He could only say "Clingy Stewage." These memories made me sad, and I wanted to cry when I thought about them, but after that first day, I didn't.

Living in the loft was beaucoup bohemian. I cooked on a hot plate, witnessed a few stabbings on the sidewalk outside my building, and could almost always smell the sticky, bready sweetness of the fortune cookies baking in the factory. In the mornings, I woke up with frost on the inside of my windows, thanks to the commer-cial heat that turned off at six P.M. and didn't come on at all on week-ends. One particularly damp morning, there was frost on my quilt. I thought the lifestyle would help me paint, or design T-shirts, or develop my cheesecake empire, but after Wagner died, my desires drained, and I found myself simply living in an overpriced dump. I started to hate the city with its dissonant non-rhythm; honking night horns and apartment building entryways that smelled like waves of foreign food every time the door opened; the coarse, slushy sidewalks; the people trudging back and forth, to work, to home, to schools and bars and stores, no one thinking of what would one day happen to them—that they would all die, one by one, with or without notice, and be replaced by generations of strangers. I also hadn't seen the sun in a month.

So I moved away from the city, out to Belmont, into the first floor of a quaint old two-decker with a big bay window seat and a real yard. The entire apartment cost less than my share of the loft, and I hoped I could save up some money and get myself home before another winter hit. Florida, with all of its familiarity and warmth and family, was suddenly looking pretty good. In the meantime, I wanted to read in the window seat, with the sun shining across my knees, a mug of coffee in my hands, and a couple of Italian lemon drop cookies balanced on my knees. I wanted to recuperate.

My landlady was made of wrinkles and had a grown son with Down syndrome who was old enough to have wrinkles of his own. I could hear him thunder back and forth from one end of the apartment to the other, and his clumsy bulk made the little chandelier in my dining room shake. They had a routine: groceries and gas on Mondays, the library on Tuesdays and Thursdays, bowling on Wednesdays, and Mass on Fridays and Sundays. On Monday nights she would bring me a Tupperware of galumpkis—pork and rice rolled in cabbage and slow-cooked in tomato sauce—which I would eat all week. Sometimes I could hear the son shouting with happiness, a throaty, unchecked, choking laugh that carried, and I could hear her laughing along with him.

The move did nothing to fix my state of mind. It is important to know that nothing external can do that for you, but at twenty-one, I didn't know a whole hell of a lot. In desperation, like so many do, I tried to pray, because alcohol was too expensive and because my grandfather, like Wagner, had once told me that there was nothing too big for God to handle. I gave it a shot and tentatively asked God to give me signs that Wagner was in heaven, that I was going to be okay. I got nothing. I kept at it. I asked Him to change my life. To make me feel better. To take away my pain and fear. Still nothing. Not a stirring. Not a feeling of hope. Just my heart-pounding fear of death. I soon grew to suspect that perhaps my grandfather was mistaken, as he had died fairly quickly after what they called a "brief battle with cancer," a fact that still angered me and caused me to doubt both my grandfather and God. I remembered Wagner shaking me and saying, "Keep the faith, you," with such blind assurance, and it ticked me off too. Some savior He was if He let perfectly fine people die all over the place. Little Somali kids snuffing out by the thousands, soldiers dying alone in deserts, families burning up in minivan accidents on the highway, blastomas, gliomas, cytomas, ICUs, NICUs, drownings, all the ways people go that are not fair, and the worst thing of all was the lie they told you about God's infinite power and goodness. I began to believe that God was like Santa Claus—a story told to little kids so they would have something to grab on to when they faced their first realizations that death would one day happen to them and to their parents and siblings, and that worst of all, their time could be up at any moment, without warning, without their having done anything meaningful.

My dark thoughts grew in scope. I had been a voracious reader as a child, and had made the mistake of reading all my mother's nursing textbooks and my stepfather's medical books and journal subscriptions from cover to cover. I knew too much, and at too young an age, with no context or reference points to keep me medically grounded. Every time I was still, I would begin to hear a wheezing in my lungs that could only mean granulomas gone bad, tuberculosis, cancer. My grieving was replaced by paranoia, and I began to check myself for bruises and petechiae, and to prod my groin and neck for swollen glands when I was in the shower. If I felt a stomach pain or blaze of heartburn through my chest, I suspected my aorta was about to tear, or there was a tumor growing that I would soon find out about once the symptoms grew too impressive to ignore.

I was so jacked up that I could hear my heartbeat almost all the time. It pounded with anxiety. I listened at night for it to skip a beat, and when it did, I panicked and caused it to skip further beats, which kept me awake even later in a swirling boil of fear, waiting for it to stop altogether, wondering if I would have time to call an ambulance for myself if something bad went down. If Wagner, who believed in God like he believed in air, had died so young, I thought, if all those trusting, faithful Somali kids with flies in their eyes were dying of starvation by the thousands, then I, a near heathen who was angry at God, could too.

I passed the rest of the winter literally cheating death by riding my bicycle nine miles into Boston, through the snow and rain, for my night shifts at the restaurant, then riding home at the end of the night, twice as fast, sometimes at two or three in the morning. I would take Massachusetts Avenue through Cambridge, then Concord Street and home as fast as I could go. I flew through the dark, dodging cars, hearing my breath rasp and my heart pound in my head, jumping snow clots and dark, red-looking puddles that reflected the choked light of the night sky. I dared something to go wrong. Every time a car did not hit me, I thought, I cheated death, and by doing so, asserted my life. *Take that, God. I'm still alive,* I thought every time I lifted my bike up onto the back porch at the end of a shift. The endorphins I produced got me high enough to finally fall asleep. I began to understand Wagner's love for feeling speed in the darkness. I did this for fourteen hundred miles until, when spring pushed through the hard winter, I didn't have cancer and my aorta didn't rupture, but I was about ten pounds lighter and needed some new pants. I ended up at the Army Navy in Cambridge, and that's where I met Kami.

I took the train into the city for our first date on a Saturday night. It was a warm spring night in May, and there was a feeling in the middle of my belly that was part anxiety, which I was used to, and part excitement, which was a feeling I hadn't known in a while. I could feel adrenaline coursing through me, and as the train shot through the tunnels in the dark, I believed that something was poised to change in my life. After so many months of anxiety and anger, it felt refreshing and hopeful and frightening. It had been so long since I had traveled by anything other than bicycle that the speed felt dangerous, and I was entranced by the rhythm of the train slicing along the tracks. It felt like we were barnstorming Cambridge, then Boston, flying recklessly, so tenuously that at any moment we could lift off and soar into space. My heart roared. I looked around at the faces in that tube with me and felt a connection with them that made me shiver. When I came out at Copley Square, blinking like a baby, the dark city lights were auroral.

I was early. I walked around the reflecting pool at the Christian Science Plaza. On Sunday mornings, before I moved out to Belmont, I would stop off at a Syrian bakery for coffee and some flat, oily bread with herbs and cheese pounded into it. Then I would walk to the plaza and eat my bread while it was still warm, drink my coffee, thick with cream and sugar, read the paper, and watch the faithful trickle into the mother church for ten o'clock Sunday school.

I had stopped going to church when I was in middle school, soon after my grandfather died. I remember childhood Sunday school classes and long sermons nursing a roll of Life Savers, looking at my mother's curvy legs in her nylons, drawing on the program and the offering envelopes with the golf pencil that was stuck in the pencil hole in the back of the pew. For a long time, I believed Jesus loved me because the Bible told me he did. My mother taught me to say my prayers when I was a little girl, and I would get on my knees at night and pray, in earnest, for everyone I knew. When I spent summers with my grandparents, they would take me to their Lutheran church on Sundays and to choir practice on Thursday nights, where I would sit with my grandfather and the other baritones while the choir sang to the hauntingly empty church. On rainy days, I would pull out my grandmother's Bible and look at the colored illustrations of Jesus sitting amidst a flock of sheep and a throng of robe-clad children, or of Moses aiming the tablet of Commandments toward the sky, or of Abraham with the knife poised over his son Isaac, about to slit his throat.

I had often wondered about the early Christian Scientists and how they thought that sickness and death were illusions caused by mistaken beliefs and that prayer would right their bad thoughts and cure the fallacy of disease, yet their children died of ruptured appendices, diabetes, and ear infections, as if they lived in the bush instead of Boston proper. Their numbers dwindled as they died out or left the Church, likely due to bad doctrine and bad leadership. After all, not taking your seriously ill child to a doctor is a dumb idea, and Mary Baker Eddy, the founder of Christian Science, had been a hypochondriac like me. In the 1980s, psychologists posthumously diagnosed her with psychotic personality disorder.

Nowhere in the Christian faith did I see what I was truly looking for as a young doubter—proof that Jesus ascended into heaven and was seated at the right hand of the Father. If God were so real, and He cared, and they believed so hard, why did He let Christian Scientist kids die when their parents prayed for healing? This feeling left me sadder still, left me wondering about where Wagner was, and for that matter, my grandfather and dead great-aunties and -uncles and grandparents and great-grandparents, and the files of dead kin that I never knew, stretching behind me, far past any landscape I had traveled. I pushed my fingers through the curl of water falling over the edge of the reflecting pool and thought about being dead, about the potential of heaven as a reality. About the fate of sinners and of the people who sin by condemning other sinners. About the availability of God. I imagined Him to be so rock star that He was off-limits to regular people, cordoned off and guarded by the holier-than-thous who had actually read the Bible, the ones who looked at you funny of a Sunday morning while they filed in to worship a God that they thought you were going to hell for not believing in.

That night, I walked around the reflecting pool and wondered about purpose. Why would a man light up the world around him and then die in a motorcycle crash, broken and bloody and alone in a hole? Did he fulfill his purpose? What was my purpose? It certainly wasn't to serve fish and chowder. There was more in store for me, but I didn't know how to find what it was. I tried again to pray, asking God not to let me down, to show me proof that Wagner was still there somewhere. I watched the pool for extra ripples. I watched the trees for a rush of wind. Nothing.

At quarter to eleven I met Kami at the Nan Ling Restaurant on Massachusetts Avenue for some late Chinese. We planned to get a quick bite to eat then go to a house party some of his friends were having. I wore a miniskirt with black tights and flat shoes because I had nice legs and because, being the girl who was too tall to take home to Mother, I wore flat shoes wherever I went.

It was no surprise that he showed up in a green Army jacket with an activity of pockets for stashing necessary urban things, such as a T pass, a wallet, maps, some extra cash, maybe a candy bar and some gum. He stood about six foot five with his big hair, which made me feel like a dainty flower—a rare pleasure—and he was as skinny as a stick. He looked like Phil Lynott from Thin Lizzy, and I also wasn't surprised to learn that he was a singer/songwriter. He was trying to break into the music business, like every third person I knew, and he worked at the Army Navy to pay the bills. We were the only ones in the restaurant. We ordered some food and talked fairly easily, ripping egg rolls and sipping cheap, bitter tea.

We were dispatching with the getting-to-know-you part of the conversation that I dislike, but that always ends up being the easiest part of any relationship, when we heard a stunning crash of metal on stone, like a demon birthing itself out of the concrete of Mass Ave and rising up to bash buildings. Kami and I looked at each other. We jumped out of the booth and ran toward the front door, the way you run in a nightmare when a monster is after you—impossibly slowly, even though you are exerting all your efforts. When I looked out, at about nine o'clock on the north side of the street, I saw an upside-down car with wheels spinning, and at about two o'clock, about fifteen or twenty yards south, there was a dark heap on the ground. The road was shiny with recent rain, and the streetlights and wet air made a mist that hung above us. The only movement came from the wheels of the car, which spun freely in the air, and the changing of the stoplight colors reflected in the asphalt.

I shouted for the waiters to call 911 and then ran outside. There was no one else on the road. I had never seen that before on Mass Ave at any time of day. Without speaking, I ran toward the heap on the ground, and Kami ran toward the car. My cheap flats slipped on the asphalt and I fell to my knees, then got up again, without the shoes, and ran across the road, which was shiny, covered in broken glass, I later found out. I slid into where the heap lay still. The heap was human, lying like a doll, facedown and twisted, and when I smoothed the hair back, I saw it was a young woman about my own age. She had jaw-length fluffy blond hair, and one side of her face was pressed into the asphalt, a place no face should ever touch. Her hands were above her, as if she were lying half on her stomach on her bed in a loose, tangled sleep. I crouched down by her to see if she was conscious. I asked her if she was okay and got no response. Then I noticed that her pelvis was twisted about ninety degrees past where it should have been, and the wrong leg faced up. I could see the rip in her back, like wet paper, that exposed one kidney and the bones of her spine. She was breathing.

This was a girl like me, a girl with a mother and father and dreams and goals, a girl who was in the impossible position of suddenly being at the end of something she didn't expect. I did not dare to move her, so I got down by her head and spoke to her. I took her hand in one of mine, and with the other, I stroked her hair back from her face. There was blood starting beneath her head, so I started talking. I said what I would want someone to say to me if I were face-down in the road, which was, "You are such a good girl. Your momma and daddy love you so much. Everything is going to be fine. We're going to wait for the ambulance. They're going to take you to the hospital and make everything better. It's going to be okay." I held her face and, on an impulse, said the only other thing that came into my mind, a song that bubbled up from childhood. I sang, *"Jesus loves you, this I know, for the Bible tells me so."* The girl's hand twitched in mine, a fast twitching, like a deaf person's finger spelling. She made a soft noise, like a breath but not quite, and when it finished, I suspected there wouldn't be another, but I was afraid to move her to start CPR. I could see the red and blue lights coming up Mass Avenue. The sound of the sirens started to register, and when they drove up and the paramedics came with their backboard and bags, they had to pull me away, make me move. I had done all I could, which felt like nothing.

I looked toward the upturned car, and I could see police officers restraining two men, one on the ground and one standing up against the wall of a business. The one standing was Kami. He was being uncuffed, yet two officers pressed him up against the wall and held him there. This confused me. I didn't know what to do, so I gathered up the girl's bag and shoes, which were scattered across the street and sidewalk. I handed them to a paramedic, then backed away and watched them drive off. I stood on the sidewalk until the police released Kami and he found me. We talked for a minute about the girl while our breathing slowed and reality came back to itself.

"Was she conscious?"

"I'm not sure," I told him.

"Was she alive?"

"I think she died when I was holding her. What was all that with the cops?"

"Yeah, well, when I went to see who was in the car, the driver tried to climb out and run off. He was wasted on something. He wasn't taking no for an answer either, so I had to stop him and hold him until the cops got there."

"And they had you up against the wall because?"

"I, uh, had a handgun. I pulled it on the driver to keep him from getting away. He hit the girl when she was walking on the sidewalk. He thought she was a pile of garbage. He kept talking about sideswiping the trash. I couldn't let him get away."

"You carry a gun?"

"Yes."

"Of course," I said. "In your multi-pocketed coat. Why not?"

"Well, I . . ."

"Can I see it?" I asked.

"They took it. I don't have a permit. They understood what I did but couldn't let me keep it. I have to go down to the station tomorrow and get it back," he said.

"Okay, then. You carry a gun illegally?"

"Yes."

"Wow. I really don't know anything about you."

"Everyone has to get past the first day. Where are your shoes?"

My legs suddenly started to sting. I looked down at the softball-sized holes at each knee in my tights and saw that my kneecaps were angry and bloody and ripped up. My tights had split at the feet, and I was barefoot. We found my shoes in the street among the crawling police and colored lights and then decided to walk back to Kami's apartment, which was close. When I put my shoes on, I noticed that the bottoms of my feet were cut and the shoes hurt, so I took them off and limped barefoot on the outsides of my feet. Kami's house was off of Huntington Avenue, a short walk under ordinary circumstances, but it took us a while to get there. We were both shaky from the adrenaline. Kami threw up in a garbage can, and I had to stop twice and sit down because my feet hurt. When we got to his apartment, it was empty and colder than the air outside. There were guitars and amplifiers, a kitchen table and one chair, and a white grand piano taking up the entire living room.

"Roommates?" I asked.

"I live alone," he said.

He poured us some orange juice, then I sat on the kitchen table and he kneeled down on the floor and dug chunks of glass out of my knees and feet, then bandaged me up. It was a touching moment, the kind of moment that would otherwise appeal to a girl's heart, except it hurt, and half an hour before, someone had died in my arms.

While I sipped orange juice, Kami picked up his guitar and started singing. He had a rich voice and a real talent. I sat on the kitchen table and wept hard while he sang, wiping my face and nose with my sleeve. It was my first cry in a long time.

"You're good," I said.

"My dad was a musician, too," he told me.

"Do you sound like him?"

"I couldn't tell you. I never met him."

"Maybe he's Phil Lynott of Thin Lizzy."

"Heard that one before. Maybe he is. You feeling better? What do you want to do?"

"I guess we could go to that party," I said.

So we did. We hopped the Green Line outbound for a few stops and then went up three flights to a typical Boston party full of college-aged people. There was a lot of beer, plenty of Dr. Martens and ripped jeans, and people were already a little tilted by the time we got there. I walked around with my bandaged feet in a pair of Kami's raft-sized flip-flops.

At first, we had to talk about it to everyone we saw. It was spilling out of us. We tried describing it.

"We just saw a terrible car crash. A girl got hit and died. We were there. We helped."

The partygoers did not care, but they saw the crazy in our eyes and listened politely for a few minutes before scrambling to change the subject or leave our company. We were wounded, too intense, killing the mood, and we realized that the experience was ours alone, and in some way, we had been set apart by it. We ended up drinking beer out back, on the archetypal triple-decker Boston porch with a hibachi, some dead plants, and an old lopsided plaid love seat with a slow fountain of stuffing coming up out of the cushions. We sat shoulder to shoulder on the love seat, and during the course of our drinking, a red welt on Kami's left cheek asserted itself and slowly turned purple.

"You have a bruise on your face," I told him. By this time, I had drunk enough beers for my hands and feet and knees to stop hurting, but I couldn't stop thinking about the accident.

"Yeah, I figured. I could feel it coming on."

"What happened?"

"Got hit." He put the cold bottle up against the mark and held it there.

"The guy hit you?" I asked.

"No, the cop did. He said he was sorry once he had sorted things out, though."

"Well, that's something," I told him. Then I said, "That girl had a life two hours ago, and now she's dead. She died in my arms."

"I know," he said. "I wonder what she did. If she was a student, or had a job, or what."

"Where she grew up," I added. "What her life was like. Did she do enough with it?"

We both drank.

"Maybe she's in heaven and dying was, like, 'Good riddance,'" I said.

"Doubt it. Right here? This beer? Us? This is all there is and there's nothing after it's gone. That's what I think."

"That's what everyone I know thinks. But what if you're wrong? What if she's in heaven, happy as a clam? What if there is more and we just don't know it?"

He shrugged. "If you want to believe the epic myth, then go ahead. It's a device designed to make people feel better."

"What do you think we're here for, then?"

"In general?" he asked. "Like in life?"

"Yes," I said. "What's our purpose? Why were we created?"

"I think we were *created*, by happy accident, to have as much fun as we can before we die, because when we die, that's it. Skulls in the dirt. The worms eat us, then people plant vegetables in the dirt the worms made. They eat the vegetables, and we live on in future generations that way. Agriculture is our only contribution."

"That's horrible," I said. "That's not enough." A swirl of fear surrounded me, and I felt a swelling of panic in my throat.

"It's the only way I can see things," he explained.

"So, there's no God?"

"Nope. If there was, why would He let a perfectly good girl that age get killed like a dog in the street?"

I had no answer. I thought of Wagner. This was the question I had been asking all along, every time I imagined Wagner, broken and dead in a construction hole with his motorcycle on top of him, or imagined my grandfather on his deathbed, or imagined myself on my deathbed surrounded by people giving me that look I dread, the one that says, *I am terribly sorry but just a little bit relieved that it is you and not me.* I realized that my struggle, my hypochondriasis, and my fear of death existed for two reasons: first because I didn't know what I was supposed to do here, and second because I didn't know what came after here. I put my head on Kami's shoulder and took a pull from my beer. We sat on the porch and watched the traffic while people came and went, then the music slowly died down, and that's when I noticed that the trains had stopped running.

"What time is it?" I asked him.

"Ten past two," he said.

"The T is done for the night. I'm stuck."

"I guess you have to come back to my place," he said simply.

"Well played," I said.

"Unless you have a friend nearby."

"No. We should go. They're cleaning up."

We stumbled downstairs and out onto the sidewalk, blinking at the night. There we stood for a moment, staring down an empty street. I took a step.

"I don't think I can walk. My feet are killing me," I said. I lifted one up to look at the sole and it was oozing fluid through the gauze.

"I'll carry you."

I doubted that he could, with his skinny musician's arms, but he scooped me up and lugged me the several blocks back to his place. A sheen of sweat started down his mustache, but he pretended it was easy. He heaved me down on the porch while he dug through pockets for his key, then the sound of the key in the lock echoed inside the emptiness of the living space. When the door swung open, I felt like an interloper in a place I didn't belong. I didn't want to be there.

"You can sleep in with me," he said. "It's a one-bedroom, so . . ."

"Not happening," I told him.

"You have a better idea?"

"How 'bout there?" I pointed to the grand piano. It was gleaming like bone in the dim light.

"On top or under?"

"Under."

"Done," he said.

He went into his room and came out with a pillow and blanket, and spread it out under the piano, then patted it and lifted his eyebrows. I kneeled and crawled under it, where he pulled the blanket around me and smoothed my hair, the same way I had done with the girl just a few hours before. I could feel my pulse in my feet, which were starting to hurt again.

"It's been a weird night, huh?" he asked.

"About the weirdest I've had."

"Me too. Are you sure about . . . ?"

"I'm sure."

"Okay. Sweet dreams. Tomorrow is a new day. That's one good thing, anyway."

Kami walked to his room, his tall, lanky body stooped over and his shoulder blades poking through his T-shirt, and I had a simultaneous glimpse of what he must have looked like as a little boy and what he would look like as an old man. He closed the bedroom door, and I was left alone under the white piano, unbearably alone, with nothing but the faint city night noises dancing in the distance, far away, outside in the street. I had not slept to those sounds in some months. I thought about Wagner and about the dead girl, and I suddenly, desperately wanted God to be paying attention to me. *Show me something,* I thought. *Show me that you know I'm thinking about Wagner. About the girl. That they meant something. Come on, God. Make it not be for nothing.* I waited for a streetlight to flicker, for a filling of joy in my heart, for something. I waited for a long time. Nothing. I thought, *I helped a girl die today. At least that's something. She didn't die alone.* I eventually nodded off, sleeping lightly in that strange, dark place.

At 5:15 A.M., when I heard the first train run past the house, I got up and limped my way out, closing the door quietly to avoid waking Kami. I had no interest in seeing him again, and in fact, I wouldn't ever. It was like an early-morning walk of shame, limping down the dim sidewalk in my party skirt with my shoes in my hand, while newspaper delivery drivers and bakery truck drivers and cabdrivers drove past me, glad that I wasn't their daughter. It was still dark and the streets were wet, the same kind of shiny they were the night before, but without the broken glass. I thought about saxophones, about what a fierce alto saxophone solo would sound like ripping through the last of the night on that empty street, blasting the dreamers awake. As I waited for the train, I saw something shiny on the ground and bent to pick it up. It was a subway token. I thought about the time Wagner had looked down by a gutter and found five shiny T tokens lined up in a row, and how he scooped them up like a gleeful child discovering a treasure. "What are my chances of those odds?" he had said in his Portugenglish, then, "Hey! Let's take the train up to Gloucester for some clams, you! I'm buying." I remembered him well for a moment, remembered some small essence of his life, not his death, and it felt okay.

An inbound train, headlights illuminating the moisture in the air, squeaked, then stopped, and I stepped carefully up the steps, found a seat, and rode the train toward Park Street Station so I could catch the Red Line home. An old woman with a pastry box on her lap glanced at my knees, then wordlessly handed me a cream-filled donut. All along, I thought, I had yearned for signs that life was not pointless, that the dead are not gone forever, that there was a reason for being here and one day we would be reunited, and in that quiet time on the train, I thought, *Be still. Just be still.* Only that voice wasn't my voice, and that thought wasn't mine either. *Okay,* I thought, *I'm listening,* and then I felt another idea that said, *You're not alone, dumbass. Just relax and trust me.*

I had been demanding of God, unreasonable. Unwilling to do my share, which was to simply believe without proof, to trust, because that's what comprises real faith. I had wanted clear signs of an after-life, dramatic ones, gothic ones, Old Testament ones—creaking floors and candles blowing out, burning bushes, an audible voice telling me that I would not die young, but would be the mother of nations. I wasn't listening for a tiny voice so small that it was a feeling, a feeling that told me to shut the hell up and stop asking for stuff, a feeling that told me I was going to be fine.

I saw the accident on the news that morning. The girl who died had been my age exactly—twenty-one years old, a beloved North-eastern University student, an American Sign Language major who had dreams of opening a school for the deaf. I wrote her name down and told myself I would call her family. I eventually looked up her parents' number, then copied it down on a scrap of paper and put it in my wallet for the next ten years. I would occasionally pick up the phone, dial the number, then hang up before anyone answered. I was afraid of myself. I was afraid of death. I was afraid I wouldn't know what to say to them. I didn't want to reopen the wound.

One fine summer day after a hard rain, my young daughters put on their rubber rain boots and splashed in the puddles while I sat on the porch holding my baby son in my arms. I thought about that number in my wallet, like I did on many occasions while watching my children do simple and beautiful things: wiping their mouths with their sleeves, or laughing at a joke, or poking a bug with a stick, or standing on tiptoe to reach something. I thought about the parents of the dead girl who had lost all those things, and who would never get them again, and decided I was doing them an injustice.

I dialed the number. A woman answered. I introduced myself, then told her that I had been with her daughter when she died, that she hadn't been alone, that I had held her and had sung "Jesus Loves Me." The woman exhaled and was silent, then she started to chuckle. I could hear laughter and music in the background. She took a breath and told me that song had been her daughter's favorite childhood song, and the day I had chosen to call would have been her thirtieth birthday. The background noise was a celebration of her life. I didn't know, I had said, and she told me, "God is kind of weird that way, but He gives us what we need, so don't forget that. You keep the faith."

GAMES I PLAY

It is a Friday night in October and, like one hundred million other women around the world at any given time (which is a fairly accurate estimation and not hyperbole), I am pregnant, the kind of pregnant where the baby is crowding your breath and it feels like you are sucking air through a snorkel, and there is no room in your thorax because a human being that is not you, yet is a little bit you, is taking up the room where your guts should be spreading out, relaxing, enjoying the weekend, the kind of pregnant where you have no idea you are about to become someone who will be filled with glee when a baby exhibits a common eructative display, the kind of person who will soon begin to call a generic, run-of-the-mill belch a "big ole burpy-durp."

My husband and I have accepted a dinner invitation from another couple he has been friends with since college. Presumably it will be the last one we can attend alone, sans baby, before I pop, and there is much merriment made over this, though this offends me slightly, as if they are implying the baby is going to ruin my life. Truthfully, I am looking forward to dining with the baby riding shotgun in a car seat, so I can have a damn beer or a damn glass of wine once in a while, like everybody else. Right now I am eating so clean I feel like it will kill me. No soda, no artificial colors, low sugar, enough cruciferous vegetables and beans to allow me to regularly crop-dust strangers with my gas, and Dutch-oven my husband under the covers a few times per hour . . . *all night long.* My husband and the other couple, Jimmy and Deb O'Toole, are career people, up-and-coming journalists headed for the top of the heap, and I am a college dropout, full to the gills with our first fetus, having nothing in common with anyone I know. Jimmy and Deb live in Providence, Rhode Island, and we live in Boston, and we get together now and again for little dinner parties sprinkled with the kind of witty conversation that comes with a measure of social pressure, continually requiring educational assertion, sometimes collective proof, that we are smarter than ninety-five percent of the population, which leaves me out of my element, because secretly, I am *not that.* One of the things I will be inclined to do is nod my head when they bring up politics of any sort, which, between me and my fetus, I don't understand and don't care one whit about. At this time in my life, I am unable to list the three branches of government, I cannot tell you about any one of the president's cabinet members or even any of the cabinet positions. When it comes to talking about Supreme Court justices, I cannot tell you the function of the Supreme Court, let alone name any of the justices. I am a late bloomer, one who can name all of the characters in every John Irving novel, who can give you Leo Tolstoy's biography in detail, who can name each plot point in *Clan of the Cave Bear,* or tell you about cross-hatching techniques in printmaking or the development of Byzantine churches throughout Europe, or how to make cheesecake on a stick with chocolate ganache, or the many varieties and reliabilities of both domestic and foreign cars, but I cannot tell you the difference between a congressman and a senator. I just don't care. That stuff is for grown-ups and I am a twenty-five-year-old child masquerading as a married woman with a bun in the oven. It is clear that I don't know what I am doing and have no business harvesting a baby.

Still, our friends are nice and it is to be a nice dinner, though my performance pressure is likely to include post-event debriefing by my husband, who is the kind of fellow to revisit things I say and behaviors I exhibit after the fact, usually on the ride home from places, questioning why I said certain things, or why I had not thought to say certain things. Because he is a few years older, because he had graduated college, and possibly because he realized far too late after marrying me—"late" being the point at which you knock up your wife and can no longer extricate yourself from a bad marriage without ruining a child—that I may not be his ideal go-getter working woman partner, he often feels free to pick apart some of my flightier comments. I don't like it but for some reason I feel I deserve it. Soon after marrying him, I grow used to being reminded of how dull I am in this way, though he does this obliquely and possibly not on purpose, and my highly tuned oversensitivity ratchets everything up a few notches and makes things worse. I live in this state as a matter of course. It does not help, in those last few months of pregnancy, that my body has shunted most of its blood supply down from my head to my giant placenta and my giant baby, which are both gorging off me like a tick, leaving me partially brain dead. So we drive to Rhode Island on a Friday night to have a little dinner party, although secretly I would prefer to stay home in bed and grow this thing so I can get it out and take a deep damn breath whenever I feel like it.

Games I play while riding on the highway: counting telephone poles to see if the number of poles per mile in Massachusetts changes when we cross into Rhode Island. Also: imagining ejecting my husband's Smiths tape from the cassette player and flinging it out of the passenger window to be snatched up by a hawk that will unravel it and thread it into a stick nest in the skies. Also: thinking of ways we can solidify our rocky new marriage quickly, before the baby is born. Also: leaving. Having the baby on my own, because I suspect we do not have the skills necessary to make a marriage work. Going back South, buying eight acres in North Florida, and raising the child on goat milk, like Heidi, or twelve acres in North Carolina, where I would make primitive crafts for a living, carving the baby a little rocker chair out of hickory, and fashioning traditional brooms and plaques that say "Home Is Where the Heart Is," which I would sell to tourists. And also: wondering if this baby is a boy or a girl, suspecting that it is a girl based on a dream I had in July, during my fifth month, the night my husband and I got in an epic fight and I refused to holler back at him because I thought the baby would hear and would get upset, so I hissed my side of the fight through my teeth. This did nothing to damper down the intoxicating cortisol and adrenaline levels that were coursing through my blood, barely filtered through the liver of a placenta before it washed the baby in it, sharing with it my elevated heart rate, my sorrow at being newly married to a man I fought with.

About thirty minutes after my husband said the words "mistake" and "marriage" and stormed out to go to work, the adrenaline I had been enjoying dipped off and I grew tired. I fell asleep propped up in bed with a book open across my belly. I dreamed of a small girl child in a smocked summer dress, bending over to smell a red flower with her hand clasped around the finger of an adult hand that wasn't mine. I was photographing this child, whose dress dipped into the shape of a feminine, off-kilter triangle, the front nearly touching the strap of her white leather sandals, the back lifting to show a pair of lacy bloomers. The baby, who suddenly received its share of my adrenaline, kicked up at its north wall and woke me. I touched my belly and called her "daughter," but told no one about my premonition, as I knew not what to do with it. I had a fifty percent chance of being wrong, after all.

At this point in the pregnancy, even entering the ninth month, I can go only so long without food before I vomit, so we must drive carefully, avoiding swerves and bumps and rapid accelerations. This child has caused fairly severe hyperemesis gravidarum, or what regular people call "nearly constant puking," and I have spent most days since its implantation trying to figure out how to keep from vomiting in front of others. I carry plastic Star Market grocery bags with me in my purse so I don't have to splash throw-up on floors. I carry flat water, or fizzy water, or water with salt and sugar in it, or crackers, or nuts, or cold noodles, depending on what I can tolerate, and expect to hurl nearly anywhere. I've got it down to a science, can do it neatly, silently, without mess. Once I start blowing chunks, everything else I attempt to get down to stop the vomiting cycle will usually come back up, too, so I have to be careful of the nuts, which will scrape my esophagus upon revisitation, and any red-colored liquid, which will look like blood and frighten me. If there is a wait at a restaurant and I get too hungry, I will run to the bathroom to heave before we sit down to eat, which will start a cycle that will ensure I will not be able to hold anything down for the rest of the night. I will eat what I can, then ask for a to-go container and bring home the rest, but often on the drive home, the smell of the seat leather, or the exhaust of a car idling in front of us at a red light, or a wobble of scent coming from the Styrofoam container, or even the sound of the container squeaking together where I grip it, will cause me to toss twenty-three dollars' worth of restaurant food right back into the to-go container, on top of the food I am hoping to eat after I get home and things settle down. A few times, I go to the doctor for IVs, which will push, by gravity, fluids I have lost back into me, transforming me from a sunken-eyed, parasite-filled shell into a rounded and ripe pregnant woman again, until the next time the vomiting cycle begins.

Somewhere near the Plainville exit, I ask my husband to pull over. He does this quickly because he is used to it by now, and I hold back my dress from the wind with one hand, push my spectacles onto my nose with the other, and throw up into the New England highway grasses, thinking, while I empty myself to the toes, about the dryness of the grass and if there can be wildfires in October, if New England even has wildfires, and about the possums that might come sniffing around after dark to snack on the vomit, and I hope I am not leading an animal to death by impact by the side of the road.

The O'Tooles' apartment is the downstairs of a typical Northeastern two-decker, complete with old, big, leaky windows, good but faded wood floors, two bedrooms, and a bathroom with 1940s tile colored seafoam green and peach, or Pepto pink and black. It is strikingly similar to our two-decker back in Boston, with a monastic wood-floored foyer, a living room with built-in half bookcases, a corner dining hutch built into the wall, and a little kitchen in the back with a gas stove and window above the sink that begged for café curtains and a house cat. The O'Tooles have decorated their apartment the same way all other up-and-coming yuppies do, with a tasteful couch and love seat, a handed-down Ethan Allen coffee table, lots of books, Irish lace curtains, modestly priced area rugs, and meaningful, middle-of-the road, placeholder art that suggests that they know what they are doing but can't afford what they truly want just yet.

Jimmy and Deb meet us at the door, yanking back their big, deaf Dalmatian, who jumps up on my stomach, scratching my bare shins with its claws on the way down. My memory of this poor dog is of one of the most unfortunate animals I have known, the regal neck and evenly dispersed spots not disguising the way the thing shrieks at its own reflection in the night glass of the windows, or tries to bolt when it sees shiny tinfoil out of the corner of its eye. This dog cannot orient itself in its world with only vision and smell. They have hired a trainer to despasticize it, spent money on teaching it sign language, and over drinks and tasteful Van Morrison on the stereo, Jimmy and Deb report their progress with the dog, demonstrate the simple signs they have learned but the dog has not, convey to us with their voices and gestures the kind of hope we will one day see emoting from parents with impaired children, the kind of hope I will one day recognize in my own voice and gestures.

Games I play during drinks: wondering what kind of birth control the O'Tooles are practicing, wondering which of us in this room has the most startling yet vaguely possible unrealized dream. Wondering if Jimmy and Deb have sex in the shower, and which of us in this room will be the first to die. Jimmy and Deb and my husband start drinking stingers while I carefully swallow a piece of garlic bread we will be having for dinner, in the hopes that the garlic will quiet the nausea I have felt since throwing up on the highway. When it doesn't work, I rummage, a little bit frantically, through Deb's kitchen for something that will, while she sympathetically guides me toward saltines, which never work but which people who have never been pregnant try to tell me to eat, or a piece of lunch meat, which might work, or some cheese, which I've not yet tried but perhaps the milk fat in it will work. It doesn't work. While they are each on their second stinger, I excuse myself to use the bathroom and vomit my body inside out. Up comes one slice of bologna, one slice of cheese, and a piece of garlic bread. Their toilet is impeccably clean, I note. I open up their medicine cabinet for some mouthwash, and it is also compulsively ordered, and I decide then that they are probably not the kind of people who would have sex in the shower, because it would be too spontaneous, as people with alphabetized medicine cabinets aren't likely to wing things, though perhaps you can schedule in sex in the shower, which I suppose some do, on Saturday morning, after walking the dog, and after coffee but before brunch and the flea market.

When I come out, my husband gives me a squint, which I understand means, "Do not tell anyone that you just threw up," and I wouldn't dare. I am tired of the sympathy. I am tired of people asking me how I feel. I am tired of people asking me if it is a boy or a girl, or if I would prefer a boy or a girl, or how many children we want to have, or if we have a name picked out yet, or when I am due. I just want the baby out of me already so my liver and my diaphragm can go back to where they belong and I can stop chunking my groceries in public.

I sit down and notice, by Jimmy's broad gestures, which the dog watches with anxiety, and Deb's higher-pitched laugh, and my husband's general loosening, that they are having a grand old time thanks to the stingers and I am, furthermore, out of the loop. How I long to drink stingers. How I long to relax my uterus with double stingers on the rocks until the weight of the baby's head softens and stretches my cervix and labor begins.

Games I play: imagining delivering the baby on their Ethan Allen coffee table, Jimmy O'Toole catching it like Thurman Munson, taking illicit peeks at my neatly trimmed hoo-ha at the same time, because when you are nearly due, the trimming of the hoo-ha can be a daily event, like keeping your landscaping up weeks before the garden club contest. I imagine the dog running off to its crate with the placenta that drops onto the Ethan Allen, guarding it to the point of biting, viciously, anyone who comes near. Before we get too tipsy, Deb says, we'd better eat.

During dinner, which is some sort of roast and Irish scalloped

potatoes with cream and dill, the smell of the dill leaving me hopeful for a few minutes that the pale potatoes will go down and stay at
best, and at worst, will come up softly and painlessly, Jimmy and
Deb grow increasingly unified and more affectionate, tipping their
heads toward each other, clasping hands, reminiscing about the years
they were together before moving to Providence, how they each
knew the other was "the one," while also reminding my husband of
wild capers and strange shared experiences from when the three
of them lived together as roommates in that rental house during
college. My husband, usually measured and reserved of countenance,
guffaws, shouts back at Jimmy, snorts humorous anecdotes of his
own. His friendship with these two has gone much further back
than his relationship with me, and this is a side of him I have not yet
seen. We have been married only eleven months, and met four
months before that. I know nothing of his previous life as Jimmy
and Deb's roommate. I have never seen him drunk, in fact. The truth
is, we don't really know each other. We guard the tender sides of
ourselves, creating polite, false truths to sink our teeth into—both
of us thinking we have one thing in the other, when really, we have
something else. We are, I realize for the first time, living a lie, and I
do not know how to be truthful about who I really am because I am
afraid he will not like the real me. The real me is insecure and com-
pulsive and tender, and needs humor and a gentle touch to ground me.
The real me likes to dream wild dreams, talk about things that will
never come true. The real me likes to drop the F-bomb and laugh at
farts. The real me likes pointing a kaleidoscope at a bright window
and saying, "Ah, look at this." The real me likes to cook the same ridi-
culously traditional foodstuff over again, like a ritual prayer: Welsh
cookies with currants, crêpes, pierogis. For some reason, I do not
think my husband will like the real me, and later, when I show him
the real me, I am right. He will never laugh at my jokes, and instead

of holding me when I need comfort, he will judge me. He will also never think a fart is funny.

Games I play while at dinner: imagining Jimmy and Deb breaking into spontaneous human cunnilingus across the dining room table, one kind of sex that does not result in a baby, shoving aside wedding-gift candles and the Le Creuset of Irish scalloped potatoes, a candle toppling to the floor and igniting their Pier 1 area rug, the deaf Dalmatian working itself into a frenzy, biting the flame and spinning until he knocks himself out against the breakfront, my husband pushing his wire-rimmed specs up his face, giving me one of his looks, heavy with implied meaning, saying, "Uhhh, I think maybe we should go." Also: imagining the tight, itchy skin on my belly splitting open like a pod, releasing the baby, along with a halo of dandelion fluff, that we all blow into the corners of the room. Also: thinking of things they might say about the things we said or did once we drive off for Boston at the end of the night: Did you see how swollen her feet were? Who wears Birkenstocks with a dress and no socks in October? I wonder if they're going to make it. Also: wondering if we are going to make it.

My husband has a wonderful time. The joy on his face is measurable, and because he is having fun, I have fun. I have never seen him this relaxed. He is lovely when he really laughs. During dinner, the dog licks my toes from underneath the table, a sensation that makes me nauseated and also reminds me that I have to urinate. I sign to him with my hands in the hammock of my lap, knees spread wide in my sacklike dress—signs that Jimmy and Deb showed us during drinks, such as the signs for *Sit*, and *Stay*, and *Go away*. Later I will teach the dogs in my life these simple signs I learned from Jimmy and Deb and this deaf Dalmatian, and they will obey, long after this dog is put down for becoming so agitated at the automobile light reflections in his living room window that he busts through it, slicing himself like a roast turkey.

After dinner, when Deb brings out a gourmet New York cheesecake that she has paid a fortune for at an upscale Providence bakery, she announces that she is quite wasted and will stop drinking to keep me company. She makes coffee, pours the men generous splashes of Sambuca in little clear glasses, plopping three coffee beans into each for good luck. My husband announces that I had better drive home, something I understood would be happening before we even sat down at the table, and I sniff his Sambuca, which quiets my stomach. He and Jimmy drink three Sambucas, growing looser and more theoretical and musing with each one, and also more relaxed in their chairs. I track their conversation from the aplomb of various managing editors they have known, to how journalism is affecting society, to the decline of the Roman Empire, and finally New York sports teams. Deb kicks off her heels and puts her tiny feet in Jimmy's lap, where he rubs them while he talks about Thurman Munson. My feet feel like mangy seal pups, swollen hot and tight and thick, and when I look down at them they look like someone else's feet. I put them up on my husband's lap, and within a minute they are back down on the floor.

Games I play during dessert: thinking about curing the obesity epidemic by inventing a drug that mimics the same hormones that are coursing through me right now, making me wish I had never eaten. Also: imagining all of the vessels in my vulva engorging, rerouting into a pipeline to maximize the blood flow in preparation for the impending baby. My vulva is so full of pregnancy blood that it hurts. What I say: It's time to go, babe. We have a long drive ahead of us, which is how we always end these dinner parties, by acknowledging the distance between Providence and Boston. What I think: We need to leave right now because my vulva is about to explode, though you won't understand because you have had two stingers and several glasses of wine and three Sambucas and don't even have a vulva.

So we say good-bye. I pour my husband into the car and begin the drive home. He turns on the radio to an alternative rock station and begins to head-bang in the abbreviated way one does in the passenger seat of a sedan. He shrieks things like, "Whoop-whoop!" and "I love this band! Love 'em!" and because happy drunks are infectious, I laugh. His frontal lobe is loosed and he is unguarded. He starts to talk about ridiculous possibilities with the enthusiasm of an eleven-year-old boy: winning the lottery and using the money to start a rally race team using only classic Saab Sonetts, building a house outside of the city from trees we mill ourselves. It will have a woodstove, he assures me, and an art studio, and a motocross track, too. He is tremendous in this light, and silly, and I love him, but also I wonder if I will see this glee again.

We pass Pawtucket. We pass Attleboro. We pass Plainville. He stops talking and grows pensive. "I am a wolf," he says. "You know that?" Then he grows quiet. Somewhere near the Foxboro exit, he decides that we need some air, because I have stopped him from opening and closing his window, so he slides the sunroof, sticks his head and shoulders out of it, and howls at the moon.

"I'm a wolf," he shouts into the night. "A lone wolf," and as he lifts his head to the sky to howl again, the wind liberates his glasses off his face and they fly onto the highway we are leaving behind. He won't remember this, I think. He drops back into the car and says, "I think I lost my spectacles," then falls asleep for the rest of the ride.

I pull up to our apartment and wake him. He fumbles for the door latch and can't find it. I get out, suspecting that my belly has grown during the course of the evening. I now feel impossibly huge. I move slowly, carefully, lumbering around to the passenger side because late in pregnancy, the weight of your uterus stretches certain ligaments inside you, which makes it feel like something is going to rupture, something that maybe feels like your aorta, so you walk gently, waddling when needed, breathing carefully, turning in Tai Chi moves because the baby is shoving its heels right up your diaphragm. I open his door and help him out. "I'm okay," he says, then stands up and announces, "I need you." He lilts as if at sea, and when I go to grab on to his arms, he says, "I'm fine," and shakes me off. He turns and vomits all over the sidewalk in front of the apartment. "Look, I'm you!" he says. He tries to laugh but it fades. He throws up some more.

"Get it all out," I say. "It's okay." I pinch my nose and look away. I'm trying to keep down the cheesecake.

I unlock the door and guide him to the bedroom, where he takes off his sweater and his shoes. He seems suddenly sober, and because I don't know better, I believe him.

"You good?" I ask.

"I'm good," he says, and gives me a double thumbs-up. He looks different without his glasses. Younger, though he is plenty young already. "I'm going to go out front and clean up," I tell him. "I'll be right back."

I walk back outside and around to the side of the building where the landlord's hose is coiled onto the side of the house. I begin to hose off the vomit from the sidewalk, and the steps and the porch, the baby kicking me in the pancreas and punching me in the bladder, and rolling its head into my cervix. When I see the vomit roll off the concrete into the leafy grass, something uncorks in me and I yurp up the several hundred calories of cheesecake I was hoping would stay in me. I hose the cheesecake into the grass and hope for a good rain.

By the time I get inside and lock the front door, I smell smoke.

I rush into the bedroom and find my husband bare-assed, passed out across the bed on his stomach, the knuckles of his right hand brushing the floor. He had turned on the space heater after I left, I notice, and discarded his corduroy pants on top of it. The pants are on fire, a slow smolder with small licks of flame beginning in the corner of the room.

I pat out the fire, put the pants in the bathtub, and run water over them. I open a window. The cold, late-fall air pulls the smoke out of the room. While my husband sleeps, I rake through the kitchen for something, anything that will stop the nausea. I rip open a red, white, and blue rocket Popsicle, which worked the previous week, though eating them fills me with guilt because they are full of chemicals. I suck on it, frantic to calm the nausea. It's not enough. My skin grows clammy. I can feel my salivary glands starting to tighten. My belly tightens in a harmless contraction, and I grab it and hold on for the ride. I think the baby wants out, though I can't imagine why. I turn the lights off to calm my system. Even looking at something wrong will spark an upchuck at this point. I fry an egg in the dark, toast two pieces of bread, slather the toast with mayonnaise, slap the egg between the toast, and bite, quickly, dropping a bolus of food down the hatch like I am dropping sheep to a Cyclops.

Tonight my husband will sleep a dreamless sleep while the hot-house of my body ripens this baby. Tomorrow he will wake up, reach for his missing glasses, and try to hide his hangover. Tomorrow we will meet and try again to forge what we are attempting to forge, but for now, I chew. I swallow. I eat. Games I play there in the dark: wondering if the egg sandwich will work. Wondering if the marriage will. Wondering if this baby will split me in two.

PIE

It was Thanksgiving week and my husband and I were living far from the South that I loved, far from deep-fried turkey, and my mother's stuffing and my mother-in-law's candied sweet potatoes, far from watching gauzy curtains wave in the breeze while the warm sun shone over the holiday feast. My family would pray over the meal, then consume it fairly quickly, after which the men would groan up and lumber like zombies for the football game while the women started coffee and headed off for the shade of the back porch where the fans were running. Thanksgiving week in the South usually afforded us some decent beach time, too, and I knew what to expect of it. But it was snowing all over this new place. In fact, New England had been blanketed by an early snow that lingered and depressed me, bringing with it a cold that stopped me in my tracks. There was no sun. I had had a baby fourteen days earlier and my hormones were starting to settle in that place you have to be careful about, the place that, if you don't watch it, will lead you into a postpartum land empty of color and joy, but I didn't know that yet, I was so bewitched by this little baby girl.

My husband's friend David Blueblood, who had a kind heart

and didn't want to see a couple of transplants spend the holiday alone, had invited us to his parents' house for Thanksgiving Day. On the Tuesday before, I called him and asked what I could bring. He reminded me that we must be exhausted, he urged me to not bring anything, but my mother didn't raise me to be rude—you don't show up to someone's house empty-handed—so I volunteered to bring a pie.

"Don't bring a pie," he said.

"It's fine. I'll bring a pumpkin. I do a good pumpkin."

"Honestly, I hate to say this, but my mother is very particular about her pies. In fact, our entire Thanksgiving dinner is homemade. Please don't trouble yourself."

"It'll be homemade. Don't worry." I had easily baked pumpkin pie a dozen times before. When I hung up, I decided that I would make it the following day, Wednesday, so it would be fresh for Thanksgiving. This pie would be a piece of cake, so to speak.

That night, the baby had her first real bout of screaming colic, the kind where a kid's face gets all stiff and dark and you can see it trying to shit itself in desperation, but it can't, so it just screams instead. I stayed up most of the night with her because my husband, who had already worked thirty-six hours in three days, had to work the next morning as well, and I could at least nap during the day while the baby was asleep. At first we rocked in the living room, where her shrieks echoed off the bare walls and funneled into the bedroom, and then we ended up in the front room office, which was unheated and freezing cold. I stayed in there for several minutes, hoping the chill would startle her into shutting up. When that didn't work, we took a drive around the neighborhood in the car, where I had my first taste of loving the baby fiercely while simultaneously resenting everything she stood for. Around six in the morning, she fell asleep, and I did too, for about two hours. By eight, she was up screaming and I had my hands full of salty, angry, drippy, writhing baby for the rest of the morning. I was exhausted beyond any previous knowledge of exhaustion, and I knew I still had to bake that pie.

I called my mother and asked what to do for colic.

"Put her down," she said. "Let her cry."

"I can do that?"

"It's called self-preservation. For you, not her. Trust me; you'll need to develop this skill if you're going to make it eighteen years."

I put the baby down on her quilt on the floor and she hollered herself hoarse while I preheated the oven of the old gas stove and chopped up the fresh pumpkin. I set the timer and baked the pumpkin chunks in the oven while I paced the dining room with the baby, clutching her like a football between my forearm and ribs. It was noon before she agreed to take the boob, but it only seemed to agitate her, and she screamed harder. At some point while she was trying to nurse, I smelled pumpkin, looked at my watch, and leaped up from the settled place we had gotten to, then ran to the kitchen with her tucked into my armpit, causing her to scream again. The buzzer on the old stove had not gone off and the pumpkin was turning a deep brown and starting to steam. The baby screamed and screamed. At around two, Sister Mary Clare, one of the nuns from the convent next door, came over to see if I was beating the baby, under the guise of asking if she could do anything to help.

"It's just colic," I said as I stood in my doorway. The baby screamed over top of me.

"Ahh."

"I've got it covered," I said. I held the baby up against my shoulder and rocked from side to side by slowly bending one knee at a time.

"I see that. Are you still in your nightgown?"

"It's been a long day." My bottom lip quivered, and something broke in me. I began to weep quietly. "Nothing I do makes it better. She won't stop."

"Give her over," the nun said. She held out her old, bent hands and I handed her the baby, who took a deep breath and stopped yelling. She rested her chin against the nun's shoulder like nothing had been wrong. The baby, whose eyes were learning how to focus, looked around curiously.

"We're going to go next door for a little while. Between me and the three old fools I live with, we should be able to pass a crying baby back and forth. Go relax. Take a bath. Come get her in a half an hour."

I did not have time to take a bath. I needed to make that pie crust and roll it out and get it in the oven, then I needed to peel and puree the pumpkin, and make the filling, then bake a pie good enough for a New England family that liked everything homemade. I made one pie crust properly, with Crisco and vinegar, rolled it out, lifted it into the pie plate, fluted the edges of the crust like my grandmother had taught me, put it in the oven, set the buzzer correctly this time, for five minutes, then went to the bathroom for the first time since early that morning. I sat there on the toilet with unease, feeling strangely alone, then I got up and brushed my teeth, and brushed my hair, then had time to put on a pair of jeans and a clean sweatshirt before I realized the buzzer had not gone off again. I ran into the kitchen and opened the oven. Smoke rolled out. I had burned the pie crust black.

They don't tell you about the level of exhaustion you will face when you have a baby. They say you won't get much sleep for the first few months, but they don't tell you that it will affect your ability to think, that you will become so tired that you will fail at the simplest of tasks, because you are so exhausted that your brain is impaired. I quickly made another crust, then put it in the pie plate, then fluted the edges, then set it on the counter while I pureed the pumpkin. As soon as I turned off the beaters, I could hear the baby screaming from next door, so I grabbed a blanket and went over to get her.

It was snowing harder. The twenty-foot walk between the two houses seemed to take a considerable effort. I could feel my thighs burning and I was afraid I was going to slip in the new snow. I knocked on the door.

"She's a pistol," Sister Margaret Mary said. I stepped in and Sister Mary Theresa handed her over. Sister Mary Clare prayed over the roaring baby while we stood awkwardly in the foyer of their little convent.

Back at the house, I put the baby in the baby sling, a bright cotton granola-head gift from a hippie friend, a gift that I had had no intention of using, and hoisted her onto my back, swaddled tightly onto me as if we were from some other country, a place where women routinely cook difficult things from scratch over hot fires with babies hanging on them like possums. She immediately quieted, and I put the pie together, rocking my way through the kitchen, singing softly, admiring my own brilliance. I gently placed the pie in the oven, set the buzzer for fifty-five minutes, then lay down on the floor quilt with the baby, who was now soundless and sleeping deeply for the first time in two days. I closed my eyes for a moment and it was a beautiful moment.

I woke to thick smoke filling the house. I left the baby on the floor, raced into the kitchen, and pulled the charred pie out of the oven and tossed it onto a snowbank in the backyard. Then I opened all the windows and doors in the house and started crying. *Screw this buzzer,* I thought. Screw this broken buzzer and this Northern gas oven that I didn't know how to control. The baby, who was low on the floor, in the only space free of smoke, woke up and started screaming. Every time she cried, it made my milk flow, and two wet circles appeared on the front of my sweatshirt and grew clammy in the cold air that was beginning to fill the house.

By the time my husband drove up, the pie was generating a

cylindrical smoke signal straight up through the neighborhood like a beacon leading him home. He found me in the kitchen weeping softly and fanning the smoke out of the open windows while the baby roared from her smoke-free space on the floor.

"I cannot seem to make this pie," I said.

"I'll go buy a pie." He picked up the baby, who yelled into his face.

"No. We can't. I said we would bring a home-baked pie. It's not that hard to do. I've done it a dozen times. And besides, if I stay in this house one more minute, I'm going to lose it." He rocked the baby back and forth and held his keys up on one finger.

At the Star Market, I was hefting the fresh pumpkins in the produce aisle, my eyes burning with fatigue, when I had a new thought: *Fuck this pie.* I went to the baking aisle and bought Libby's canned spiced pumpkin pie mix, and a ready-bake crust already in the pie plate, covered sweetly in a circle of wax paper to protect the tender, unbaked crust that looked every bit as good as the one I had spent forty-five minutes making two times over. My problem was solved, even if it was a hinky solution.

That night we almost called the nuns over for an exorcism. We passed the baby back and forth while she screamed so hard she vomited. We waited for her head to spin around. She writhed in our arms and hollered until each of us wanted to fling her, at which point we would pass her off to the other person and go and stand outside on the back porch in the snow, thinking of pre-baby days where we could do the things we wanted, normal things, like reading the paper sitting down, or taking a shower, *or baking a pie.* At two, the baby finally fell asleep on my husband's chest, and I put together the canned pie mix and baked it in the prepackaged crust. I sat in the kitchen and watched the clock, checking the pie every ten minutes while I drank several cups of coffee. It took fifty-five minutes from start to finish and I was pleased with myself. By this point, I had slept perhaps three hours out of the last sixty and I had never before felt so odd without having been ill. In the few moments before I finally fell asleep, I saw briefly, out of the corner of my eye, a small giraffe bending down to take a bite of the area rug in my bedroom.

We awoke the next morning to the memory of the previous day's storm, to rays of sun passing through the lace dining room curtains, to a peaceful, pink-cheeked baby, a dirty kitchen that still smelled like smoke, and one perfect, deceptively un-homemade pie in the fridge. I had slept four hours in a row, straight through to six A.M., for the first time since the baby was born.

That afternoon we left Boston and drove to a nearby town with rolling hills and old colonials, a town I had never seen before, to break bread with the Bluebloods, the kind of proper New England family most people only read about. This was a family that went way back. A family that had a summer place in Maine or maybe on Cape Cod. A family that used different sets of silver for different occasions. A family that liked a completely homemade Thanksgiving. I held the pie on my lap like a Fabergé egg while the baby slept in the backseat like an angel. The snow that covered the Massachusetts hills turned the region into a series of postcards, and for a few minutes, I didn't miss the South.

You don't have to talk much when you show up to a place with a new baby. They take your things quickly, unburden you of your coat and your diaper bag and your baby. They shove you down in a chair and begin drilling you with questions, while holding the baby improperly, in ways you know she doesn't like. But you are so happy that you are not holding the baby for once that you let it happen, you ignore the thought of germs marching up their hands and arms and onto the baby's face, and you sit back. They ask you questions about the baby that one might ask about a new pet: How much does she sleep? How much does she weigh? What does she eat? Does she do any tricks?

These Bluebloods, eight in all, were gracious and proper and well educated. They read the classics and talked about them. They loved tradition and their vocabularies far exceeded mine. I felt like a hillbilly at the White House, and in situations like that, I knew to keep my mouth shut, so I sat quietly and smiled, and drank whatever aperitif they handed me in Great-Great-Great-Grandmother Blueblood's sherry glass that had come over on the *Mayflower*. The baby slept sweetly. Before I knew it, I had downed two Lillets and a Dubonnet, nibbling on salted nuts while they talked about things I didn't understand but grew increasingly interested in as the alcohol took effect. When the baby woke up and mewed politely, I asked to be excused and Mrs. Blueblood guided me into a room not too far off the living room. When I walked, I felt my body pitch, and realized I was buzzed for the first time in many months.

Alone in the dim, well-appointed Queen Anne office, I sat in a wingback chair and nursed my daughter. All traces of yesterday's demon baby were gone, and she pressed against my bare chest and placed her rosebud fingers on my swollen breast. I touched her tiny nails. I could feel her relax, and the relief from the pressure of my boob while she drained it was magnificent. My body had begun to reward me with the hormones it gives new mothers—warm, happy, satisfied hormones—and I sat back in the chair, reminded of a nursing sow lying flat out on her side in an oxytocin-induced stupor, drunk with pleasure. While she nursed, I cried silent, happy tears that leaked out of my eyes and rolled down my cheeks. About fifty percent of the time we did this I cried in this way and it, too, was not unpleasant.

Another thing they don't tell you about when you have a baby is the amount of leaking there will be, and not just from the baby. Any time the baby cried, my breasts leaked milk. If I heard a baby cry on television, my breasts leaked milk. Occasionally when I simply thought about the baby, my eyes leaked tears, though I was not unhappy. Once in a while, when caught unawares and I didn't tighten up in time, I peed when I laughed. They make products for each of these things and, in fear of losing control of something, either myself or the baby, I bought them all.

Breast pads are round, white pads made out of the same material as menstrual pads. They stick onto the inside of your bra and absorb the milk that leaks out of you every time you think about your baby. When the baby nurses from the left breast, the right breast leaks like a faucet, and you usually need to hold a breast pad up to it, or face squirting your lap, or the baby's legs, or anyone else in the room with you. I bought these breast pads, along with pads for leaking pee when I laughed, and extra tissues, and baby wipes for all the leaking the baby's back end did, and the rubber bulb for sucking up all the leaking the baby's nose did, and the plastic pads to put the baby on when changing her diaper, and many, many diapers, and the bibs to catch all the leaking that came from her face, and the spit-up towels to throw over my shoulder to catch the prodigious, spontaneous, post-meal mouth leaking. I kept all these things in a giant soft-sided trunk they called a diaper bag, and carried it everywhere I went, in case of emergency.

The baby was tiny enough to have no room in her digestive system for both new food and waste, so whenever she ate, she crapped, a full gastro-colic reflex, like a bird or a fish would do. I finished nursing her, then changed her diaper on top of the plastic baby-changing pad that came with the new diaper bag. In the dim light, I folded a tiny triangle out of the baby wipe, and I cleaned the poop out of the folds of her labia and her belly button. Baby poop moves forward, too, as well as back, and often leaks out of the top of the diaper, another thing they don't tell you. I rolled the soiled wipes in the old diaper and put the rolled-up diaper in its special pocket in the diaper bag. Then I snapped up the baby's little green velour footie suit, folded up the diaper-changing pad, and changed my breast pads. It was growing dark, and I fumbled with all of the equipment while joggling the baby, whom I wanted to keep happy. Outside the door I heard the stirrings of polite conversation, the kind you might hear through the door of a probate attorney's office, and a clinking of glasses and appetizer plates.

I adjusted my nursing bra, reswaddled the baby, stuffed everything into the diaper bag, and headed out with the baby over one shoulder and the diaper bag over the other. Eight Blueblood faces met mine with interest at first, and then I noticed my husband's eyes grow wide. In fact, when I stepped toward him, I saw him glance down at my long, black skirt, and then back up at my face, frantically. I understood this to be some sort of message, but I couldn't process it fast enough. David Blueblood, his hair perfect, his white shirt crisp, who had been walking from the kitchen into the living room, reached for my skirt, pressing his tie into his chest as he bent down, and said, "Hullo, what's this?" Then he plucked a used breast pad, which I had missed, off the hem of my skirt. He held it up in front of the group, turned it in the light, and squinted.

"It's a breast pad, David. I'll take it," I said. My face felt purple, and I would like to have died right there, but probably not as much as David Blueblood, who blanched, and attempted to fling the pad out of his grasp, but was unable to because the sticky side was stuck fast onto his fingers.

"Oh, God!" As soon as he said this, the baby flinched and urped up the contents of her stomach over my shoulder, down my black sweater, and onto the Bluebloods' expensive Persian rug. I peeled the breast pad off David Blueblood's fingers and stood there with it. The baby started to scream.

From the squash and sour cream soup, through the turkey and stuffing, the gracious Bluebloods passed the angry baby around the table, from person to person like a hot potato. They joggled and rocked her, switched her positions when she fussed, ignored her matter-of-factly when she was good. They talked over her as if it was a matter of course, and perfectly natural to be sharing a holiday meal with a tiny, screaming troll. The alcohol I consumed had long since stopped me from being embarrassed, and by the time they were making coffee and setting out the dessert sherry, I was cockeyed with dinner wine, feeling no pain, and in love with the Blueblood family. *I could become a New Englander,* I thought. *Things are so practically handled with a rolling of the shirtsleeves and an opening of the hands, with earnest emphasis on the homemade, the traditional, the family. They aren't even bothered by this baby, who is ruining everything. They have a wisdom,* I decided. I was looking forward to pumpkin pie, to my pumpkin pie, to sharing my pumpkin pie with these kind people, who had only given of themselves graciously and asked nothing in return.

By now it was dark and the table was ornamented with small crystal glasses that caught the light of the chandelier, fine little spoons, round, feminine bits of silver coffee service, and thin, see-through porcelain plates. The women of the family began to bring out the dessert lineup: a dark chocolate cranberry tart, a pound cake that weighed over a pound, a light, puffy Marlborough pie, a bronze apple pie so perfect it looked like a photo, a chocolate pie, chocolate-dipped candied ginger sticks, and my desperate, criminal, fake-homemade pumpkin pie.

"Almost every recipe on this table came from one of our great-grandmothers," Mrs. Blueblood said. "It's important to keep the tradition going." Everyone agreed. They went for the pumpkin first. They held their plates out.

"This looks good," they said. "Who did this pie?"

"I did." I sipped my sherry.

"Homemade and with a new baby, too? This is wonderful. You didn't have to do that."

I smiled around the table. This *was* wonderful. They weren't going to know a thing.

"You are a marvelous young woman," someone said. It echoed around the table. I felt warm and accepted. My husband looked at me, raised his eyebrows, and stirred his coffee. The baby sat facing outward at the table, leaning against David Blueblood's chest, blinking calmly, her tiny fingers grasping his. They sliced my pie and passed it around. They dug in. Mrs. Blueblood took the first bite, chewed for a moment, then pulled something long and white and pulpy from her mouth. Everyone else chewed and pulled from their mouths something long and white and pulpy. I quickly cut into my pie with my fork and pulled it apart. Inside, between the crust and the filling, was the white circle of protective wax paper that had come in the store-bought pie crust packaging. I had been too tired to notice it when I was cooking, and had baked it into the pie. As they extracted the wax paper strings from their mouths, they looked at me, eight pairs of pale New England eyes, steeped in tradition. I was too tipsy to cry at this point, but the baby wasn't, so she started right up again and did it enough for the both of us.

FEAR OF FALLING

Soon after the birth of my first daughter, I developed a fear of flying; more specifically, a fear of dying in an airplane crash. The airplane ride itself: fun. Fine. The crash, if it must happen . . . okay, I suppose. They say it's fast and everybody has to go sometime. As long as your affairs are in order, it's better than withering away in a hospital bed or being eaten by a pack of dogs. It was the idea of falling toward Earth before the crash that scared me, because I know what my imagination does to me. It is impressive and unchecked, wide open and resistance-free, like a superconductor, complete with sights and sounds and smells and goose bumps and decision-altering, conceptual baggage that rarely materializes. I had a baby now, a responsibility to raise a child up in the ways she should go, until she no longer needed me. The thought that I would have time to ponder, in those few minutes of free fall before we hit the ground, all the things I would leave behind undone, was too much.

    This fear developed out of the blue when my daughter was six weeks old, on a return flight home to Boston after visiting family down South. We were settling into our row, which was near the toilet, and I could hear the metallic flush of waste and smell the eau de colonic leftovers each time someone opened and closed the thin-paneled bathroom door. That door was so flimsy, I thought, as I watched a fat man close it shut behind him. It wobbled. It looked like it was made of fiberglass, like it would crumble with the slightest of challenges. I looked out the window. What was this plane made of anyway? It appeared to be metal, but what if it was fiberglass, or worse, the same kind of plastic they had started making car bumpers out of? What did they even make planes out of, and why hadn't I taken the time to learn how two stupid engines could keep a seven-hundred-thousand-pound bullet in the sky for hours at a time? I understood no physics and my lack of knowledge felt extremely limiting all of a sudden. I began to sweat. My husband helped me to settle our daughter's car seat into the middle seat between us, and when we clicked the seat buckle, I was stricken by the thinness of the belt, the impossibility of a scratched metal buckle to protect this baby in the event of a crash.

Panic swelled up in my throat and I had a quick, startlingly detailed image of the airplane at thirty thousand feet, sun glinting off the metal wing etched with thousands of tiny scratches, ripping in half and plunging out of the sky. My husband, because he is a tall man, was quickly decapitated by a sharp piece of debris that flew across the top of the seats, and the baby's car seat was sucked out of the hole. I had no choice but to leap out after it, pointing and rocketing down toward it, then wrapping my arms around it, watching my howling daughter's perfectly oval face while we fell at 120 miles per hour. This thought worked at the speed of a neuron, and before the flight attendants could sit down, I was up, tugging at the car seat, and headed for the closed-off door of the plane.

"I can't do this. I have to get off." I announced this to no one in particular. Two flight attendants shot up the aisle after me, and my husband pushed past them. He wrenched the baby out of my hands, pinched me in the crook of the elbow, and said, "Everybody's staring at us. Get back in your seat."

"This airplane's going to go down," I said. "I'm going to die before I get a chance to raise this baby." I remember saying that out loud, which, I must say, was articulate of me. I could feel the stares while we walked back down the aisle, but I didn't care. This was before 9/11 and heightened security, and I was simply a nutty young mom, not a security threat.

"You're embarrassing me," my husband said through a fake smile.

He put the baby in the window seat, buckled her up, sat in the middle between us, then buckled me, then himself. He put a hand on my forearm and gripped it so tightly that I couldn't get up.

"Let me off this plane," I said. "It doesn't feel right." He gripped my arm tighter. At six weeks postpartum, hormones can be unstable, and lead women to believe things that may not be true. In my mind, I was rational.

"Stop it. We're going home. You're flying." The baby and I both started crying. He looked at the seat back in front of him and didn't speak to me again. Of course we made it home with no trouble—planes don't crash from anxious, accidental telekinesis—but there was a distance between us after that. I had shown a side of me that neither of us had known existed, an irrational side, a weakness, yet a strange, primal urge for survival that had nothing to do with my husband. It wasn't attractive to him.

After the trip, I felt unsettled and sad, though my baby was healthy and beautiful and perfect. Often, I would daydream while nursing her, seeing, instead of her losing her first tooth, or carving a pumpkin, or doing the long jump, or going on her first date, images of starving children with flies in their eyes, rotten meat, acres of garbage, beatings, immolations, bloated whale carcasses washed up on the shore. I would feel a spinning in the room that would cause me to hold tight to the baby, lest she be torn out of my hands. Because my husband had shown he was not interested in my irrational thoughts, I did not tell him how I felt. I was ashamed and afraid of what would happen if I did share them. Gradually, things got better, but it took until well after my daughter's first birthday. I toughed it out because I didn't know any better.

When my daughter was seventeen months old, I got pregnant again. My hormones minded themselves this time and I felt wonderful throughout most of the pregnancy, but within a few weeks after the birth of my second daughter, I began having trouble thinking clearly and I felt worse than I ever had in my life. I developed intrusive thoughts that wouldn't go away, largely based on a belief that something I accidentally did would kill the baby. Unlike flying, an event-based fear that I had solved by deciding to never fly again, these thoughts were with me every day.

Around suppertime, I would put the baby in the wind-up swing in the kitchen, crank it up, and let her swing while I cooked. My older daughter would play with her toys nearby. Within a few days, I had to move the swing several feet out of the kitchen because I had recurring thoughts of the butcher's knife, which I had used adroitly for years, somehow tumbling out of my grip and piercing the baby through her fontanel. I was afraid to walk her outside because we lived at the top of a large hill and I had thoughts of losing my grip on the stroller handle and sending her plummeting down into traffic at the bottom of the hill. I was also afraid to bathe her, because I was sure that, despite my good intentions, and despite my two years of baby-bathing experience, I would lose hold of her soapy body and she would slide down under the shallow water of the baby bath and drown, and if she didn't die right away, the bathwater she inhaled would set off a pneumonia that would kill her.

Worse than this, I was afraid to tell my husband, or anyone else.

I was afraid that they would take my children away from me, or put me in the nuthouse, so I managed it by force of will, with the irrationality of it bleeding outside the lines of normalcy like a stain.

During this time, the monster of my hypochondria reared its nasty head, like it does when I have troubles of any sort; I also became obsessed with the beginning of my own end. I began to prod my breasts for lumps. Every day I found several—I was breastfeeding after all, and the ducts were impressively lumpy because they were full of milk, not tumors. These lumps would cause a spinning fear that would take over and ruin, several times per day, whatever I happened to be doing—coloring with my older daughter, watching the baby make funny faces, reading, hanging laundry, stirring a sauce. When this happened, I had a sensation of falling that made me break out in a sweat, and called for me to grab on to things.

I compulsively inspected my skin for mole changes, felt my groin and armpits and clavicles and jawline for swollen glands. I was exhausted from being up in the middle of the night with a new baby, but hormonal logic, an oxymoron if there ever was one, told me that it must be leukemia, or lymphoma, or lupus, and not simple exhaustion. Every headache that developed was a brain tumor, but not a minor-league, benign one—a mac daddy astrocytoma that would leave my daughters to one day button up their own wedding dresses. I did not know to diagnose myself with what I really had, although I did learn to stop sharing my feelings with my husband. I was too embarrassed, and my husband had no room for crazy in his marriage.

"You're too sensitive," he would say when I tried to bring it up, which is what everyone in my life has always told me. "You have two perfectly healthy daughters and all you do is worry about ridiculous things. I don't understand." I would try to explain how I felt, but when I did, he stopped responding to me. He would turn his back on me in the kitchen, or in bed, and I was left alone with my thoughts, embarrassed and ashamed of my weakness. Besides, I did have two healthy daughters and a nice life, and I felt guilty for having these thoughts.

I would read *Goodnight Moon* to the girls before tucking them in for the night, weeping quietly in their dark bedroom because I was about to lie down for the night myself, and I might get a blood clot in my sleep, because Margaret Wise Brown, the author of *Goodnight Moon,* had died from a blood clot after flinging her leg in the air while abed. At night, I would crawl into my bed afraid that I wouldn't wake up the next morning, and what was worse, my daughters would be raised by a man who wouldn't say nice things about me to them after I was gone.

One night, when the baby was almost twelve weeks old, I awoke with a strange pain in my abdomen that caused me to think suspiciously about the obscene mound of baked cauliflower I had eaten for supper. Cauliflower usually ignites in me a prodigious, occasionally debilitating gas factory that I freely use as a weapon against others, but if this were gas, I had outdone myself. Although there was nothing vague about the pain—it was acute and very real—I could not pinpoint its origin. It was high enough to be a pancreas or gallbladder, yet low enough to be an appendix. In my misery, I executed my German grandmother's trick of lying on your stomach with the buttocks in the air—the gas rises and you soon have the relief you are seeking, at the expense of anyone else in the room—but in this instance, nothing helped. I switched position, and took a deep breath. Nothing changed. I shook my husband awake.

"Something's wrong," I told him. "I have to go to the hospital."

"What is it?"

"I have a pain in my side. It's bad."

"You're joking."

"I'm not."

"What do you want me to do, drive you?"

"I don't think I can drive."

"Well, we can't get the girls up in the middle of the night, and we can't leave them alone."

"Something's really wrong. I've got to go in. Where are the keys?"

"On my dresser."

I crawled over him, and pulled pants on under my nightgown, hunched, unable to stand up straight, or even place my feet on the ground without pain shooting through me.

"I have to leave for work by eight." He rolled over toward the window before I left the room.

Real pain will quickly eclipse any sentimental thought of suffering and death. I was in too much pain to cry, in too much pain to worry that my husband didn't seem concerned, and in too much pain to worry about dying. In fact, the pain was so severe that I quickly began to believe that death was a better option than feeling the way I did. I drove down the dark, empty, shiny Boston streets, hollering out loud in agony, the echo of my voice filling the empty car. My goal was to stay in the right lane and not crash. I followed the subway tracks to Beth Israel Hospital, pulled up to the emergency room main entrance, left the car running, and walked in through the double doors, where I managed to notice a terribly shiny measure of seafoam tiles and chrome chairs. For some reason I had time to think, *I don't want to die here; it's too reflective,* before vomiting all over the waxed tile floors and passing out.

I woke up on a gurney in a room to the smell of rubbing alcohol. A thick, red-bearded man bent over me to start an IV. I thought he was Jesus. I rolled my head and vomited off the gurney.

"Am I dying?" I asked.

"No, ma'am."

"Oh, God, would you please kill me then?" The pain would not allow me to sit still, so I tried to crawl up the back of the gurney. I draped myself over the top and vomited again.

The nurse pushed a button and an intercom came on. "Page housekeeping, please," he said. "Hold on there, little mama, I'm going to give you some morphine as soon as we get some information from you."

The next five hours were spent giving blood and getting tests. I would sleep in a lovely morphine stupor filled with crystal snowflakes rotating and falling, then turning, without warning, into sour faces that bit out at me. I would wake periodically to revisit the pain, retch into a pan, then fall back to sleep, only to feel like I was falling backwards, headfirst off the gurney, before the snowflakes started up again. The nurse came in periodically to check on me. A CT scan had identified a very tiny stone in my right kidney. It was my job to pee it out, they told me, and they gave me several quarts of IV fluids and a strainer. I hobbled up every fifteen minutes to either throw up or whizzle bloodred urine into the toilet. Around sunrise I peed out a grain of dark sand, which, when I looked at it closely, looked like a jagged, knife-edged moon rock with an evil face carved in it. I had a hard time believing this was the stone.

"That's it?" I asked the nurse. "It's a speck."

He peered into the strainer. "Looks like it. Lucky you."

"So I'm not going to die?"

"Why, do you want to?" He winked.

"Sometimes," I said, and he stopped what he was doing and looked at me. Maybe the morphine had loosened my tongue, but I told him about the perseverations, about the fears I had of accidentally killing the baby, about crying every day, about how I spent the previous afternoon in the rocking chair holding the baby with two hands, the house getting dark in the early-spring light, my older daughter playing in the cold fireplace with a shovel and a bunch of ashes. I told him I was afraid that the house would burn down when I turned on the stove, and that when I sat quietly, I could feel the Earth spinning on its axis, and that if I let go of the girls, they would fly off and fall into space.

"How old is your baby?" he asked.

"Three months."

"You probably have postpartum depression, sweetie. Women get it all the time. You'll get over it when your hormones regulate, but you need to tell your doctor. Call them as soon as you get home. Will you do that?"

I drove myself home, against the doctor's advice, in a morphine haze, just in time for my husband to meet me at the door and hand me the baby.

"You okay?" he asked.

"Kidney stone," I said. "And postpartum depression, I think." I handed him back the baby and went to lie down on the couch. Aftershocks of pain shot through my flank and down my leg, and I was weak and shaking. The baby started a low cry that rolled into a full boil within fifteen seconds.

"Is it out? Good. Here, can you nurse her? She's about to blow." He handed her back. She screamed in my arms and rooted for my breast.

"I can't. They gave me morphine. I have to pump and dump for twenty-four hours."

"There's a bottle on the counter. Sorry, but I have to leave." And he did have to leave. I knew this. He was very dependable and took his work deadlines seriously, and to my recollection, never missed one.

I cried when he left, grateful that there was a name to what I had, and oddly happy to know that I wasn't the only one it happened to. If there were others, I thought, I could find them. I could tell a doctor and they wouldn't take my children away from me. Maybe my husband would understand. I slept randomly and dangerously throughout the day. I woke once, during lunch, with my head on the kitchen table, to my two-year-old trying to see if a green bean would fit inside the nostril of her tiny sister, who was at least in the baby swing, and not out in the yard somewhere. And most important, I called my doctor and made an appointment.

My husband and I made it three more years and one more baby before we said the word "divorce," and though we both tried hard to make it work, we were terribly ill-suited for each other. I think the beginning of the end was that day on the airplane when I was so afraid of falling out of the sky, of losing control. The day I showed the vulnerability that comes when you give birth, the vulnerability that comes when your body takes over by creating a baby inside of it, then turns you inside out, then rights itself again, as if it had been through a storm. What my husband could have done that day was ask me why I was afraid. What he could have done was hug me, and tell me we weren't going to fall out of the sky. What he could have said was, "You're not going to die, hon. You're scared because this is new. You're a little kooky because your hormones need to get back to normal. We're going to have a great life. Besides, it's not the falling that kills you, silly. It's the landing. Here, hold my hand."

FM D&R—1-10.06

*Field Manual—Divorce and Remarriage: Suburban Ops
Headquarters: Department of Suburbia, USA*

Distribution Restriction: Distribution authorized to the DOSA
(Department of Suburban Affairs) and DOFF (Department of Fractured Families) contractors only to maintain operations security.
Other requests for this document must be referred to HMFMWIC
(Head Motherfucker Mom What's in Charge), US Suburban Ops Combined Arms Center 1 Rue de Cul de Sac (Building X), Fort Lauderdale,
FL 33301.

Destruction Notice: Destroy by any method that will prevent disclosure of contents or reconstruction of the document.

PREFACE

PURPOSE

This Field Manual establishes doctrine for nonmilitary operations
in a divorce and remarriage (D&R) environment. It is based on

existing doctrine and lessons learned from recent combat operations. Additional D&R doctrine is being developed.

SCOPE

To make this text useful to agents involved in D&R operations re-
gardless of where these operations may occur, the doctrine con-
tained herein is broad in scope and involves principles applicable to
various D&Rs. This FM is not focused on any region or country.
Most divorces have some common characteristics, but their ideo-
logical basis may vary widely. Fundamental to all D&R operations
is the need to help local agents establish safety, security, and stabil-
ity, because divorce thrives on chaos and instability.

APPLICABILITY

The primary audience for this manual is conventional-force leaders
at division level and below. It supports Suburban Ops Education
System instruction on the theory and conduct of D&R operations.

1. THE DETONATION OF BOMBS

1.1. It was the day after Halloween and I was still finding green
      greasepaint in the ears and neck folds of my two-year-old, who
      swore she had wanted to go trick-or-treating as a witch, though
      when she saw her Hulk-green face in the mirror she scared her-
      self to tears. It was raining hard outside and I was exhausted
      from being up nearly all night feeding the four-month-old, who,
      due to his cleft palate, ate every two hours around the clock. My
      husband had gone to work and to class, and I was looking at a
      long day alone with the kids in a tiny apartment. I sat down at
      the computer and moved the mouse. The screen opened up to a
      series of e-mails from my husband's coworker, who I realized,

after reading the e-mails, wasn't simply his coworker, but perhaps the love of his life. It explained a lot. When he got home that night I didn't say anything. I didn't say anything the rest of the week. I didn't say anything for almost a month, until Thanksgiving week rolled around and he had decided to stay in town for a few extra days while I went home to South Florida. I told him I found the e-mails and we had the conversation that started it all and ended it all at the same time, the conversation that wrapped the children up in little duct-taped bomb vests, set the timer, and began the countdown.

"It's either her or us," I said. "Your choice."

"Her," he said simply. Three. Two. One.

Boom.

2. MANAGING THE DECOMPOSITION OF CASUALTIES AFTER BATTLE

2.1. We had moved to Florida for my husband's graduate school, which I suspect was a last-ditch attempt at keeping the marriage together, and we were living in married student housing provided by the university. So many times, right before a couple breaks up, they either move to a new place, or, if they have means, they renovate or have a house built, as if this fresh start will wipe the slate clean of all the war crimes committed in the name of love and jealousy and immaturity and misunderstanding, as if a move across the country, or the building of a custom home, will take the weight off the big one that is poised to detonate.

Over Christmas break, my husband moved to another apartment the university had temporarily allotted for our breakup, and one night, after I had gone to bed, he came over and packed his half of our property, and his own clothes and personal belongings, in liquor store boxes. This made sense, I thought, as I listened to him bang around. He had an early flight the next morning, back up north for New Year's Eve, and had likely wanted to pack before he left.

The baby woke me at sunrise the next morning. I lifted him out of his crib, and carried him into my room, where I changed his diaper and kissed his little feet. Then we went out to the kitchen for breakfast, where I noticed that before he left, my husband had stacked all of the packed boxes nearly to the ceiling, blocking the front door and the front windows, effectively barring us inside. I couldn't even get to the door. Everyone knows divorce makes people do things they would not ordinarily do. I called my mother, sobbing.

"He blocked us inside the apartment, Mom," I said.

"Jesus, who does that? Come home for New Year's," she said.

2.2. We left for my mother's right after breakfast. During the five-hour drive, I fantasized about pulling over on the side of the road for a long nap. Whenever the girls talked to me, I could think of nothing to say, so we put in CDs and sang all the songs we knew. When I got home, I handed the baby to my mother and lay down on the living room floor, where both my mother's dogs and my other children climbed on top of me.

"God help me," I said through the pile.

"It'll be all right," my mother said.

The next day I stretched out on the couch and cried whenever the kids weren't looking.

"Why don't you go take a shower or something," my mother said, when she saw me stifling a sob into a couch pillow.

I sat down in the middle of the shower and let the water run over me until I could catch my breath, then put my head on the

bathroom tile and watched a row of sugar ants walk a complicated path of grout line, and out a tiny crack in the sliding glass
door. I thought, *I could die right here and it wouldn't matter. I
would be a simple war casualty. People would absorb the kids.
They were young. They would get over losing me.* I lay there and
waited for the sugar ants to find a hole into my brain and jump-
start the decomposition process by carting my parts back to their
place. Eventually, my mother knocked on the bathroom door.

"Are you okay?"

"No. I think I'm dying," I said.

"I'm coming in." She opened the door and helped me sit up.
I sat there wrapped in my towel, too spent to cry, and she sat
next to me on the floor and held my head.

"You're not dying," she said. "You're just going through a
divorce. It's not the end of the world. You'll see."

"I don't believe you," I told her. "What am I going to do with
these kids? They're wrecked. I'm wrecked. No one's ever going
to love me."

"Sure they will."

"I'm never getting married again."

"Sure you will," she said. She laughed and patted my arm.

"Watch me not," I said.

That night, I got dressed up, went out with some old friends,
and the world rang in the millennium while my mother put my
children to bed. As we started the countdown amidst clots of
clutched lovers, amidst rockets of streamers, and spilled champagne and crooked hats, amidst sloppy, drunk kissers and
donkey horns, it occurred to me that I was out past midnight
and my children would be getting up as soon as the first bird
squawked in the tree outside their bedroom window. It would
be months before I stopped telling people that love was a farce,

that I would never marry again, that anyone even thinking of partnering up was a fool.

3. FRATERNIZING WITH THE ENEMY

3.1. Our uncoupling was ugly in all of the ways of war, full of distrust, head games, threats, spies, broken treaties, battles, and roentgens of fallout. I suppose there are other kinds of divorce, but I haven't met anyone who has had any other kind than this. Perhaps if two childless, wealthy sociopaths without the ability to emotionally attach, or two childless Buddhists with lovingkindness in their hearts, were to get divorced, there would be another kind of divorce, but the only kind I know makes you hurt for a long time, and what's more, you can see the people who rely on you going down with the ship through no fault of their own. Highlights of my divorce include being evicted from married student housing with three kids under the age of six, moving into a broken-down rental house in a shoddy neighborhood with money my father gifted me, applying for welfare and food stamps, which I was told could take months to kick in, and waiting for the assistance with the sort of pre-panic you feel when you are on the highway and you notice the car is almost on E and you have miles to go before the next exit.

3.2. My newly exed husband was in the process of moving back up north to where we had lived. The divorce was final in April, three weeks before Easter. A few weeks after we signed the paperwork and walked crying out of the courtroom, he had a U-Haul packed and was ready to leave. He came over to have supper with us at our new spooky house before he left, bringing Thai food in the little cardboard boxes the girls loved. We ate together one last time, though we were no longer a family, then he tucked the children in for the night, which must have been confusing. I told them, "Say good-bye to Daddy. When you wake up in the morning he will be driving his truck to Boston. When you wake up in the morning, he will be halfway there." What I should have said, so they would understand, was, "When you wake up in the morning, Daddy will be gone."

3.3. While the children slept, we moved to the living room for an emotional debriefing. We listened to music while lying in the dark on the living room floor, getting drunk on an expensive Schorschbock beer made from 30 percent alcohol, almost powerful enough to take the sting out of what we were doing. We talked about music, specialty beers, and anything but the disaster of our marriage, or the children, or our separate futures, topics that felt off-limits in the way they are off-limits during a first date. Not looking at each other felt fine. We went to my room and lay down together for the last time, fully clothed, on top of the covers. My heart, which always had an independent streak, immediately started to beat funny, and later, I would look back on this as the first night I experienced an arrhythmia that would plague me for years.

"Do you feel that?" I asked, though I hated to bring it up. My hypochondriasis was always one of the hardest things for him to take about me. He was behind me, with his arms wrapped around my rib cage.

"Yes," he said.

"I don't know what that is," I said. We lay there in the dark, without words, eyes wide open, feeling my heart gallop wildly until it was time for him to go. Then he left.

In the morning the girls woke up and started running around the house looking for their daddy. My oldest looked out the front window for his truck. My middle girl woke her brother.

"Daddy's gone," I said. "Remember?" And all four of us started to cry.

4. BANDAGING THE WOUNDED

4.1. After blowing you up, divorce will run you down. People who say that children are resilient and will recover well from divorce are on the pipe. I don't know anyone who has gone through a divorce who isn't fundamentally changed, and my children were no exception. Even as young kids, when they were supposed to be unburdened and malleable, they were affected by the combustion, and I am certain it still affects them. My oldest child became immediately distrustful of anyone's intentions; my middle child, who barely talked as it was, spoke about half as much; and my baby, who didn't seem to know any better, *somehow knew everything* and was sick all the time. In fact, the three of them seemed to be perpetually open for business to every bacterium or virus that floated through their airspace during that first year, and you can't tell me that their burning fevers and diarrhea and constant runny noses were not a statement of protest, physical proof of their susceptibility to an onslaught of all sorts of attacks, both physical and psychic, rolled up into one ball of nose pus or a virulent enterovirus, or chronic, dry hack of a cough that left their throats hot and croaky, and woke me in the middle of the night.

4.2. During the Fourth of July weekend, my middle child developed a wet cough and told me her chest hurt.

"Where, baby?" I asked.

She pointed to her heart, and while I had melodramatic thoughts of both pericarditis and the metaphoric emotional pain of having her family ripped apart, logic said it was a simple virus. I pulled her onto my lap and put my hand on her breastbone. It was summer, too hot for a fever, yet she had one.

"I'm going to call the doctor."

"Dust put a Band-Aid on it," she offered, with her little lisp. "Band-Aids make it better."

This child was Band-Aid obsessed. She put them on her baby dolls, she put them on bruises, she put them on me when I was napping, she put them on her little brother. Once I found one on the wall, covering some crayon scramble she had surreptitiously drawn. She could go through a box a day like an addict, if I left them within her reach. I got out my stash, peeled a neon green one, and asked her where she wanted it.

"Wight here." She pointed to a spot where there was already a Band-Aid. I pulled the old one off and pressed the new one gently into the middle of her chest. During this year, I put Band-Aids on anybody who wanted one, wherever they wanted them, no questions asked.

4.3. All three of them fell sick with the virus on the Fourth of July, which was also my birthday. I made some red, white, and blue cupcakes while they barfed their guts out. At dusk, I propped them up in the side yard with some sparklers, then put them to bed. They were asleep before sunset, the fever riding through their dreams like a dark horse, while Kurt Vonnegut and I ate cupcakes alone in my room. I read until the sun came up because I was afraid someone would break in through the sliding glass door in the bedroom and murder me in my sleep on my birthday.

5. RATIONS AND DELIVERY OF MRES

5.1. It is hard to get a job in a college town, especially when you are one zombie in several thousand shuffling around with a use-less BA tucked under your inked-up arm, advertising your tutoring service on Craigslist or competing with undergrads for all the part-time Starbucks and Home Depot and FedEx jobs. I had finished college in a hurry while pregnant with one, two, then three kids, once I saw the marriage circling the drain, but now that I had the degree in my fist, I could not find a job, as my only work history was in the restaurant business and in baby making. My children were also so physically and emo-tionally needy that I couldn't seem to make it to an interview. Every time I landed one, a kid would magically get sick right about the time I was putting on lipstick and giving final in-structions to the sitter, with whom I had to barter house-cleaning because I had no money. I rescheduled one interview so many times they told me I had used up all the sick days allot-ted to an employee for a year simply trying to make it to the interview.

5.2. We spent our days drawing and coloring, reading library books, splashing in a baby pool I set up in the carport, and hanging laundry on the line so I could keep the electric bill down. On windy nights, the old, untrimmed oak trees scraped the sides of our house and my oldest daughter, who was six, would run cry-ing into my bed, afraid that someone was going to break through her bedroom window and murder her in her sleep. I knew where she got it, but I couldn't tell her that I had similar worries. I had to pretend her idea was ridiculous.

5.3. I knew we had hit bottom when we started eating soup I made from Ramen noodles and hot dogs that we got from a food pantry, possibly the least nutritious thing you can feed to a child besides bark and roots. The children called it "bird's nest soup," and I sliced the hot dogs sliver-thin so the baby wouldn't choke on them.

5.4. We made our own Halloween decorations. We cut out pumpkins from the comic pages of the Sunday paper, and put faces on them with old buttons and other bits of cutout paper, then taped them all over the house. We made ghosts from tissues and dental floss, and hung them from the walls until they frightened my middle child and we took them down. On Sunday, two nights before Halloween, right after dark, there was a knock on the door.

I answered it to find seven or eight brown bags lined up on my porch without a human in sight, nor a set of brake lights on the road. I was frightened. I imagined a prank involving clowns, of which I was phobic, or rabbit carcasses, which, frankly, we would have eaten, but would have initially spooked me nonetheless, but when I peeked into one of the bags, I saw two boxes of cereal and a bag of apples. Another one had cans of tomato sauce and dried pasta. Groceries. The girls helped me carry the bags in, and we unpacked fruit, a gallon of milk, a bunch of carrots, frozen hamburger, juice, Bisquick, peanut butter, and frosted windmill cookies. I remain grateful to this day for those mystery groceries. I wouldn't have made it the rest of the month without them, but it was embarrassing to know that other people, to whom I had not spoken about our poverty, could recognize it.

6. SUBURBAN OPS FOR CLEARING A BUILDING

6.1. When we drove to my mother's house for Thanksgiving, it was a relief to sit in a room with other grown-ups and watch the children play. I had help. My generous family had extra laps, extra hands for diaper changes and for screwing on sippy cup lids, and enough patience to read aloud *Go, Dog. Go!* many more times than is psychologically healthy. We watched *Holiday Inn,* which was our family's official start-the-holiday movie, and the girls swirled around the living room in baggy T-shirts and panties, copying Danny Kaye and Vera-Ellen by gliding across the tile in their socks, while my son toddled around in his diaper, weaving in and out of my mother's lace curtains, which were willowing out from the windows in the South Florida breeze.

Thanksgiving Day was a blur. There was cooking, and kid minding, and a houseful of family and friends, and unusual foodstuffs to navigate. One of the girls demanded extra pumpkin pie after dessert, then vomited it right up onto the tile, where the pie held the shape of her esophagus for a brief moment before one of the dogs ate it. After we put the kids to bed, I slumped at the table and picked the turkey carcass clean of meat, then gave it to my mother to boil for soup. I was too exhausted to go to bed. My mother pulled me up out of the chair and led me to my room, as if I were a child.

6.2. On Sunday night we left for home, though I wasn't ready to go back, and my mother drove behind us to the gas station so she could pay for my gas. It was dark and chilly, and the kids were bathed and in their jammies and ready to sleep in their car seats, so when we got home, I could transfer them easily to bed after the long drive.

The lights of the gas station were unforgiving and bright enough to make me squint. I saw my own future face in the wrinkles around my mother's eyes. While we were filling the tank, she put her hand on my arm and said, "Why don't you come home for a year? David and I talked it over. We want you to. You can save some money, start over. We can help with the kids."

"I have a lease, Mom," I said. "I can't."

"Think about it," she said.

6.3. On the drive home, we rolled down all the windows and yelled out of them for "fun." I was trying to keep the children awake until close to their regular bedtime, so they wouldn't start their day at four the next morning, which is what happened after long road trips and disrupted sleep schedules. The cold air blew around the car and made the children frisky, even though they were locked inside their car seats and could only move their hands and their feet and their heads. We sang "The Fox" by Burl Ives twenty-seven times until I nearly screamed the last verse. After the children fell asleep, I thought about moving back home to South Florida, with its traffic, and ugly, flat landscaping, and rude people. *I can't do it,* I decided. I had already escaped it once, and I doubted that, with its viney, gripping tropical plants and ferocious climate, one could achieve that kind of thing twice. Besides, I liked our little college town. We almost had seasons. My oldest was in school. My food stamps had just kicked in, and I had a business idea brewing. The landlord might sue me if I broke the lease, and I didn't have any money to withstand a lawsuit. Besides, I believed that moving home to your parents' house after a divorce was a certain sign of failure.

6.4. By the time we hit Fort Pierce, all three children were sleeping deeply, and the coffee I had drunk to stay awake had metabolized to my bladder. We had hours left to go and I knew I was in trouble. I was going to have to hold it unless I wanted to wake all three children and drag them into a rest stop. I was too afraid of being hit by a car to stop and squat by the side of the road, so I held it. By around ten-thirty, I knew I had a few short minutes before I blew, so at the next rest stop, I found the darkest corner, under the biggest tree, cut my lights, and silently, like a thief dancing through a series of laser lights, crawled past the children in their car seats, past a stray arm cast into the air, past splayed feet, and toys, and a box of food, to the back of the minivan where the luggage was. If those kids heard a car door slam or felt my skin on theirs, they would wake up for the rest of the trip, and it would be no fun for any of us. People without children should know that parents will go to ridiculous lengths to keep their kids from waking up once they have gone to sleep for the night. We will pay money, we will compromise ourselves in many ways, we will lie, we will do whatever it takes, which is why I pulled out one of my daughter's size-five night diapers from her bag, unfolded it, pulled down my jeans, and urinated into the diaper while squatting in the backseat of the minivan. It was a relief until the diaper reached maximum capacity, and I ended up spraying the remaining quart of wee everywhere, soaking the luggage, the laundry basket of clean, folded clothes, the carpet in the minivan, and my own pants and panties. I crawled up and drove the rest of the way home, wet and stinking of urine.

6.5. When we pulled into the carport at one in the morning, I gripped
the baseball bat I kept in the car, my neck and arm hairs pricked
up in fear, pushed open the front door of our shoddy, low-rent
house, and cautiously looked around, prepared to bash out the
brains of anything that moved in the dark. I checked behind all
the doors and curtains, the shower curtain, and inside the closets and the toy box. It was terrifying. When I was sure the place
was clear, I carried my children in one by one, laid them in their
beds, my oldest daughter waking briefly in my arms to say,
"I smell pee," before falling back to sleep. I stood in the kitchen
and realized how empty and dark and ominous things felt. How
alone I really was. I changed my pants and then called my
mother, who was always up at one in the morning. I thanked her
again for her offer, and said that we would be glad to take her up
on it. We were moved in two weeks later, just in time to put up
the Christmas tree.

7. USING PROPAGANDA TO MANIPULATE CIVILIAN EMOTIONS

7.1. My mother and stepfather set the children up in my old bedroom. It was large enough to fit three twin beds, bookcases, and
a variety of low shelves for toys. It was tiled, which was good for
cleaning up the kinds of messes their little bodies were able to
produce: vomit, retched-up red Robitussin, or purple Dimetapp
sneezed through the nose at the wrong time, diarrhea leaked
through the elastic of a night diaper. The emotions of what we
had been through were coming out of their orifices, like shrap-
nel working its way out of the skin.

My mother had given up her home office for my own room.
I pushed the bed into the corner to create enough space for my
desk and computer and fifty-pound tubs of lye and oils for the
handmade soap business I was trying to start. At night, I would

put the children to sleep and make soap until late, before collapsing on the bed and trying to fall asleep myself. Despite being surrounded by little souls who held their arms up for hourly hugs, and a family who rearranged their lives and took my children and me in, I felt like a discard, like a lonely cat, especially after midnight, when my mother's own cats cried forsaken night songs into the sky, and then fought each other against the back-fence line outside my bedroom window.

7.2. Things have to be done after a divorce, no matter how inert you feel. For instance, you need to wake up in the morning and get out of bed. You need to continue to speak to the children, who, despite their confusion, have extraordinary levels of energy and require constant interaction. You hold one child on your hip while you help the other down the slide, then you put one down to push another one on the swing, then you leave that one swinging to help the second one brush his knees off after a fall, then you help the first one back up the slide. You clap and fake-smile. You say "wheeee!" You answer all the questions, you wipe all the noses, you fill all the cups, you give all the baths.

Also, you must manipulate their emotions by telling them how much fun it will be to do things you have no interest in, such as eating a meal, or going to the grocery store, or decorating the Christmas tree. You must lie often in those early months. There is nothing I could ever say to make a newly divorced parent feel better. The first couple of years are the worst.

7.3. My mother and stepfather came home with an extremely tall, thin Christmas tree wrapped tightly in twine. We slid it into the house without knowing much about it, though my stepfather predicted it was going to be too big, like he did every year. We placed the tree in the base, aimed the top for the center of the vaulted ceiling, and screwed it in, while the girls ran around throwing tissue paper from the ornament boxes, singing "Jingle Bells," the "Batman Smells" version, and my son, who had recently mastered the stiff-legged toddle-run, bounced off all of the low objects in the room. I snipped the twine girdling the tree together, and when it exploded several feet outward, the bottom branches knocked my son off his feet. Wrapped up in all that twine was an enormous fat lady of a tree, a tree so magnificent it belonged in a church, or a department store in a midsized city. We started laughing. I picked up my son, who had begun to cry.

"Look at this thing!" my mother said.

"It's too goddamn big is what it is," my stepfather said.

"Watch your language, David," my mother said. "The children."

"It *is* a goddamn big tree," said my oldest, who had just turned six.

"Don't cuss," I said, and she asked, honestly, "Why not? You told Daddy 'Merry fucking Christmas' on the phone last night. I heard you."

8. BASIC RECONNAISSANCE

8.1. The dating site dude's name was Keith. Forty-two, retired navy captain. Divorced, no kids. Lived off his investments. His photo was nice and I liked the idea of career military. It showed that he could follow rules, stay the course, yet I still looked up everything I could find about him without paying for a subscription database. After a week of e-mails, which I used to check his grammar, and another week of phone conversations, which I used to discern if he had the voice of a psychopath, I agreed to meet him at a high-end restaurant/bar in Fort Lauderdale for drinks and a bite to eat. He told me he would be wearing a white linen shirt. Like Jesus.

8.2. I wasn't trying to date because I was lonely. Technically, I wasn't lonely, because I was never alone. Every time I sat down in a chair, children would climb up in my lap. When I went to the toilet, there was a knock on the door from someone who had to ask me an important question right at the glorious crowning moment that makes a bowel movement worth it. Nearly every morning I would wake up with my face pressed against the wall, sleeping like a plank because the three-year-old had snuck in when I wasn't looking and was spread like a snow angel in the middle of the bed. Sometimes a child would be spooning me. Sometimes the bed would be wet with pee and I would be sleeping in it. I wasn't lonely at all. Far from it. What I was trying to do by attempting to date was to prove that I wasn't worthless. Rejected. Unlovable. Unwanted. Unwanted is the worst.

The alarming thing about this is that I had no business dating with young children and no career, and a heart and soul fresh out of the marriage ICU, a big battle scar in the place where relationship knowledge should have been. Anything you do, either with or without your kids, will eventually affect them anyway, so you need to be extremely careful. You must tiptoe through the rest of your life. I shouldn't have tried to date, but I didn't know it then. I was young. I was dumb. I felt so unwanted.

8.3. I put the children to sleep and got dressed up in a skirt for the first time in a year. I put on real earrings, not the puffy Ariel stickers the girls pressed onto my earlobes when I fell asleep. I hugged my mother good-bye and drove into town. The bar was decorated with party store Valentine's Day kitsch, pink and red hearts with strips of plastic bursting forth from them, hanging like fake fireworks from the ceiling tiles, big X and O letters scrawled on the mirrors in lipstick. Everything looked shiny. Keith stood to shake my hand and lilted sideways briefly, and then steadied himself with one hand on the edge of the bar. I could see the beginning of an unfocused glaze in his eyes. Behind the bar was the kind of bartender you would want to hire if you owned a bar—crisp shirt, bright teeth, compassionately tipped eyebrows, cheerfully drying glasses with a white towel. We sat down.

"What are you having?" Keith asked me.

"A cranberry juice," I said.

"She'll have a vodka cranberry," Keith said to the bartender. "And I'll have another Manhattan."

The bartender looked me in the eye as he gave us our drinks. He looked at Keith, then back at me. He raised an eyebrow.

"So," Keith said. "Tell me all about yourself."

"Well, I'm starting a handmade natural soap business and—"

"Imma stop you right there. You know what I like about you? Your legs. They go on forever. You play basketball?" He looked me up and down.

"Not so much," I said. "I'm more into cycling."

"Me too," he said. "I love to cycle. Love it."

"What kind of riding do you do?" I asked.

"I don't actually have a bike right now, but I love cycling. Anything you love, I love." He put his hands on my knee. I looked at the bartender.

"Please don't," I said, and I pushed his hand away.

"Imma go to the head," Keith said. As soon as he left, the bartender leaned in and said, "Did you drive here?" I nodded.

"You need to go. This guy's a creep. A drinker. He brings women here all the time." This scared me. I stood up, but before I could gather my purse, Keith was back, sliding his hand around my waist.

"Listen," I started, "my son is sick. I have to leave." I peeled his arm off me, and walked through the crowd of people to the door. Keith followed me. I walked toward my car and he followed me, bumping into people as he walked. I hadn't realized he was this drunk. At my car, he said, "I made a mistake. I had one too many. Can you drop me off at my house? It's three blocks away."

8.4. I didn't say no when I should have. It was a problem of mine. I unlocked my car door and let him in. He couldn't give me clear directions to his house, so I drove him around for twenty minutes while he babbled about the babies he was going to put in me, and when we found his house, he wouldn't get out of the car. I had to go around to the passenger side and pull him out by his arms. I raced back around to the driver's side, locked my door, and had begun to back down the narrow road when he pulled out a handgun from inside his waistband, pointed it into the air, and shouted, "Nobody tells Keith when the date is over!" He shot once into the air. I peeled out.

8.5. I was still shaking when I unlocked my mother's front door. *You're an idiot,* I thought. *You have children. You have no business ever dating.*

My mother was in the family room, reading. "You're home early," she said. "How was it?"

"I'm an idiot," I said. I stomped past her and went straight to the computer in my room to unsubscribe from the dating site. Right as the arrow of my mouse hovered over the "Delete Profile" button, a new message popped into my inbox. The photo was handsome. Athletic. Ruddy cheeks. He looked like a coach. *Nope,* I thought, *do not click on that,* but something seemed to guide the mouse arrow over to the inbox and I clicked open the message and fell into it like quicksand, though I still don't know how. It was the last week of January, three weeks before Valentine's Day.

9. BREAKING THE RULES OF ENGAGEMENT

9.1. I met the coach at a Mexican restaurant. There was a waiting list, so they gave us a small plastic box and told us to come to the hostess desk when the box began to buzz. We sat outside on a bench and talked while we waited. He showed up dressed like a coach: khakis with sneakers, polo shirt, a windburned, sunburned face, and a ruddy red neck. His hair was also parted on the side, but it didn't matter. We talked so much that we didn't notice we were the only ones left, that an hour had passed and everyone else had gone in and our buzzer never did buzz. We found the hostess and she sat us right away.

9.2. After dinner, we went out to the parking lot and sat in his car, an '86 Mustang, so we could look at the interior. I love car interiors. It's an odd interest of mine. The smell of them, the dash design, the shape and feel of the seats, the color choice, the door handles: All of this makes me happy. It's the closest to being in a spaceship that most of us will ever get. We talked about car upholstery, cars we had owned and loved, our kids (his two and my three) and where we grew up, and sports, and other things. We sat there so long we watched the dishwashers leave out the back door, and the restaurant manager lock up for the night. We agreed to see each other again.

9.3. After our work was done and the kids were asleep, we would talk on the phone, often late into the night, long past when we should have gone to bed. We talked as if we had a lifetime of talking to catch up on, but I was wary. I didn't want to like him too much. There was my own heart to protect, but there were also five children. I didn't want us to do anything rash. At one point, I tried to discourage him from seeing me.

"I'm a disaster," I told him. "I live with my parents in a back bedroom. I don't even have a job."

"Very smart. You're taking some time to regroup."

"I have chronic anxiety," I said.

"I don't ever have that," he said.

"My kids are so little they're a liability."

"A month after meeting me they are going to like me more than they like you," he said.

"I'm telling you, I'm a disaster," I said.

"Well, I'm an engineer. We love disasters."

9.4. Valentine's Day was a Wednesday night. We were scheduled to go out on our third date the following Friday, but he dropped by after my kids had gone to sleep to bring me a chocolate bar. He said he could only stay a minute, so I walked him out to his car. I wanted to kiss him, but I didn't say anything. We had not kissed yet.

"Happy Valentine's Day," he said.

"I didn't get you anything," I said.

"I don't need presents," he said. We lingered by the garage door for a minute.

"Well, I'll e-mail you tomorrow," he said. E-mail is also how I first checked his grammar and punctuation, but it became a way for us to talk during the days when we were busy with our families.

"Okay. Good night," I said. "Thank you for the chocolate."

"You're welcome," he said. I watched him walk toward his car, and when he reached the bumper he turned and walked back to where I was standing, grabbed my face with both his hands, and kissed me until my knees buckled. I had to lean up against the garage door to recover.

"I wasn't quite ready to say good night," he said. "Now I am. You good?"

"I think so," I said.

"Good night, then," he said, and he drove away.

9.5. Two months later, we stretched out in the hammock on my mother's back porch and held hands while we looked at the light pollution in the South Florida sky. We talked until we couldn't keep our eyes open. It was time for him to leave. He turned to me all of a sudden and said, "I love you."

I didn't know what else to say, so I said the first thing that came to mind.

"Thank you."

We were married a year later.

10. CLEARING THE MINEFIELD

10.1. Second marriages have a low rate of success. A statistic I found from one of those imperfect, yet snooty psychotherapists who gets a book deal and thinks he can save the planet with his impartation, says that two-thirds of them fail. That's worse than first marriages, and first marriages are a liquid love minefield, simmering with all sorts of malignable potential, and when they go wrong—kabloom! I don't think children of divorce can survive a second detonation. To survive a second marriage, you must completely demine the field of any explosive remnants of war, however slow, expensive, and dangerous the process may be. Along the way, if all goes well, the protocol itself will change from military to humanitarian, and the children will once again begin to feel safe.

10.2. Because we had each been through a divorce, my second husband and I should have been frightened of the ways our new marriage could explode us and our assemblage of children, but we chose to be proactive instead, deliberately unfurling our hands from the grip we had on failure, misperceptions, bad patterns of thought, and the very idea of what a family should be. We rebuilt something new from the ground up, out of the rubble of two destroyed families, from swords of bone and flaps of muscle, from misalignments, and fractured loyalty, from the stumps that are left after you step on a land mine. We cleared the field. We built the fort back up and lived in it fiercely. We hung our flag.

MEN I WOULD HAVE SLEPT WITH

Disclaimer: I am happily married.

BATEMAN, JASON

Because freckles. And because he is the kind of guy who would probably like to be on bottom. The kind of guy who, being in this position, *could* watch you, but wouldn't. He'd just close his eyes, clasp his hands behind his head, and let you watch him, which is strangely intimate. Also, the fact that it is easy to imagine being in a relationship with him based on characters he plays in the movies, which is what every straight woman who has seen Jason Bateman says. I've never denied being basic.

BRUNO

The French exchange student when I was a high school freshman and he was a senior and he flew back to France at the end of the year without having known I existed. He wore a tiny biracial Afro when everyone was wearing fades, and tight pants when everyone was wearing baggy. And his polo shirts were of a European fit, which means I could see his latissimus dorsi when he turned his back on me, shifted his books in his arms, and walked down the hall to chat up the cheerleaders who attached themselves to him like ticks. He looked so very French, although he is probably bald now. Sometimes you can forecast things like this by high school hair patterns, but for me, baldness is not a problem. *See also* Levin, Tony.

BUCKLEY, JEFF

Because he used his knowledge of Bartók to create atypically phrased, elongated rock arrangements and because his last good-bye was something only Mark Twain could have drummed up: drowning in the Mississippi River. He drowned in a river while sober and while singing "Whole Lotta Love" by Led Zeppelin. Who does that? If it were up to me, I would have been f%*ing him silly that night instead of letting him walk alone at night by a river.

BULL, SITTING

I fear people will think I am adding him to build a dimension of diversity to this list, which I am not doing. He was hot and I'm an equal opportunity sex fantasizer. Because cheekbones. And because I would have tanned hides for him. And watered his horse. And disrobed for him under the night sky.

CARSON, BEN

Because hands that hold tiny tools that separate people who are stuck together at the brain, and because soft-spoken, though putting Ben Carson on this list is like saying I want to know Jesus in the biblical sense. Carson is a devout man and as such, it feels wrong, but look what I'm doing here as a whole: You're not reading any prize-winning advancement of modern literature, you're reading a fantasy sex list. *See also* Tebow, Tim.

CENA, JOHN

Because cancer kids, and perhaps a low-rolling sexual rage that only comes out during the full moon, and because I am an unabashed muscle slut who dreams of feeling like a tiny, delicate flower for fifteen minutes. *See also* James, LeBron.

CHEADLE, DON

Because a thousand times yes, although I fear I would squash him like a bug.

CHEKHOV, ANTON

Because beard and because he wrote *Ivanov* in two weeks, while also working full-time as a doctor, while also treating the poor free of charge, which speaks to a kind heart. No lip kissing the lungers, though due to Chekhov's Generalized Hotness Factor (GHF) of 8.2 on a 10 scale that rivals even the best of the Pinterest inked-up hipster beard boards, this would be the kind of nearly impossible primal challenge hot-blooded teenagers battle during religious retreats. You know you're not supposed to do it, but you want to so bad you could crush a mason jar in your fist. *See also* Holliday, Doc, and Irving, John.

CUSTOMER IN WHEELCHAIR—LEGAL SEA FOODS, COPLEY PLACE, BOSTON, MA

Again, not trying for any inclusivity awards here. This list does not use universal design. So what, the wheelchair? I don't care about that stuff. You don't need working legs to be sexy. The man had massive shoulders and a presence that caused me to sweat inside my bra, and I made another waitress switch tables with me so I could wait on him. He ate a cup of clam chowder, a roll with butter, and a steamed lobster. Then he ordered coffee and one profiterole, of which he ate one bite. The economy of that—that measured self-control—made me want to intimately know him. This was before the Internet, so I would have had to put out some effort, riding my bicycle to the library, then looking up the phone number to a major teaching hospital with a spinal cord injury center, and requesting literature on sexual positions and special considerations for wheelchair-bound populations, et cetera. Then I would have studied the literature. Then shaboinked this man with the lights on.

DE NIRO, ROBERT

Because as a straight woman, I am required by the Union to put him on my list, although I fear I wouldn't stand a chance with him because he has a type and I am not it.

DOCTOR, FIRST-YEAR RESIDENT, EMERGENCY ROOM, NORTH FLORIDA

Because the medial sides of his eyebrows tilted up and saluted each other with amusement when I vigorously described the color, consistency, and value of the copious collegiate diarrhea from which I was suffering. This diarrhea had dehydrated me so much that I fainted and shat my shorts, and still I sat there on that gurney at three A.M. trying to look pretty. And because his skin looked like biscuits and gravy in the fluorescent lights, but his shoulders rolled muscularly under his stained white coat. And because, although he admitted to sleeping only four hours every other day, he still had a bruise on his cheek from slam dancing at a Red Hot Chili Peppers concert. I know this because I am the kind of person to ask strangers personal questions such as, "What's with the crutches?" or "How did you get that bruise on your face?" or "Do you date patients?"

DOUGLASS, FREDERICK

Because his upper lip was shaped like a crossbow, and because he was an abolitionist, and because suffrage. What a badass to be one of the first men to go for that when no one else was touching it with a ten-foot pole. I would have brushed his coats, blued his shirts, oiled his head, massaged his scalp, and rubbed the worried furrow in his brow away, and loved him till death did we part. And taken it out in trade.

FEYNMAN, RICHARD

I had a dream once that I was a reincarnation of his first wife, Arline. After I woke, I believed it for ten, fifteen minutes, preparing breakfast wearing nothing but my aura, imagining sending him coded letters, rubbing my pinkie in the curve of his philtrum, quieting the clammy, busy flutter of his hands. Thinking of him before I died of TB, stopping my bedside clock at 9:21 P.M., leaving him something to puzzle over. Waiting many years to reincarnate into the body of a tall, anxious overthinker with both an irrational fear of catching tuberculosis (*See also* Chekhov, Anton, and Holliday, Doc) and an unsung desire to build an emergency nuclear bunker in my backyard. I would have this man's baby just so I could raise a child who would understand theoretical physics.

GILMOUR, DAVID

He owned me the first time I heard the second guitar solo from Pink Floyd's "Comfortably Numb." Plus, I'm not scared of a little belly. It's what happens when men who don't work out get older and keep eating the carbs and don't stay on top of their T. Also, men should not worry about going bald. If they do something very well—run a business, parent their children, make decisions, play the guitar, stage sieges against governments trying to take away their land, or perform cunnilingus—it is possible to be masterful with a crowning glory of forehead. *See also* Hackman, Gene, and Levin, Tony.

GOLDBLUM, JEFF

Both before and after *The Fly,* because I am equal opportunity nerd-ist and muscle slut, though I must share some concern about this one's potential chat factor. Sometimes I don't need them to talk. I just want them to sit there and look pretty. I think this one would be interesting, at least at first; the kind of interesting where you lose yourself for hours, philosophizing far into the night, the Bob Marley playlist on repeat, even though your eyes are watering from exhaustion and your stomach is empty and the birds are starting to sing in the trees and the sky is getting light, and you realize that, in order to shut him up, there is nothing to do but have another bit of how's your father in hopes that he will fall asleep.

GOLDMAN, MR., PRIVATE ROOM, MED-SURG UNIT, MT. AUBURN HOSPITAL, CAMBRIDGE, MA

Because he was eighty-eight years old with muscles and had a well-kept thirty-eight-year-old wife who worshipped him, and because his eyes were ice blue and sparkled with humorous things unsaid and he was vital as all get-out. Don't ever let a few wrinkles and a sixty-year age gap set back your opinion of someone. He had prostate cancer (*See also* Zappa, Frank), which he said was less likely to kill him than boredom, and he also had insomnia. Sometimes during night shifts, after my work was done, I would sneak into his room and pull up a chair and he would talk, mostly about crazy things he had done in his life, speaking without wistfulness or regret. He had been a wartime soldier, then a merchant marine. He had made and lost and remade three fortunes. Once in a while I would put a blanket down on the floor and he would do push-ups. He told me once, "If I were single, I would snap you up." "But I'm half a foot taller than you," I said, to which he replied, "I like a big girl." *See also* Kravitz, Lenny.

HACKMAN, GENE

Old enough to be my father or grandfather in certain cultures. So what? This list defies chronology and exists as a fantasy where both the man and I would meet in the prospective primes of our lives. And because older guys are fine as long as they can still alpha. And because Gene Hackman, though technically a 4.2 out of 10 on the GHF scale, due to an imbalance of the facial features, is overall a 9.5, largely owing to his *je ne sais sex quoi*—that unnamable thing that makes a guy with an average face and zero provable gym hours still extremely f%*kable.

HAMM, JON

Because a primal part of my hindbrain can name the ways in which his day-old beard growth would make my cheeks sting, and sometimes, when I'm having a bad day, I scroll through pictures of him on the Internet and it's like rolling up a nice, sticky, fat marijuana cigarette. I can almost smell him, though who am I kidding? I don't smoke. If I did, I wouldn't be calling it a "marijuana cigarette."

HOLLIDAY, DOC

Micoplasmically risky. Dusty. Potentially epic, yet stifling experience, likely above a noisy saloon, or in the storage room of his dental office. Again, no lip kissing the lungers (*See also* Chekhov, Anton), but you aren't required to kiss in order to knock the boots.

HOWARD, TIM

Because goalie. And because no other explanation is needed. Just watch the soccer.

HURT, WILLIAM

Because he wouldn't need to use words to tell me what he wants. He could just use eyebrows (*See also* Doctor, First-Year Resident), and perhaps sign language, though when I watched *Children of a Lesser God* forty-two times in high school, I wasn't watching it for the sign language. I was watching it for that scene where he takes off his shirt.

IRVING, JOHN

Because Irving has a humorous way of applying the exclamation mark! And because sometimes—though not often—writers interest me. Generally, writers don't spend their days logging or boxing or hiking, but writing, for hours at a time, their asses spreading slowly over the years, like glacial goo, to envelop their desk chairs. Their bodies are often grublike, soft, and thick in the middle, and even the men are larger at the hips than at the shoulders. And we all know that reduced firing of the muscles reduces HGH, which can affect testosterone levels and potential alpha drive. And I am not a fan of soft keyboard hands on men. But John Irving works out to offset this! He lifts weights! Lifting weights gives you rough hands. So does pounding away on an old-fashioned typewriter, which I imagine he does. And he writes autobiographically in his earlier novels so I feel like I know him (*See also* Bateman, Jason). Examples: An easy Google search shows that he wrestled in college, like some of his characters (*See also* The Redhead in My Neighborhood), and that his borderline protagonist, Trumper, in *The Water-Method Man* was at a Midwestern college in Iowa (read: *Iowa MFA program where Irving attended!*), finishing an advanced degree in literature (read: *MFA in Creative Writing, which Irving obtained!*). Trumper has a fling with a dainty student named Lydia, who wears "Pretty Piece Underthings," which I imagine I might have worn in a different life, at a different age, had I been short enough to have ever been a coquette (*See also* My Husband). John Irving also pays the kind of inner attention to detail that I do, so perhaps conversation, or lack thereof, would be ideal, with each of us spending hours in silence, a nearly constant desire of mine, and meeting up in the evening for a light meal and some nookie. Admittedly, I often fall prey to either the potentially false persona, or the lip shape, which, again, speaks to my basic, predictable nature.

JAMES, LEBRON

Yes, all day long, but must use constant condom, in case he even sneezed in my direction. Any potential children created would be too freakishly tall to survive, though I imagine his big hands would have a nice, strong grip. On my wrists. Or my ponytail. *See also* Cena, John.

JONES, TOMMY LEE

Because I like a man with acne scars on his face and because He. Doesn't. Bargain. If I tell you the number of times I have watched that scene from *The Fugitive*, you would think something is wrong with me. He is also the kind of actor you think shows his true self in the roles he plays so it's easy to imagine what it's like to have coffee and bacon with him in the morning, or wait with him in an airport, or inspect with him a fence line on a ranch. *See also* Bateman, Jason.

KRAVITZ, LENNY

I'm not afraid of a short man. Horizontality: the great equalizer. *See also* Goldman, Mr.

KLEIN, FELIX

Because I, too, am interested in the interface between math and physics, but in an obtuse, borderline-average-IQ way. What he liked, I'd like, because beard. And because big thinkers make me want to have their babies. *See also* Feynman, Richard, and My Husband.

LEVIN, TONY

I once got six-degrees-of-separation close with Tony Levin, as my then-husband worked with someone who knew him. He sent me a card right before the birth of my first daughter, when I was filled up with another man's baby and also married, and also not hot. The card said, "Have a nice baby. Tony Levin." It wasn't enough. If I were given a get-out-of-jail-free pass for one night I would use it on Tony Levin.

MY HUSBAND WHEN WE WERE YOUNG

Chronologically, it is possible that he could have been my high school math teacher. If he started teaching at twenty-two while I was a high school senior at seventeen, we could have broken the law in the Xerox room or the backseat of his car, or a dinky motel near the highway, even though he was married at the time. I would have been the kind of girl to fall madly for him, doodle his name in my notes, look up his phone number in the phone book, and call at night, hanging up when either he or his wife answered, then make myself sick crying about him when I went away to college. I would have been his Lydia Kindle (*See also* Irving, John!). Alas, we didn't meet until years later, when I was a grown-a$$ woman and he was divorced and no longer teaching math.

ONE OF MY NAMELESS BOSSES

Because oddly hot. High intellectual prey drive, though. He was curious about everything and that was sexy. So were his eyes, which were small and both dark and bright at the same time, and his lips curled up on the sides as if he knew a secret about what you looked like naked. We fought all the time and I didn't like him as a person because he was a tool. We once had a three-day argument about whether the comma should go inside the quotes or outside. His rationale (for everything) was that he went to Oxford for graduate school and *that's how they did it in England*. I still would have pounded the duck with him, probably in his office, if we had both been certain kinds of people, which we weren't. Don't $h*t where you eat and all that.

PRIMA, LOUIS

Because he sang loose and funny and slid his notes and always hit them when you thought he wouldn't, and because he had a good sense of syncopation, and you'd think, after the show is done, he would have a couple of drinks and then slay you speechless with him stripped down to his wifebeater, his lips still swollen from playing his trumpet, and you on your belly and grabbing the iron bedstead in his French Quarter rental. He'd talk, too, and ask you what you liked, or better, *tell you what you liked*. He died before I was born, and as such, deserves a special time travel category. *See also* Bull, Sitting; Douglass, Frederick; Holliday, Doc; Klein, Felix; Rorschach, Hermann; Tesla, Nikola; and X, Malcolm.

THE REDHEAD IN MY NEIGHBORHOOD

Because redhead. And because freckles all over. And because he was a gentleman. He was leaving for college when I was an incoming high school freshman, so the age difference would have been alarmingly illegal, but we had a nice, platonic summer of us listening to music in his bedroom and me taking long walks around the neighborhood hoping to catch him washing his car in his cutoffs. He had meaty forearms and thick hands and fingers, and a slightly lupine slope to his shoulders, likely because he was a wrestler, and I like wrestlers. *See also* Cena, John, and Irving, John.

REZNOR, TRENT

All day every day at any point in time.

RORSCHACH, HERMANN

Because every time I take a Rorschach test I see things so dirty I scare myself. I'm betting he did, too.

STUDENT, UNDERGRAD ANATOMY AND PHYSIOLOGY CLASS, UNIVERSITY OF FLORIDA

Because he was extremely competitive and we were neck and neck for the highest grade in our class of several hundred, and if you think I would have gotten a 99.6 as my final grade on my own, you are nuts. I'm not the kind of person who *needs* a 99.6. A 94 or 95 is fine in most instances. I studied extra hard for this class because it gave us something to talk about, and because trying to beat his scores on tests and quizzes was what I did instead of f%*king him. Sometimes I beat him and sometimes he beat me, which is kind of a metaphor for how repeated rolls in the hay go. We developed an intimate semester-long camaraderie that confused me, as he was twenty years old and lived in a trailer park with his eighteen-year-old wife, who wasn't even in college and who worked as a checker at a grocery store and read gossip magazines. The logical end to that life bomb is so clearly this: He should have been with me, his intellectual and athletic equal, and not her. Incidentally, this man had a nose so big you could hang a nightgown off it, but he had the body of a triathlete because he was a triathlete. When we sat together in lecture, sometimes his flexor digitorum profundus would brush my flexor carpi ulnaris and I would not be able to concentrate. There were no hairs on this arm. Just smooth sheets of skin covering his muscles, all of which I could name by heart.

TEBOW, TIM

I'm sorry but I can't help it. I keep trying to delete him from this list out of respect for his purity, but my computer keeps putting him back on, as if by some sort of sexual autocorrect. *See also* Carson, Ben.

TESLA, NIKOLA

Because I would f%*k him in his laboratory with the power on. Fully dressed, him in a linen summer suit, and me in enough petticoats to choke a chicken, bent over a desk or a chair, metal hairpins scattered on the floor, my updo ruined to where anyone on the street would know what I had just been up to when I later walked outside. And because he is a mechanical engineer and I like watching guys work with tools and I am literally unable to apologize for it. *See also* My Husband.

VAN HALEN, ALEX

An extraordinary drummer and I am interested in extraordinary drummers. If this were an unabridged list it would contain perhaps fifteen or twenty drummers, even though a list that long, especially one full of drummers, would run the risk of making me look like a slut. Alas and alackaday, to Tina Fey's earnest prayer for her daughter to be the drummer so she need not lie with drummers, I must reply the following: What can I say? Sometimes you just want to lie with the drummer.

VAN HALEN, EDDIE

I know. Brothers. Something wrong with this, but I am attracted to expertise, especially in the areas of the hard sciences, music, and athletics, and also to men who have oddly shaped lips. (*See also* Douglass, Frederick, and Van Halen, Alex.) I would be the kind of person to choose one brother over the other and not look back, because

I am an extremely loyal person, if a little Walter Sex Mittyish in my mind, but yes to this brother, as well, though there is likely a significant size discrepancy. *See also* Cheadle, Don.

WHITE, JACK

Because he holds the neck of his guitar like a boss, and because I once drove an extra hour by accident—nearly to Homestead, Florida—instead of getting off at my exit in Miami because I was listening to *Blunderbuss*. I think part of why women like musicians is we pretend to believe that the unchecked passion they display in their lyrics or while playing onstage is a representation of how they would act in a relationship, even though we know this cannot actually be true. They forget to flush like everybody else, they get depressed, they lock themselves up in studios for hours, they spend weeks or months alone with other musicians, they go on tour and sleep with copious numbers of other women. We don't fall in love with them, we fall in love with what they create. It's a farcical crush train from which it is difficult to disembark while young. Still: Jack White six ways to Sunday.

WILDER, ALMANZO

There is suggestion of some sort of genetic defect here, perhaps MTHFR, because he and his wife, Laura Ingalls Wilder, my favorite childhood author, didn't produce very strong children, and he developed an unknown illness that he never quite recovered from, but that never fazed me. (*See also* Chekhov, Anton, and Holliday, Doc.) The bottom line is that he worked hard and was extremely good-looking. And he married a writer. I'm a writer.

WILLIAMS, PHARRELL

Because lips in "Money Maker," though things between us might go the way of poor Don Cheadle. *See also* Cheadle, Don.

WINTERS, DICK

Because war hero, though this is not *necessarily* why I like him. (*See also* Yeager, Chuck.) I like him because cheekbones, and because he did a "French wash" with ice water and a razor every day during that awful winter in Bastogne.

X, MALCOLM

I like a guy with glasses and an overbite. I would make him leave the glasses on.

YEAGER, CHUCK

Because flight suit. And war hero, and balls the size of coconuts for breaking the sound barrier as a test pilot, but mostly flight suit.

ZAPPA, FRANK

As with many of the men on this list, this one is much older than me (*See also* Hackman, Gene), but because ink-black mustache, and because he sweated on my forearm at a show once where I had front-row seats. I'm not the kind of creeper who refuses to wash after getting sweated on by a famous person. I don't ask for autographs, and I don't get starstruck. I just wiped the sweat away, but it was cool, because he looked at me like he noticed he had dropped some sweat on me, which shows both a kindness and a sense of humor. I don't know how Frank Zappa and I would have gotten on, but I know that I would have made sure he ejaculated far more than the twenty-one times per month needed to reduce his prostate cancer risk by thirty-three percent.

KICKING THE SNAKES

Pain and drugs got me into graduate school. Not angst, mind you, but real, true, physical pain, the kind that makes your loved ones look at you with *that face,* the face that is part pity, part fear, the kind that makes them, quietly, when you aren't watching, hide the home-defense goods: the oily antique .380 handed down from a relative, the shotgun whose barrel is just long enough to reach your face if you put the butt of it on the ground and use a spatula to reach the trigger. I'm talking about the kind of pain that changes your world-view and makes you into a different person, and I'm talking about the kind of drugs doctors prescribe that ordinary people get hooked on all the time, the kind of drugs that, if you get hooked on them, will make you flush your own family down the toilet. Narcotics are no joke, but without experiencing an intolerable level of pain that required high doses of them, I would never have applied to an MFA program, because I was essentially an anxious coward afraid of rejection.

Quick disclaimer here: I apologize in advance for bringing this up, because there is nothing more annoying to me than writers writing about writing, especially writers writing about how writing makes "the soul sing." Seriously, if I could bring myself to get on an airplane, I would rather sit in front of a seat-kicking kid with an ear infection for the entirety of a transatlantic flight than read or write about writers who write about writing. But here it comes, my soul-singing desire, spit up like a fur ball: I wanted to be a writer.

It started when I was ten, after we moved to upstate New York in the middle of winter, where the cold weather was physically painful. I stayed inside until spring, huddled up with a blanket in the torn vinyl Barcalounger the previous owners had left behind in our unfinished basement, reading a forgotten box of *Reader's Digest* issues from the 1970s. I was thrilled by the humorous bits, and true-life accounts of danger written by regular people. I was thrilled by the idea that I could earn twenty-five dollars writing a "Life in These United States," if only I could find something funny enough to write about. Back then, especially to me, twenty-five dollars represented a grandiose sum of money. I practiced writing in a little notebook I never showed anyone, hoping to come up with a hit. I never did.

Later, in high school, even though I was uneasy about showing my writing to others, I joined the school literary club. Three weeks in, I was sent to the principal's office for writing a satire of Poe's "The Raven" from the perspective of a serial killer who kills all his victims in a shower scene like the one from the film *Psycho,* which I had recently watched, though I shouldn't have. (I don't do well with movies like that.) My argument was that the poem was a copycat exercise intended to improve my writing skills by studying the style of another writer. They didn't understand. I was expelled from the literary club and rejected by the other students for being too intense.

In college, even though I wanted to be a writer, I studied anything but writing, because people told me it was frivolous, and because I wasn't sure you needed college to be a writer. I studied printmaking, and literature (also frivolous), and anatomy and physiology (not at all frivolous), with some vague goals of doing something scientific, then I quit college to "become" a writer. I thought that if I just holed up and wrote a lot I would get better. I handwrote three terrible novels about subjects you might find nineteen-year-olds discussing while drunk at a party. Later, I had one of my roommates read my work. He declared it terrible, and when I reread it, I realized he was right. I threw all three manuscripts into a fire. Then I stopped trying to write and got married.

Later still, when I got my act together, I did study writing. I got a degree in it, then went to work doing various forms of professional writing. I wrote Web content for a few different companies. I developed courses for online high school and college programs. I wrote a few academic children's books, and lots of advertising copy for a scientific publishing house, most of the time from the comfort of my own home, and mostly at night while the kids were sleeping. In a way, I was *kind of* a writer. When I told people I was a writer, their faces lit up as if they had discovered I was a famous actress and could maybe get them an agent or a part in a movie. They literally leaned into me and gave me all their attention. When I told them I wrote Web content, it was as if I told them I did porn. Web content was no more interesting than insurance adjusting, and they were right.

What I secretly wanted to do was go back to school and get a graduate degree in creative writing, mostly because I wanted to make room in my life to write creative work and that would give me an excuse to do it. I thought that by getting an MFA I would become, with the same earnest desire as Pinocchio, a *real writer.* I wanted to let my soul free to write the things I wanted to write.

There was a school I had my eye on, only partly because it was in the city where I lived, and I wasn't able to relocate. It was a good school. My mother had gone there. Every year, for perhaps six years,

I would print out an application, fill it out, prepare a writing sample, be overcome with doubt, and throw the application away in fear. You see, writing Web content and science copywriting had nothing to do with revealing myself, which is what I was afraid of. I was afraid of rejection. I was afraid of not being good enough at what I really wanted to do, so that each time the deadline rolled around, I choked. I could imagine a panel of people passing my manuscript around and shaking their heads, their noses squinched slightly, politely, as if someone in the room had just opened a jar of kimchi. I could imagine getting the form letter rejection, saying that the competition was particularly tough that year and they had many qualified applicants and only a few slots, et cetera. I knew that rejection came with writing, but I couldn't face the ultimate insult of pre-rejection, that uber-proof that I was not good enough to even *get into* a writing program. I couldn't bring myself to apply. It simply made me too anxious.

But then I went surfing on a windy day. I mistakenly let the surfboard act as a sail and rip my right shoulder back, tearing my labrum somewhere deep inside the socket. It hurt and weakened my shoulder, but because I wasn't enthusiastic about having surgery, I walked around like that for a long time before getting up the guts to have it fixed, because I was also anxious about having surgery. I had read on the Internet that shoulder surgery was particularly painful, but I had not been told that the recovery for this kind of surgery is so terribly painful that most people can't sleep lying down for several weeks. You have to sleep in a chair. A surgeon will not tell his patients how bad a recovery will be, because if he did, no one would ever schedule surgery; they would walk around all third-worldly, wearing slings and limping and popping pills and keeling over now and then, and surgeons would be renting apartments like the rest of us.

I had had some experience with real pain, in the form of kidney stones. I seem to be able to produce kidney stones the way a chicken lays eggs, and every time I get one it is the worst pain I have ever experienced and my husband gives me *the face* and hides the home-defense equipment. Kidney stones are demonic, excruciating, worse than childbirth and twenty other clichéd pain comparisons, and apparently, though I walk the planet like an Amazon, I have tiny, delicate, shrinking violet ureters that are not big enough in diameter to pass even the smallest of stones—I have only passed one on my own—so each stone I develop gets repeatedly stuck trying to go down the water flume and slams itself, over and over, into the entrance to my ureter, like trying to shove a golf ball through a garden hose.

When I get a kidney stone, I require the placement of a cruel device called a ureteral stent, which a doctor will tell you is a soft, malleable, harmless piece of plastic, but which is actually a tube with two coiled springs, one that sits lodged inside your kidney and one that floats around in your bladder. The tube that connects the kidney end to the bladder end helps keep the ureter from closing due to inflammation or scar tissue, and, if all goes well, allows the stone to pass. The bladder end of the stent is attached to a string, which comes out your very sensitive flower of a pee hole and gets taped to your thigh. Stents themselves are terribly painful, and for me, cause severe bladder spasms, sometimes from simply switching positions in a chair. They are so bad I can't sleep. Every time I feel a spasm, it makes me groan and weep loudly. I can't get through one without waking my husband up at night, or if it is in the daytime, without making the kids come running into the room, wearing that face . . . the face they get when they see their mom doing something they should not have to see, like sitting on a toilet screaming in pain, or weeping and begging to be put out of her misery. I usually keep a stent in for nine days or so, just long enough for me to feel defeated about humanity, and all of this requires copious levels of narcotics to get through it. And when the stent is out, and the pain eventually ebbs away, I must get myself off the narcotics, which I grow to enjoy.

In order to remove a stent, the doctor grabs ahold of the string, lies through his teeth about how it won't hurt very much, and yanks the stent out like he is pulling on a fighter kite. The spring quickly leaves your kidney and travels down your ureter and out your urethra. They don't tell you how this is going to feel. There are no words. If people knew, they wouldn't come back to the office to have their stents removed. They would avoid it at all costs, walking around all third-worldly, until they keel over and die from the stent growing into their tissue and causing a deadly infection.

I believe there is a level of fundamental purity you maintain, no matter how tainted you are by pornography, or crime, or cruelty, or poverty, or violence, when you haven't experienced a certain level of physical pain. I believe some people are able to avoid it for a lifetime: careful people, or lucky ones, or people with congenital analgesia, who walk around with this type of innocence, and it is a rare gift. Though I have had three babies three separate times without anesthesia, which does sting the hoo-ha mightily, the day I go to have my first stent removed is the last day of my true innocence. The doctor, whose name is the same as a brutal founder of a famous empire, greets us like he has had a wonderful weekend. He is tan and rested and acts like he wants to get this over with because there is a nice club sandwich, or maybe a high-class call girl, waiting on the desk in his office. He shakes hands with my husband. I have worn a skirt so I wouldn't have to change into a paper robe, so I lie back on the table and hike it up self-consciously, in front of this slightly wolfish man, while my husband watches.

"This might sting a little bit," he says.

"What do you mean sting?" I ask.

"I mean you might feel a little pinch."

"Okay," I go. "Whatever. I'm ready to get this thing out." I am not worried at this point, because I am an innocent, an innocent doped up on narcotics. While we are talking the doctor spreads my legs and aims a bright light on my hoo-ha.

"You might want to hold her hand," he tells my husband. "Here we go." He rips the tape from my thigh, causing me to remark, in my innocence, "Wow, that *did* sting," and then grabs the string and begins to pull out the stent, the coil stretching out and putting pressure against the tender things that should never be touched by anything, pressing against my ureter, and out my violated urethra. This takes perhaps seven seconds, but in those seven seconds, the universe implodes behind my eyes. I see the corruption of all mankind, Adam raping Eve in the garden, children suffocating puppies, my grandparents wading through a landscape of vomit, my daughters pole dancing on a stage of snakes and skulls, Aretha Franklin's backup singers humming generations of lies brought to life in an echo of falsetto. My eyes roll back in my head and I nearly lose consciousness. There is a white sheet in my field of vision and I start crying hard.

"You sonofabitch!" I shriek. "That wasn't a pinch! You are a damn liar!"

"They always do this," he says to my husband. "I have to lie. If I told you how bad it was, you would have worried about it. But now it's over." He peels off his gloves, turning his back to face the sink, which was when I first realized that doctors lie, and also, that life is very, very short. It got me thinking about all the things I had been too afraid to do, but should have, because stupid things like war or infection or crank-ass random accidents can finish people off without them doing what they were put here to do. That one stent was enough pain for a lifetime.

So, when it was time to have my shoulder repaired, I was uneasy enough to want to get the truth out of the orthopedic surgeon.

"What's the pain level going to be like after this?"

"You'll be uncomfortable."

"How uncomfortable? Because usually when you guys say 'uncomfortable' it means I end up crying. And besides, it's Christmas. I want to make sure we have a good Christmas."

"Define 'good Christmas.'"

"I mean, we have kids at home. I want to make Christmas cookies, wrap presents while drinking cocoa, go shopping, and decorate the tree."

"Yeah, it won't be your best Christmas," he says. "But your kids are old enough to understand. Look, it's a surgical procedure. You're going to be uncomfortable, but I'm going to give you pain medication, so you'll be fine."

"So, some pain meds and I'll be fine?"

"Everything has a price. You're an active girl. You want the shoulder fixed for the rest of your life, you're going to have to go through a little discomfort."

I wake up from surgery with blood all over my face. It is dripping down from my eyes, down my cheeks, and into my neck. I am in excruciating pain, right out of the gate. I hear a voice.

"How's the discomfort, sweetie? Give me a number from one to ten." It is the recovery nurse.

"Eleven," I whisper. "My face is bleeding. Why is my face bleeding?"

"It's tears, sweetie. You're crying. I've never seen anyone wake up crying from surgery before. Congratulations, you get morphine."

So I go home that day with a prescription for some hard-core narcotic pain medication and Ambien, a powerful sleeping pill.

"Trust me," the nurse says. "You're gonna need these. Patients who have this surgery find it difficult to sleep for a long time."

"I think the doctor lied again," I hiss to my husband on the way home. I sleep through dinner, the children's homework, two soccer games, and all three remaining kids coming in to say good night, but after that, I didn't sleep more than four hours at a stretch for the next two months. I would take an Ambien around nine, fall fitfully asleep and dream of monsters, things with triangular teeth in red, angry gums biting me, only the teeth were loose, they stuck in my skin, left a poison in my shoulder that streaked red, up to my brain. Or I would dream of being led on a tour around a gracious old house, when all I really wanted was the bathroom, opening door after door, looking into closets, bedrooms, studies, libraries, shops, and finally seeing a door marked "toilet" and opening it to find one of those dreaded windy air bendy giant nylon sock people that used-car dealers put in front of their lots popping out at me, making me wet my pants in front of the dangerous, desperate president of an economically unstable nation. It was his house that I was touring, I found out in that moment, and I was some sort of ambassador. A lot rode on how I carried myself through this tour.

I would wake up to pain, soaked with pain-induced sweat, yet be unable to change my nightgown because my shoulder hurt so much that I couldn't dress myself. I would ease myself out of the recliner I slept in, take more narcotics, and walk around like a ghost in my wet nightie, billowing it around me until it dried out, sitting on a chair for a few minutes, then when the pain got too bad, moving to the couch to watch infomercials until the meds kicked in. I watched so many tantalizing infomercials that if we had had any money, I would have spent it all on their promises. Then I would do a few slow laps around the dining room table, then amble outside to the front porch, then back inside to wrap a Christmas present with one hand, then over to the computer to surf for something to distract me. Anything to keep moving, because sitting still is what made the pain build until it made me cry. I did this for weeks while my husband's and the children's lives went on without me.

There are two things to mention about narcotics here. The first is that, like postsurgical shoulder pain, the strength and power of narcotics should not be underestimated. I am sensitive to drugs of all kinds, and I don't like them. I don't even drink alcohol anymore. I get a taste in my mouth the moment a Tylenol hits my system. I have uncommon, often severe side effects to medications, and prefer to not take them. Still, I was sucked into the allure of narcotics. They do something to the brain that makes you crave them, and once you no longer need the drugs, you still want them. You love them and you want to be loved by them, so your brain tells you that you must have them.

Another thing is that narcotics are the only things I have found to date that have taken away my anxiety, which I had enjoyed for most of my life. I didn't know how badly anxiety affected me until I no longer felt it. On Percocet, I did not give one flying fork about what anyone thought about me, I did not overexamine the things I said or did, and I stopped worrying about things that would never happen. I became a different, more neurotypical person when I was taking them, and I loved every bit of how they made me feel. I could think about driving to the grocery store without getting a knot in my stomach. I could answer the telephone without butterflies, I could imagine my kids growing up without getting leukemia. I could picture my daughters' wedding days without seeing my own tombstone. Narcotics did what Valium and Xanax and Bach Flower Remedies and homeopathy and psychotherapy had never been able to do for my anxiety. They hobbled my personality, but made me, in a way, into a better, more functional person. The only anxiety I felt was when I thought about living without them.

A few nights before Christmas Eve, when the rest of the house was sleeping, my meds wore off and I couldn't sleep. I popped my pills and went online while I waited for them to take effect. I checked on my eBay motors watch list . . . I was watching a 1967 Volkswagen Beetle, a 1978 Volkswagen Westfalia camper, and a 1982 Ford Bronco II, because I always watched old cars. Then, while I was checking my e-mail, I started to really feel good. I went through my Facebook feed, looked up an article on shoulder pain, and by the time I thought to check the writing program Web site, which I did every year in December, I was plotzed out of my gourd. I realized I only had a few more weeks left if I wanted to apply.

I loved feeling high. It was such a relief to not worry about ridiculous things that might not happen, or to not have an anxiety attack while sitting alone on the back porch with a magazine. I didn't overthink. I printed out the application and made a hand-scrawled, wasted checklist of things I needed to do to apply. Then, for the rest of the week, in fifteen-minute increments while my family was sleeping, I popped pills and worked on my application until it was done. I was unapologetically, heavily shit-canned during the whole process, including writing the sample of my work, but my nerves were Rico Suave, sitting at a bar wearing a Panama hat and a vest with a pocket watch, drinking Southern Comfort Manhattans. I mailed the application without fear, and then I waited. I don't remember if we had a good Christmas.

Over the next few months, I started to scare myself when I realized that I was looking forward to each dose of Percocet, and I loved the fifteen-minute high the Ambien gave me right before I fell asleep. I thought I might be in trouble when, after a hard day, I took an extra pill to feel better emotionally, and it worked. Then I did it again the next day just to see if I was right. Then I started taking two per dose and then I started taking a second Ambien in the middle of the night after the first wore off. To steal a phrase from Kurt Vonnegut that I have seen tattooed on no fewer than forty-seven hipsters: *Everything was beautiful and nothing hurt.* There was no pain and there was no anxiety. Parenting was a delight, because I simply didn't care about much, and because the drugs also made me a little stupid. I said yes a lot and the children loved me for it.

We all know how pill-heads ruin their lives. We have all heard the stories of normal people: schoolteachers, or bank managers, or housewives, et cetera, who get in a car accident and start taking Percocet and muscle relaxants, and end up crushing and snorting black market oxys on the back of strangers' toilets, or giving sexual favors in exchange for pills, losing their jobs and their families in the process of the decline. Talk to any police officer and he will tell you that pill-heads are dangerously numb—empty zombies who operate with the singular goal of obtaining more pills. And don't let them lie to you, the sleeping medication Ambien is addictive. When taken together, Ambien and Percocet make even a common, garden-variety housewife panic when she thinks the prescriptions might be getting low, or worse, that there are no refills left, and worse yet, leads her to ruminating on some experimental ideas, such as how far one could go to get more of these drugs when the prescription runs out. Sell the wedding ring? Dip into savings? Leave the children home alone to go meet some guy named "Toothless Tim" in an IHOP parking lot?

At this point, I didn't technically need the drugs anymore, but I wanted them very much. I liked how I felt just a little numb, numb enough to not feel the worry that had dominated my personality for most of my life. I knew I was treading in dangerous water, the kind of water with a big undertow that was waiting for me to go to the doctor and fib about my pain levels, or find an ER resident I could lie to about back pain, an undertow that was waiting for me to hide a bottle of pills from my husband, or hide an addiction from myself. One Friday after the kids were asleep, I grabbed my pills and took them to my husband, who was reading in bed. I handed him the bottles.

"I need to stage my own intervention. I'm getting too dependent on these."

"Okay," he said slowly.

"You know I have an addictive personality."

"You do."

"I need to stop these now," I said. I was embarrassed to admit this kind of weakness, especially to a man who, besides a small, nagging issue with Monster energy drinks, doesn't even have a vice.

And here is part of the beauty of my husband. He got out of bed, grabbed the bottles of pills, took me by the elbow, and led me to the bathroom. He handed me a bottle.

"Open it," he said. I did. "Now flush it." I did. He handed me the other one, and I dumped it and flushed, watching my pills swirl down the drain to drug fish and other wildlife all over Southeast Florida.

"Are there refills on these?" he asked.

"One on each."

"Give me the bottles," he said. I handed them to him and he put them in his pocket so I wouldn't be able to use the prescription number to call in a refill.

"Thank you for telling me," he said.

"You're welcome," I said, and this is another beautiful thing about my husband: his ability to allow me to feel generous and beneficent as a result of things he does.

It took me weeks to get back to a normal sleeping pattern without the drugs, and within a few days of quitting, the anxiety started creeping back up past Defcon 4, to Defcon 3, and finally, Defcon 2, where I could hear my own heart beating in my ears as a matter of course and push myself into an anxiety spiral simply by poking my imagination, and I realized, clearly, cleanly, in an unimpaired way, that I had applied to graduate school while I was on drugs.

Around the end of March, a few weeks after flushing my drugs,

I began to feel queasy in the hours before the mailman delivered the mail each day, or when I opened my e-mail in the morning. I began to check the school Web site several times per day, the mailbox on my porch several times per day, and my e-mail several times per day. When I thought about the MFA program, I would sometimes get a nervous colon, which led me to fool myself into believing I didn't want to get in after all, that graduate degrees did not matter. The market was flooded with baristas and middle school tutors with MFAs behind their names, and besides, I had important things going on at home. There were some soffits that needed scraping and repainting. I was thinking about starting to sew the kids' clothes again, because they were in high school and the fashions were more challenging, and I was sure they would love looking different from all their friends, and think of all the money we would save. I had also watched an Internet video on how to paint a faux mahogany look on a garage door and I had a mind to do it. Maybe I would even start a home business painting faux wood garage doors for people in wealthier neighborhoods. I told myself I put the program out of my mind, but I couldn't. I wanted it too much.

The thing that drug abuse and anxiety and pain flirt with, bat back and forth like a badminton birdie, a crocheted hacky sack, a psychological hot potato, is *loss of control*. Nobody wants to lose control. Before I had my first child, the thing I was afraid of more than the pain of natural childbirth was accidentally having a bowel movement in front of the midwife while I was pushing. And now, years later, when I think of the pain I can't remember its particulars, but I do recall shitting myself while pushing, and the midwife wiping my bottom with a Chux, saying, "Oopsie, a little poopsie!"

So we develop anxiety to brace ourselves for adjustments we are afraid to make due to things we don't want to happen. We develop hypochondriasis in anticipation of the ultimate loss of control—death.

We drink at parties so we can try and control how we are viewed, so we can be seen by others as interesting and entertaining. We avoid pain because we fear it becoming worse, unbearable even, to where we want to jump off a bridge or shoot ourselves in the heads to make it stop. We take drugs to protectively numb ourselves from an accumulation of lifelong pain of all sorts—physical, psychological, and psychic. These things, especially when they work in concert, weave in and out of each other. We take drugs to avoid pain, we avoid pain because we are afraid of losing control, and we lose control trying to not feel pain. The pain eats the drugs, the drugs eat the anxiety, the anxiety eats the pain, and we are left with a roil of snakes shaped like a Celtic knot, each with another's tail in its dirty little mouth. Everything has a price.

Sometimes, perhaps even for one day, during that fresh, drug-free, postsurgical state, when my pain was improved, and my shoulder injury was healing, I felt a tiny bit of control that came on me of its own volition. It wasn't drug induced. It felt hopeful—there wasn't an anticipation of pain in my immediate future, save the possible rejection from the MFA program, and honestly, fuck them, right? Who were they to tell me I would or wouldn't "be" a writer? I was feeling a little giddy, a little silly in the way that someone who just cheated death feels, so the kids and I planned an April Fool's Day prank on my husband. My kids loved April Fool's Day and often concocted elaborate ruses to fool other family members. We once called my ex-husband and told him that our fifteen-year-old had gotten pregnant and he believed it for almost a minute. We were pros.

I curled up on my bed. The kids ran out to get my husband, who was outside doing something manly that would have been inconvenient to stop, like digging a fence-post hole. They said, "Something's wrong with Mommy. You have to come inside." I waited, snickering inside my armpit. When I heard his footsteps on the bedroom floor, I groaned.

"I think I have a kidney stone," I said.

"You're kidding me."

I got up and paced across the room bent over, yet on tiptoes, the way I walk when I have a kidney stone. I groaned again like a goat, my kidney pain sound.

"Jeezy Petes," he said. "Looks like we're going to the ER," and this is where we burst out laughing, shouting, "April Fools! Ha ha! We fooled you, didn't we?" The kids jumped up and down, delighted with their win. My husband, who doesn't appreciate pranks, wasn't amused.

The next morning, in the ultimate payback, I woke up with a real kidney stone. I kid you not. We drove to the ER, where I vomited on the floor and passed out, while the tiny stone slammed against my ureter, trying to escape. They admitted me. I had surgery. They gave me another stent. When I woke up pissing iron filings and razor blades, filling the toilet with blood, they mercifully whacked me out of my skull with a morphine drip. My husband had brought my laptop, and I was able to fool around on it between the hallucinations I had of Chinese men with Fu Manchu moustaches floating down from the ceiling, lips a'pucker, to kiss me about the face and neck. I checked my e-mail and found one from the director of the MFA program telling me I was accepted for the following fall with full funding. In fact, thanks to the morphine and another prescription bottle of hydrocodone, I don't remember my hospital stay, I don't remember the nurses, and I usually make friends with the nurses. I don't remember my doctor, and I don't remember opening that e-mail and getting one of the best pieces of news of my life. My husband had to tell me I read it.

But when faced with a new thing, we always get a choice. We can turn back to what we know is safe, or we can take a chance and do the thing, even if it scares us. I got out of the hospital, had my stent removed, and this time, when I stopped needing the drugs for pain control, I stopped taking them. Instead of looking forward to an imagined, always apocalyptic personal future, I looked forward to something real that was actually going to happen. I kicked the knot of snakes into the dirt and moved on.

TWO VIEWS OF A SECRET

Some people believe there are two kinds of people: those who believe in God and those who don't, those who eat animal flesh and those who don't, those who burn the midnight oil and those who get up with the sun, those who fantasize about space and time travel and those who don't read sci-fi, those who pick their scabs and those who don't. Or as Tom Robbins said, "Those who believe there are two kinds of people in this world and those who are smart enough to know better." I'm not smart enough to know better, because I believe there truly are two kinds of jazz music lovers: those who think that Jaco Pastorius was the best bass player who ever lived, and those who are misinformed.

Because I live with a scattered mind, and because my prefrontal cortex could probably use a hoarder intervention, it helps me to think this way. I envy clean thinkers who can follow a logical map in their mind to a thought they have stored there, who can make sense of the volumes of information that are thrown at them every day, those who are not daunted by caretaking their memories and knowledge. But that's not how I roll.

Classifying things into sets of two is not sophisticated. My life is structured around things of two: two piles on my desk—things to do right away so I don't lose my job or house, and things that can wait. Two orders of kids—the ones on autopilot who have left home, and the ones I still have to remember to feed. My old marriage and my current one. The sheets that are on the bed, and the set that is hanging on the line out back. I am willing to consider that my simplistic view might be a sign of inferior processing, as I recognize that I am unable to categorize things logically without blending in unscientific pieces of information, such as feelings and memories, and for me, even colors.

I am a lifelong music lover. One of my earliest memories is of lying in my crib with my favorite stuffed elephant, who had a windup music box where his heart should have been. At night, when I couldn't sleep and the darkness lay ahead of me like a long road, I would wind the key in the elephant's back and listen to "Brahms' Lullaby," manipulating the sound by pushing it into my ear, or pressing it against the mattress to make the notes bounce off the springs and create an echo that felt like an empty room. Sometimes I would hold the key to slow the song down, or speed it up. When I did these things, the sound manifested as colors in the dark, either behind my eyelids, or in the space before me when my eyes were open. I could see the music. And for many years, I assumed this was what all people experienced.

When I was six or seven, my parents bought me a portable white plastic record player. My father taped a nickel onto the arm to keep it from skipping, and sometimes, on Friday nights after payday, he would bring home a 45 record of whatever caught his fancy. I spent hours playing records alone in my room, memorizing the songs of Steve Miller, the Beatles, Elton John, and Kiki Dee, and a discarded fifties doo-wop collection that must have belonged to my parents.

When I visited my grandparents, I tagged along to their weekly choir practice. I leaned against my grandfather while he sang, so I could feel his baritone vibrations moving through my body while I followed along to his part in the hymnbook with my finger. The sanctuary would become a dance hall, where visual echoes of the pipe organ and the Latin praise songs ricocheted into the high-arched space and showed me their colors.

When I was nine, my grandfather bought me a tabletop organ. It spanned two octaves, and had a red plastic covering and bright white buttons that played real chords. He built me a little table and bench and my parents put it in the upstairs dormer room. I sat on my little bench in front of that organ for many hours, teaching myself how to read music by trial and error using a booklet that had come with the organ. The organ sounded terrible and I made it sound worse, which I think is why my parents set it up so far away from the rest of the house. No one could bear it. When I was eleven, my parents rented me a clarinet, a real instrument, and I thought I was on my way to becoming a real musician. I loved that clarinet so much I rubbed it with special wood oil, and each time I took it apart, I placed its sections gently in the case as if they were parts of a rare, fragile artifact. At night, I slept with the case on a pillow beside my head, like a favorite pet.

My first sound was an open G, which on the clarinet was a no-fingered note that came out wobbly and wretched and leaky and squirting with spit. Not joyful. A day later I tried an F, then an F sharp, each of which used one different finger to produce, but which somehow made perfect sense, like identifying each sibling in a set of fraternal twins. As I gathered speed and built up an embouchure, I learned more notes, then slowly began to put them together as scales that made clear visual, as well as auditory, sense. The notes had their own positions, their own identities, their own colors.

In beginning orchestra, we began with simple compositions in C major—sixteen-bar pieces composed of whole notes and half notes that no one, not even the kids who didn't practice, could screw up. C notes and C-major chords are thick, sunny yellow lines, with the color variations a satin ribbon might have. They felt good and were easy to understand. By middle school, we played classical music by real composers, which produced explosions of color that were hard to describe or recollect, yet were consistent each time I heard them. When I then learned to play the saxophone and moved into complex jazz compositions, the vague collection of colors and images that I had always associated with music became a lexicon, or better stated, persona for me. It became a filter through which I saw the world—all parts of it: the kindness of my friend Jim, an alto saxophone player, who died of leukemia in college, is a sandpaper-colored B-flat note he sustained during a solo, the breath he took before he played. The feeling that I had always had—the choking, black, anty scramble in my throat when I listened to a distorted electric guitar sound, or Mozart's Concerto 34 in D Minor—was the same feeling I had when I felt anxiety about something, which was quite often. The pinching in the bone and muscle behind my ears leading down my neck is the orange anger that rushed my field of vision when cymbals crashed, and became what I heard or felt when I got in an argument with someone. The slow swing of a Glenn Miller song was soft, pastel ribbon candy folding over on itself, and also the love my grandmother and grandfather shared with each other. Music, which had always been a palette of feelings and images, took on an arrangement of order that made sense, though I still stand by my classification of two when I say that there are two kinds of people in the world, those who can see what music sounds like, and those who cannot.

———————————

I've never denied being obsessive. In fact, I'm annoying enough about it that people either humor me, like they would a mentally ill relative, or they end up angry at my fundamental makeup and stop spending time with me. I don't keep a lot of friends, and my husband's application is currently being reviewed by the Congregation for the Causes of Saints, but my mind is a playground, or perhaps a laboratory, and I have grown used to managing it. By the time I was in high school, I practiced both instruments many hours per week, ignoring the Florida life outside of my bedroom windows, children shouting and riding by on bicycles, the sprinkler system turning on and off, cicadas in the bushes, and the breeze parting the tree branches and making the leaves hum. My stunted social life revolved around music, and all my school activities were band related. I entered state competitions and competed in solo and ensemble performances. For a while, even as a freshman, I was one of the best.

I joined our award-winning high school jazz band, but although I enjoyed playing sax, my heart wasn't in it. I never connected with the greats: Sonny Rollins, John Coltrane, Stan Getz, Lester Young, Charlie Parker, and others. The sound didn't look or feel good to me. It was pebbled and sandy, and made me sad to listen to it, sad like a dark Sunday afternoon in winter, where there is nothing to look forward to except tomato soup, a grilled cheese sandwich, and early bed. Plus, I felt extra dorky. The case was heavy and I sweated when I carried it in the Florida heat. Also, the lead tenor sax player was a child prodigy and, with him in the picture, my lack of skill was evident on a daily basis, and what's worse, I saw a photo of myself once with my cheeks sucked in, blowing on that saxophone, and it reminded me of a pornographic photo I had once accidentally seen at too young an age.

When I needed a break from the classical and jazz, I would listen to rock and folk songs, sometimes looking for "new" stuff in my mother's old records. I accidentally stumbled upon Jaco Pastorius playing bass on a Joni Mitchell album, and within a few minutes, his sound changed everything about how I looked at music.

I don't remember where or when I first heard Jaco play with Weather Report, but I know the song was "Birdland," and I listened to it hundreds of times in a row, exclusively, for months. Weather Report's "Birdland" sounded perfect. It was the suds in a washing machine on high, the green taste of a new reed, bitter and slightly tangy on the tongue, the feeling in the teeth when you play a metal mouthpiece and you know there is too much air in the note, paint splattered on a white wall, a sexy girl with laryngitis telling a boy "yes."

Within a week of hearing "Birdland," I was messing around on someone's bass guitar, and within a few months, I had bought my own. I had begun to practice, starting where I had with the clarinet, learning my way around the scales, awed by the sight of the vibrating strings, which I looked at as closely as I could while still keeping my eyes in focus. The golden vibration of the strings is what I saw behind my lids when Jaco laid out a long note. It besotted me. The desire to own this feeling drove me to learn as much as I could about Jaco, and, for the first time in my life, I trolled for information like an obsessed fan, indiscriminate of source.

Someone told me that Jaco was classically trained and knew music theory like a beast, and that he developed his talent by transposing classical guitar arrangements for the bass. I began to do the same. When I found out that Jaco was from Fort Lauderdale, it thrilled me to know that on some level, even theoretically at least, when I went to the beach with my friends, or to the music store,

I could possibly run into him. He lived where I lived. He was from where I was from.

There are two kinds of people in the world: the lucky ones who always seem to win raffles and lottery scratch-off tickets and T-shirts, and the rest of us. As my interest in bass playing grew, I often seemed to almost run into Jaco, but not quite. One summer day, I took the bus down to Peaches Records and Tapes on Sunrise Boulevard in Fort Lauderdale. I had some sweaty cash rolled up in the pocket of my cutoffs, and was prepared to part with a good chunk of it to find a live recording of Jaco and Weather Report playing a certain Jimi Hendrix song in Europe. Peaches was a valuable resource for the music lover in those days. They had an inventory that, unless you were into some obscure stuff, usually yielded you a good find or two on every visit. They staffed employees who knew music, and who could help you find what you were looking for. Jaco's portrait, a photo from his first solo album, was also painted on the front of the building.

That day I went straight to the jazz section and started thumbing my way through the Ws. An employee strolled over.

"Looking for anything specific?"

"Weather Report. 'Third Stone from the Sun.' Live. You know it?"

"Jaco, huh? You know, he was *just* in here yesterday."

I gnashed my teeth.

I also used to frequent a music store on Oakland Park Boulevard called Modern Music, which was the best music store in South Florida at the time. Modern Music was where real musicians gathered, where the best repairs were done, where you could get the latest gear. We just called it "Modern," as in, "I'll be back later. I'm going over to Modern to see if they can tweak my pickups." I would find my way there at least once a week, sometimes to take a bass lesson, but mostly just to hover, looking at instruments, listening through the thin walls to students playing in the small side rooms, thumbing through music books, and watching instruments go in and out of the repair shop. One day, when I walked in for a lesson, my bass teacher said, "You should have gotten here fifteen minutes earlier. Jaco was *just* in. I kid you not."

Fort Lauderdale in the early eighties was a simpler place than it is now, and a little more magical. We moved at a slower pace, possibly because it was the last echo of a time before guaranteed central air-conditioning in every house and business. It could take all day to get a thing done. You could fill an old milk jug with water and wrap some sandwiches up in tinfoil and ride your bike to the beach, and stay until the mosquitoes started biting. If you had to be at work by four, you somehow had time to practice, meet up with friends, read the paper, take a swim, do your chores, and still take a bus to your job, and then maybe catch the tail end of a show afterwards. No one I knew had any money, but we were richer then—we had time to give away, and we were generous. Older, wiser musicians would take a few moments and tell the younger folks a story, or show them a riff, or listen to one. Guys would gather and debate the virtues of a new arrangement of an old song, or talk about a recent concert with simple appreciation, and without malice or envy.

It was also a time when musical Nephilim walked among us, without molestation or entourage, playing phenomenal sets at small venues. It was a time when everyone with a regular babysitting or lawn-mowing job could afford a ticket. A time when you could safely camp out in line at Sunrise Musical Theater the night before ticket sales opened for a show, and if you were first in line, you got the front-row seats. You didn't need to be a member of royalty or sell a kidney to afford it. I saw Al Di Meola from the second row. Al Jarreau from the first row. I shook Peter Gabriel's hand. I sat so close to Frank Zappa at one of his shows that he sweated on me. I saw the great jazz drummer Pete Erskine play at a venue so intimate that it didn't need amplification. I met Boots Randolph's band at a Denny's on a weeknight, forty-five minutes after seeing them in concert, and waited on Geddy Lee, the bassist for Rush, at a restaurant where I worked not too long after. It seemed odd that, since I went to the same places Jaco went, and listened to the music of some of his peers, I would not have run into him.

I upgraded and got a copy of a '62 Fender Jazz bass because Jaco played one, and I was trying hard to get his sound. For several months I listened to Jaco's new solo album, *Word of Mouth*, exclusively, then I bought a cassette for the car. I memorized the album and entertained myself for hours with the thematic echoes that wove in and out. I listened to "Three Views of a Secret" every night while going to sleep. This song was a reckless run through every emotion in a relationship, from first meeting to death, so multilayered it was like the Bible. I tried to imagine what Jaco was thinking when he arranged it, tucking in little secret vocal tracks I could barely hear, matching a bass sound with an angelic falsetto, building in slow intensity toward the end of the song like the pot builds up heat with the frog sitting right in it.

I also imagined Jaco scoring the horn parts to "Liberty City" while sitting at the beach with his kids—the same beach I went to. I thought of him listening to his favorite music before falling asleep, like I did, wondering if he saw his own musical experimentation as a form of time travel, with how he molded a typical big band sound into another realm of big band, in essence, taking listeners to a musical place none of us had been, nor should have gone for another seventy-five years. Jaco's brilliance was never more apparent to me than when I studied this album. I was awed by his ability to push the envelope, flex his genius, while at the same time making me feel like I knew a part of him that no one else knew. That's what Jaco did—his music made everyone feel like they knew him, or had a right to.

I would often catch a ride down to the Musicians Exchange, a strange little club on the seediest part of Sunrise Boulevard in Fort Lauderdale. It was kind of a dive—a two-story place with a dark, dangerous-looking parking lot in the back of the building. When I crossed that lot on the way to the entrance, I would imagine getting stabbed or abducted there, and could see the cops knocking on my parents' doors, delivering the news, and perhaps my personal belongings, to them—my Velcro Ocean Pacific surfer's wallet, with Jaco's picture tucked behind my driver's license, a bass pick from my pocket, and my Sony Walkman with a Weather Report cassette inside. Once, when I was desperate to see Buckwheat Zydeco live, I took the bus down and stayed out late enough for the buses to stop running and got stranded on Sunrise Boulevard, among the pimps and working girls and drug dealers and nightwalkers trying to score some temporary pleasure in the middle of the night. I had to call someone to come get me.

One night I had menstrual cramps and declined an invite to go down to the Exchange with some friends. The next day I spoke to one of them.

"How was it?"

"Amazing. I met Jaco in the men's bathroom. I peed right next to him."

By the way, there are two kinds of women in the world: those who take Tylenol and get on with things, and those who let cramps ruin their opportunities.

I think Jaco was a guy who pushed the limits with how he lived. He certainly did on a musical level. I didn't know him. I can't pretend to know much about him. The legend that surrounded him on the street was often just gossip from people who heard from a friend who was in a session with someone who knew someone he went on tour with, gossip that probably fueled many inaccuracies about him. I heard from my bass teacher that he was starting to go crazy. Or do drugs. Or both. Someone told me he shaved his head while on tour in Japan. Someone told me that he stood in the middle of a river and threw his favorite Fender into the water. Someone told me he jumped out of a window. Someone else told me he slashed all the tendons in his left forearm and would never play again.

I think the reason people talked about him with such malicious vigor is because he was the closest they would ever get to someone with a truly extraordinary mind: a Miles Davis, a Richard Feynman, a Michelangelo, a Mary Cassatt, a Marie Curie, a Carl Linnaeus. I often dreamed of going back in time and seeing them in action. Often before falling asleep at night, I imagined elaborate and vivid scenes where I would simply stand in a corner, perhaps as a maid, or a laboratory cleaner, or a backstage witness, while they did whatever it was they did best. Sometimes we had conversations. My admiration for these people was based on recognizing a kind of genius that comes rarely within a field. Their bodies of work would be studied by generations of students and fellow experts. They broke through constraints of time to master concepts others weren't ready to handle. People want to be part of that. There are the fans and the students and the hangers-on, but there are also those who look for the angel to fall so they can feel better about their own commonness, about the truth that is their average contribution to the world, which brings me back around to the idea that there are two kinds of people: those who build others up with the things they say and do, and those who tear them down. In loyalty to Jaco, I stopped listening to the rumors.

One night I went down to the Exchange to see a local band. I borrowed my mother's car and drove down on a Thursday night after helping with the dishes, after studying for a biology test and walking the family dog. I parked as far away from the Dumpster as I could so I wouldn't get abducted and put into a snuff movie, then walked inside and up a narrow flight of stairs. I settled somewhere in the middle of the room, alone at a table with a teardrop-shaped candleholder covered with plastic mesh. The band was finishing up a song, and as I let my eyes adjust to the dim light, the song faded away and the guitarist said, "Jaco Pastorius on bass guitar." Jaco put down the bass, and stood up, grabbed his drink, and went toward the bathroom. The band started up another song. I choked on my spit.

There are two kinds of people in the world: those who wait for things to pass them by, living a life of regret, and those who grab the world by the tonsils. I was a shy girl. I had a history of cowardice, often letting things, valuable things, slip away. I couldn't raise my hand in class. I couldn't make eye contact with the cute boy. I could never take a solo with the band, or even play any kind of improvisation in front of other people. I froze instead, and scrambled for the sheet music. Improvisation is about sharing secret parts of yourself on the fly, without controlling the content, without controlling what people know of you, and without caring what people think. I couldn't do it. I couldn't put my soul on display for others to understand raw things about me the way Jaco did.

My heart started to pound in my throat and I felt dizzy. When Jaco came back he walked around the room and mingled with a few people. I did nothing. I waited. Waited. My heart was wrecked—a tympani hijacked by a manic psychiatric escapee. I was going to collapse if I didn't breathe. I would kick myself if I let this opportunity go, so when Jaco stood, I leaped up and called out, "Mr. Pastorius!" waving like a child on a Ferris wheel. Jaco saw me, appeared to think twice about it, then walked sideways over to my table, as if he were on a boat with an uneven keel.

"Mr. Pastorius, I play bass, too!" I shrieked, though he was close enough for me to no longer need to holler. Calling him Mr. Pastorius was nerd maneuver number one, and declaring that I played bass out of the gate like that was the most dorkalicious thing that I could have declared, aside from "I play clarinet." You don't lead with that. You say something introductory, like, "Great set." I shrank down inside my tall bones. Jaco squinted at me with his head tipped to the side. He looked older than any of his pictures, and was a little heavier, and had cut his long brown hair short. He was my height.

"You play bass, huh? That's great." I saw his eyes move somewhere else.

"Do you have any advice?"

"Who do you listen to?" he asked.

"Everyone. I listen to everyone," I told him, and I meant it. I wanted to mention Glenn Miller and Yes, and Rush and Art Blakey, and John Lee Hooker, and Joe Walsh and Scott Joplin and Miles Davis and Mozart, but there wasn't time. I could tell my window was closing.

"That's good," he said. "Let me see your hands." I held them up and showed him my stretch.

"Not bad." He pointed at me and winked. "Keep practicing. Get your harmonics down." And then he walked away. He mingled a few minutes more and then walked out of the Exchange and I never saw him again.

I was excited for a few minutes, and when the letdown came, I was surprised. I thought that because Jaco's music had resonated with me so deeply, meeting him would be pivotal, crucial to my life in some way. But it wasn't. It reminded me that the music that I loved so much, the music that I could see move behind my eyelids—that was my own experience. Part of music was for sharing—the part that people can experience together—a live performance, a mix tape, the kinship you feel when you make music with other people. But part of it was private—the love you feel for it. The surging swell of emotion that you can't name when it plays, the way it is almost religious, wordlessly so, in its power.

I went home and practiced my harmonics until two-thirty in the morning, then got up four hours later and earned a C-minus on my biology test. Jaco died suddenly not long after, a sealed book, unclassifiable under anyone's system, taking with him all of the music he had yet to make, leaving us with not enough. He was my first and last celebrity obsession.

There are two kinds of people in the world: those to whom valuable, tender secrets are whispered in music, and those who just hear the music. Although I had wanted to meet Jaco for so long, I learned that the part of his musical existence I had hungered after was the private part, the part I had no right to, the part he couldn't explain to anyone anyway, just as I couldn't explain mine. What he could share stood alone like good art should, to be experienced. His music, like the music of other truly great artists, speaks a truth, the truth that music, with or without words, can be a type of philosophy, a branch of science, a form of classification, a fanning of genius, and a strain of time travel.

When I listen to Jaco's music now, I can send myself back to South Florida in the early eighties. I can hear a whisper of how South Florida used to be, salty and hot and open, a place that was relaxed and electric at the same time, a place that is only a memory. Sometimes when I listen, I get a glimpse of a packed concert hall, or stadium, or sixty-seat nightclub spilling over with sound, or a music stand alone in a bedroom, or of Jaco, tan and shirtless and smiling at the beach. I get a whiff of bus exhaust, or feel the echo of a sixty-four-bar solo that I will never forget, played by someone whose name I don't remember at a warehouse show in 1984. In this case, as with all my favorite time travel, backwards is best.

And here are my time-traveling particles realigning with his, a phantom double of myself popping out of thin air to see Jaco in his creative prime, playing with Joni Mitchell at Red Rocks in 1976, at the start of an acoustic song with just Joni, when Jaco would walk offstage for a few minutes, spot me, and say, "Hey! Come here. Hold this for me, wouldja?" He would hand me his bass, then bend down to tie his shoe. Then he would stand up, lean into me, and say, "You can see it too, can't you?"

"What?" I would say.

"The music. Just look at it. It's perfect, man." And it would be there, bending in our field of vision, yielding to the sandstone, these sound-bent colors of Joni's guitar, and lines and textures that were our shared, private language.

"It is," I would say.

"Things are going great, in case you're wondering. I'm up to some serious shit. No one in the world can do what I'm doing right now. You have to believe you're the best if you're going to be the best. You can't pay attention to what anyone else is doing. You can't worry about what people think. You have to just do your thing, man."

"Okay."

"Listen: I'll be writing a solo album in a couple of years."

"I should be telling you that," I would say.

"No need, man. I've already been there. I time travel, too. I understand everything. But there's a song called 'Three Views of a Secret' on there and it'll be crazy. You're gonna love it. It's gonna blow your mind."

"I know," I'd say. "It already did."

FOSTER DOG

We once thought we were *all that* when it came to behavioral training. My husband and I had successfully trained our five children and
our two dogs using many of the same methods, so it made sense
that, when our egos inflated to an overstuffed and inappropriate level
of pomp, we thought we were good enough to make a difference in
someone else's life. However well intended that kind of thinking is,
there is usually a measure of conceit and danger that comes with it.
Keep in mind that most of the time when I say "we" here, I mean
"me." My husband was not necessarily on board. Our dogs had settled down into adulthood, our children were on autopilot, and
things were relatively quiet for the first time in a long time, and my
husband liked it that way. I, however, felt a little restless and thought
we should take in a foster dog. It would be a collaborative family effort, I declared, though my husband put his hands up in the air and
walked out of the room when he heard this. Our job would be to
train a surrendered dog to behave in the house, teach it some man-
ners, and give it the social skills it needed to be attractive to potential
owners. Because I loved terriers and had success in training other

members of the breed, we got involved with a regional Bull Terrier Rescue League.

Our dogs were not particularly complex. We had a thick, clumsy, loose-lipped black Labrador who liked to nap, and a grubby cairn terrier who ran around looking like he had just licked a light socket. Both were happy dogs who knew their place in our family.

In my naïve mind, a bull terrier would be no harder to work with than any other kind of dog, though they had a reputation of being difficult to train. It is true: Bull terriers have a rare countenance. They mostly look like they've aspirated a huge snort of nitrous oxide and are commencing to ponder, while high, one of life's unanswerable questions, while at the same time planning a nasty prank. They are a helix of both yin and yang—purity and wickedness cohabiting in a fur furnace.

Soon the organization had a dog for us. He was called Moose, a snow-white bull terrier with a string of former homes. We were told he was owned by a busy veterinarian who needed a behavioral intervention so she could rehome him to a family that had more time to devote to him. Aside from being neglected, Moose also had a neurological problem common to that breed that caused him to compulsively spin in circles, and he was also completely deaf—a double whammy. We thought we might be able to teach him a few simple sign commands that would help his behavior. What the rescue organization neglected to tell us, but should have, was that our attempt at training him was a last-ditch effort to keep the dog from being euthanized.

When his owner dropped him off at our house, she brought a crate, a food and water bowl, a choke collar, a prong collar, a barking shock collar, a dog seat belt for rides in the car, and two hundred dollars' worth of drugs that a body could be stabbed for in certain social circles, including phenobarbital, Valium, and Xanax.

She also provided a list of instructions on how to drug the dog, when to drug him, and under what conditions we were to add more drugs or lessen his dosages, and oh yeah, she told us, he was an uncontrollable barker. It was here that I had my first wobble of doubt. In fact, I considered backing down from the deal and asking the owner to take her hairy little addict back, but I watched him frolicking with the children in the living room, and in my naïveté, simply couldn't do it. He *looked* okay. He sure was cute. Perhaps he wasn't as bad as his meds made him out to be. Perhaps it was, as it so often is, a problem with the dog's human leadership and this situation would be something we could fix.

"He's cute," I told my husband. The dog nosed my son so hard in the crotch that it launched him into the air.

"He looks like a demon," my husband said. "Are you sure this is a dog?"

The owner drove off shouting, "I'll mail more meds if you start to run out!" And, "He's not picky! He eats anything!" And, "Oh yeah! He can't swim!"

"What?" we shouted.

"Bye!" And she left us with a fistful of barbiturates and a panting, pink and white anvil.

Five minutes later he was at the bottom of the pool. We had taken him to the back patio to show him the lay of the land and also to let him relieve himself before he went inside. We watched him sniff around and explore our yard. He circled the pool, looked sideways at something that caught his eye, and stepped over the edge. My teenage daughter, fresh from the shower, leaped in after him and dragged him out. He snarfed water and shook his head and immediately started to circle the pool again. He appeared to have the balance of a drunkard, or a big-headed baby. He bent over the edge to bite a flower that had blown in and went in, face-first this time. We all leaped up again.

"Wait!" I shouted. "Let's see if he can swim at all." We watched the dog sink to the bottom, spine first. He righted himself and then began to walk on the bottom of the pool toward the deep end.

"Kids," I said later, "this dog has the molecular density of bohrium. He cannot be alone outside, and must always be leashed." The dog trotted over to the yard and squatted. He looked at us out of the corner of his eye and birthed a flaxen-haired Barbie head inside a large soft-serve pile of stool.

Moose was a beautiful dog, if you like the look of a pink-tinged goblin with a head shaped like a football and a body shaped like a hot, steroid-injected potato. The heat that came off him made him feel as if he'd just popped out of a toaster. My daughters fell in love with him within twenty-four hours, and it wasn't because of his good looks. It was because his nose was heart-shaped, and because his belly was bald hot and naked and he groaned when you rubbed it, and because when he couldn't communicate, he would stare at your face and deaf bark at you, "Wark! Wark! Wark!" as if he were trying to impart something critical, and because when he put his twenty-pound head in your lap and you scratched gently under his chin, he would close his tiny, pea-sized eyes and smile. Plus we felt a little sorry for him, something you should never do with a dog, or with children.

Moose quickly became engrossed by the swimming pool. He circled it with enthusiasm, tiptoeing around the six-inch coping as if he were on a tightrope, often biting floating flowers or bubbles. He would submerge his nose up to the lower rim of his eyelids, and bark underwater. He fell in fourteen times per day. When we pulled him out by his leash, he wagged his tail, and started another lap around the edge of the pool, scraping the pads of his feet pink, until he fell in and we had to haul him out by his leash, as if we were yanking up a lobster trap. We rubbed his pink nose and legs with SPF 50 sunscreen before he went outside. We played ball with him to develop a relationship with him. We walked him to discharge his energy. We played training games to build his trust, and it appeared, once in a while, to work. When my daughters took him out at night, he stood protectively between them and any unknown threats, such as the sweaty, shirtless, almost handsome teenage boys playing basketball up the street.

Because he had no awareness of the pool's boundaries, and had the buoyancy of a Neanderthal, and seemingly no balance whatsoever, Moose was in danger of drowning on a daily basis. His owner mailed us a canine life vest, which we strapped on him whenever he was outside. He wore the vest with pride, like a superhero cape, launching himself over the edge of the deep end at a full sprint and swimming to the shallow-end steps, over and over. With the vest on he was able to fulfill his dream of swimming like a buoyant piglet.

Moose was the pinkest dog we ever saw. Outside, he was happy, and when he was happy, or at least when he was cardiovascularly active, he turned pinker, a rose blush starting at the tip of his triangular nose and traveling up his Roman snout, and from the bottoms of his toes up his thick, muscled legs. He radiated heat. When he jumped in the pool, steam floated above him. After a few laps, his berry-colored belly cooled briefly, but his jowls still blushed like the cheeks of a German milkmaid. We threw the ball to him in the pool and he swam and swam. He showed little interest in any training or sign language. In order to get his attention, we stomped on the patio deck or the floor so he could feel the vibrations. Then we gave him a sign. After four weeks of signing "sit" and reinforcing it with treats or a toss of the ball, or a dip in the pool, he sat sporadically, when he remembered. If he felt like it.

Inside the house, it was a different story. Moose followed my husband around constantly. He appeared to love men, but it was an anxious love, an annoying love with furtive glances and boundary issues, the love of a stalker. He galloped across all terrain, including the dining table, beds, and the other dogs' backs. He spun compulsively in the kitchen, knocking into the backs of our knees until they buckled, causing us to spill plates of food, mugs of coffee. We kept him leashed in the house, and he was attached to one of us whenever he was outside of his crate, but this did not seem to matter. A few days into his visit with us, I was cooking dinner with Moose leashed to my belt loop. He stopped tangling himself in my feet and turned toward the patio, then gazed out with a look on his face I had never seen before, like he was scratching a deep itch. It took a moment to realize that he was filling our Labrador's food bowl with urine.

"Help me, here," I said to my husband. The fish was beginning to burn in the pan.

"This is not my project," he said, but he unhooked Moose from my waist and led him outside, where the dog leaped into the pool, skin hissing, leash still attached, the fire inside him dampened for a few moments.

Several times a day, possibly when medication doses were waning, Moose would begin to shark around the house and yard, looking for something to destroy. He enjoyed ripping apart whole coconuts, eviscerating "indestructible" dog toys, and plucking the laundry off the clothesline with an exuberant, slightly nasty, glee-filled smirk. He purposefully waited until we were watching to defecate on beach towels the kids dropped on the patio.

One evening we were sitting at the outside table enjoying dinner. We speculated that Moose might be settling down.

"He sure is cute," we said. "Look how he enjoys being around us when we do things together." The dog trotted jauntily around the pool wearing his life vest, nearly lost his balance, then recovered. He stood for a moment facing the canal, taking in the evening air. Then he looked over his left shoulder at us with a glint in his eye, hunched forward, and shot a hot horizontal stream of diarrhea five feet across the deck into the pool.

"Nice!" said my husband.

"Give him time," we said.

Moose loved his toys so much that he killed them and consumed them. Then whatever of the toy was not in his colon, he left in a pile, and turned a cold nose to. Occasionally he would revisit the pile of old toys and upset himself. He would bark at it, possibly regretting his decision. No matter, there was always something else to do—knock down a garbage can, vomit in my shoe, eat a worm. Our own dogs looked on in horror, but the girls thought he was on the verge of a breakthrough. If he could just realize that we loved him, they said, that our sign language had meaning that would help orient him to the world, Moose would turn a corner, like Helen Keller had. The girls held this hope tight to their hearts, faithful that love would be enough, though I was beginning to worry.

"I feel so bad for him," my daughter said one day, as we watched her sister trying to teach him a simple sign.

"Don't," I said. "It isn't good for him."

"Isn't he cute?"

"Sure is, but I don't think we're the right people for this job."

"You always tell us never to give up, Mom."

"I understand this, but I think it's time to consider that he might be a psycho," I said. My younger daughter signed "sit," and pushed

Moose's bottom down for the fifteenth time that session, then he broke away and leaped to the patio sliding glass door, and threw his shoulder into it until the glass shook. He barked his crooked, stifled, slightly shrill bark: "Wark! Wark! Wark!"

It became clear that the training was going poorly. After six or seven weeks, Moose still did not sit regularly, or show a glimmer of interest in obeying the simplest command. He had no desire to please us and did not care what any of us were doing. Apparently, the phrase "he eats anything" applied to anything that wasn't food. Moose could swallow a pair of panties or a Beanie Baby and out it would come a day later, encased in fully formed stool the shape of his large intestine, but adding a dot-sized squirt of fish oil to his kibble caused a two-day bout of diarrhea and midnight crate crapping that exhausted me, and caused me to fantasize about swiping the canine Xanax for my personal use. In fact, it was constant work to make sure Moose was okay hour by hour, and we were tired. Maybe he was crazy, I thought, as I put him in his crate one night, and watched him gnaw on his bed until his night dose of meds put him to sleep. If Moose was like this on phenobarbital, and Xanax, and antidepressants, what kind of dog was he au naturel? I was afraid to find out.

The owner, who promised us every day for two weeks that refills of his meds were in the mail, stopped taking my calls, and I knew something was wrong. I began to talk to the children about giving him back, an idea that my husband applauded. I suggested that the dog might be too neurologically damaged to be rehabilitated, at least by us. The girls cried and presented arguments. They begged me to give him more time. All he needed was love, they said, and I wanted this to be true, both for my big-hearted girls and for the dog. We had read *Chicken Soup for the Dog Lover's Soul*, as well as five or six dog training books, and we tried to love him as much as we could, while giving him our attention, our time, regular training, firm bound-aries, exercise, and every bit of effort we had. It wasn't working.

I began to halve Moose's pills in order to conserve them, calling both the rescue organization and the vet daily. No one returned my calls. As soon as his medication blood levels dropped, his energy level doubled and he became obsessed with the pool in an unhealthy way. He no longer wanted to come inside at all, but instead ran cir-cles around the deck until his skin showed pink and sunburned under his thin white fur, and he scraped his paws so raw that he left bloody footprints on the pavers. We slathered his hot body with more sunscreen, and tried to keep him inside, but when we didn't let him out, he wark wark warked until we opened the back door. His only pleasure seemed to be swimming.

Finally, we ran out of meds, and the dog turned. The first night without them, he chased his tail uncontrollably, which looked ador-able and clownish for about five seconds, until he began to hurl him-self into the front of the stove and the lower kitchen cabinets. The hot energy coming off him was sickening, desperate, and frantic. We could feel it in the air. He attacked our cairn terrier, who had been minding his business in the corner, then, a few minutes later, went for my son, who had gotten up off the couch to walk across the living room, and sunk his teeth into the boy's narrow butt.

"Hey!" my son said.

"It's a dermal piercing," my daughter told him.

"It hurts," my son said. "I hate Moose." We lunged for the dog, and wrestled him into his crate, where he spent the evening chew-ing a hole in his own abdomen while I left voicemails for his owner every fifteen minutes.

"He's got to go back," my husband said. "He's chaos. He's going to get someone in the face." I agreed. When I put his floatation vest on him to protect the wound, he bit me in the forearm, and later, in the middle of the night, he ate through the vest and bloodied his gums chewing the metal sides of the crate. The unfocused, desperate look he gave me while I sat by his crate helped me to realize he was suffering beyond what should be allowed, and beyond what we, or anyone, could fix. I hated this.

At around two in the morning, once Moose had finally fallen asleep, I got online and tracked down the owner's work address.

The next morning, while the girls alternately wept and gave me the stank eye, I packed Moose into his crate.

"Where are you taking him?"

"To his owner."

"The vet?"

"Yes."

"Is she going to help him?"

"I don't know. I hope so."

"Are you giving up on him?"

"I don't know. I hope not."

"Can we come?"

"No."

I didn't look at the girls' faces in the living room window as I drove off with the dog, locked in his crate and shoved into the cargo area of my SUV. I cried myself an hour and forty-five minutes through rush-hour Miami traffic to his owner's vet clinic in Kendall, Florida, a flat, overcrowded sprawl pocked with "apartment homes" and leased Japanese sedans that is so far south, you lose meaningful chunks of your life just driving there and back.

I wondered how this would end. Would the vet give Moose a shot that made him all better? Would she embrace him, unchanged? What would be the point of taking him back to her? To surrender him? To get more meds so we could continue to slap coats of paint over the rusted depths of his disabilities?

The traffic on the way to Kendall was what you would expect it to be: similar to battling your way down a long, hot, overcrowded road to hell. On any given day, I would rather rub honey on my bum and sit in a red ant pile than point my car toward Kendall, Florida, but here we were, and the traffic had slowed. Outside, car engines groaned, and tires gobbled the road with a hollow, feverish, unhealthy hum, and all I could feel was ten kinds of wrong. Moose lay panting in the back, the wound in his side oozing. He wouldn't look at me.

As I drove closer to our exit, I realized that nothing good would come of confronting a woman who dumped her helpless dog and stopped taking my calls. Moose would be euthanized, despite our best efforts. The weight of what I was driving to do pressed on me until I screamed and pounded the steering wheel. Around me in other cars people wore looks of sour discontent as they drove, unhappiness wafting off them like the migraine waves of heat coming off the asphalt. No one had seen my tantrum, or if they had, they hadn't cared. The traffic slowed to a crawl and my mind wandered.

I would have to tell the children, I knew, though it would break their hearts. Children can hold hope for a long time without it burning their hands, far longer than adults can, which is what allows them to complete the act of growing up in a world where people lie, where people let you down all the time, a world where love isn't always enough, a world where, sometimes, you have to give up on someone else in order to save yourself. Yet, losing this kind of hope can break a child's heart. This is why parents lie to their kids. Because they aren't ready to see them lose hope. I understood this, which is why I decided I would lie to my children about Moose. I would lie the consummate dog-death lie that parents all over the world use: Moose had found a home on a farm. Perhaps a farm with deaf owners who were also certified dog trainers. This was an excusable lie, a lie without malice, a lie I would like to believe, a hope I would like to hold, for the truth was breaking my heart, too.

I saw an exit I had never noticed, and wanted to take it, this exit I dreamed would turn into an empty road, a country road, one that would lie protected from the sun by a curved canopy of bending trees, trees that don't grow in Miami, soft sunlight dappling the dash, the car weightless on the gravelly dirt, the sound of the tires fading into a peaceful hum.

We would drive west, this sick dog and I, toward the Everglades, a magical part of Florida where the air felt new, and zummed with ozone and post-rain plant juices, mosses, and paisley-shaped, snake-made eddies, swirling quietly in watered curves, the slicing of wind in the grass, where the shaded undersides of things took away your heat, put out your fire.

I no longer heard the car engine, or the radio, which I had played to drown out the whimpering of the dog and the sniffling wrench of my own tears. It was silent. Deaf-silent, as I thought about flying, without even the whisk of the wind in our ears, to a farmhouse under a live oak, with a wide porch and acres to roam, where a gentle man with the scent of meat and egg rubbed into his hands would meet us on the steps and cup Moose under his hard, white-hot jaw and cool him into deep belly breaths, and hold him in his arms until he slept, and when he awakened, his nerves would be untroubled and still, and he would be loved by a soft-skinned toddler, and stand nose to nose with her, kissing slices of pepperoni from her pursed, pillowed lips, until the cries of delight from long-legged, slow-moving birds would call him to the yard, where a puddle of water and a muddy hole awaited him, and he would dig and splash and play, and he would hear the breath of his own lungs fill his ears, and when he barked, he would hear his own joy.

And I told myself I was driving him to this place, told myself that Moose was going to a farm, he was going to a farm, the best farm there was, praying to hold that hope in my hands for as long as I could stand it, though it burned me through and through.

SOCCER MOM

There's that embarrassing mom thing where, if you're like me, and you're at a soccer game watching your children play in, say, a tournament, and your soft, delicious little child, the one who still sleeps at night with a stuffed horse, is making a drive toward the ball, and she reaches it, pulling ahead of several lesser children, feigning out a slow-thinking defender, putting out an arm to steady herself against the face of said slow thinker, squaring up to shoot, and you are watching her from the sidelines, wearing shorts short enough to allow you to survive the oppressive heat yet long enough to cover the ugly purple thigh veins your pregnancies gave you, pacing and tripping over a cooler full of Capri Suns and orange wedges, and at the same moment your child is about to make contact with the ball, your own foot reaches out and kicks the air like a marionette. You cannot help it any more than you can help gagging the first time your baby has diarrhea, or yelling "fuck" in front of your preschooler when you grate a hunk of knuckle skin into the pile of Monterey Jack cheese on taco night.

Then there's that thing where, if you're like me, after you've watched a number of children play soccer for a number of years, and although you have never once played soccer yourself, you begin to believe you have developed a nearly psychic coaching gift, and in a series of brilliant illuminations of strategy that assert themselves only after you shingle your hair into the bobbed, highlighted helmet the other soccer moms are wearing, you realize you know exactly who needs to come out and who needs to go in in a given game to win it, and you see your husband on the other side of the field, *coaching the game,* and you pull out your cell phone and dial him up. You watch him reach into his pocket, check to see who is calling, see that it is you, and decline the call. You call him again.

"What?" he says. You can hear him scream this from the other side of the field a portion of a second after it comes through the phone.

"Pull Kristi out. Put Maya in goal. Move Alexis to midfield."

"Right," your husband says, and he hangs up. He makes no substitutions and ignores your frantic waves, then as your daughter makes another run for the ball, you kick your foot in the air again, this time screaming, *"Shoot it!"* as if your telling your child to shoot the ball is what will make her do it, as if she, who has played soccer for five years, would never think of this on her own when running up on the goal. There is another battle for the ball and you involuntarily kick the air a third time, as if you are a frog on a dissection table in Bologna and Luigi Galvani is electrifying your muscles with a charged scalpel. You can't stop yourself from looking like a sideline fool. You cannot not kick. It's a thing soccer moms do, and nearly against your will, you have become one.

When is it you realize you have allowed your children's accomplishments to begin to replace everything you have ever done? Oh, it's now. It's right here on the sidelines of this under-watered, crispy field in the sports complex designed with the maximum legal square feet of asphalt parking lot and minimum legal number of trees.

It reaches nearly one hundred degrees here in peak sun, and your naked neck broils like a steak while you watch twenty-two children burn a collective 6,600 calories. You haven't seen the inside of a gym in three years because you have been too busy washing sports uniforms and returning them to the proper bedrooms, and checking gear bags, and feeding your progeny supper at four in the afternoon in time to get them to their various practices, which you must stay and watch, because that's what the good soccer moms do. You must appear to be a good soccer mom, even though you are barely holding it together, and you just want to go home and take a nap and pick the kids up after practice is over. But the good soccer moms will notice if you don't stay and they will judge you for it. You know this because you yourself judge the "bad" moms who drop their children off, firing bitter darts of jealousy from your eyes as they drive away to meet a friend for coffee, or grab a massage while they know their child is safe at practice. Even though they tell everyone they have to go "pick up a prescription," or "take another child to math enrichment," *you know* and you judge them.

Your soccer mom status is cemented by a few other behaviors. First, there is the belief that your daughter is an irreplaceable anchor—the star, if you will, even if only in your own eyes—on any given team. Or your son is the star. Or your stepson is. Or it's not soccer, but lacrosse, or it's not lacrosse, but football, or basketball or baseball or softball or dance, and at any given moment, two or three or four of your kids play on several different sports teams and you spend your afternoons, evenings, and weekends coordinating practice times and carpools with other mothers whose children are not as good as yours, mothers you would ordinarily have no interest in spending time with, though it's not because their children are boring or average, it's because their mothers talk too much. You drive to windswept fields teeming with hundreds of other children, and plunk your ass in a folding chair while your children exercise, watching them with the same obsessive interest slower members of society have in reality TV shows. Sometimes you bring snacks. For yourself.

Next is the unhealthy obsession with outfitting your children like professional athletes. Sporty kids need gear, so if you are a regular person like me, you fork over whatever you can swing, handing down cleats and outgrown gloves and gear bags to your smaller children in the gear queue, occasionally shopping at Play It Again Sports in a neighboring town where no one you know will see you buying used sports equipment. You forgo new clothes for yourself, or luxuries of any sort, in order for these children to have the extra-thick shin guards, or properly fitting Under Armour, even though you remember playing childhood softball and basketball in sneakers from Kmart and cheap, silk-screened team T-shirts without any ill effects, except for the fact that you did not get a college sports scholarship. You begin to believe that your children need this gear in order to have the athletic opportunity they *deserve*. If you are rich or a sociopath who cares not one whit about running up the credit card bills, you buy the best of everything you can find at Dick's or Soccer Max, thinking, almost against your will, that a $160 shell-out in football cleats for a nine-year-old now might translate into a professional football career that will allow your little QB to one day buy you an upscale house and a silver Escalade. As if a pair of cleats will be the thing that turns your child into a winner.

Then there is the schedule juggling. If you are at all like me, after you recover from the cost of the gear, and the league entrance fees, insurance fees, uniform fees, and conditioning coach fees, and your children are safely ensconced on their various teams, you use the last of your money to purchase a master organizer they sell for moms who are trying to get a handle on a schedule every bit as complicated as a teaching hospital's surgical schedule, or the daily flight schedule managed from an air traffic control tower of an international airport. You spread out all the practice times and game times for the Bombers, the Eagles, the Blazers, the Knights, and the Intimidators on the kitchen table and begin to input data into the organizer, carefully orchestrating who has to be where when, and what time dinner needs to be on the table on various nights, and which sports events coordinate with school events that can't be missed. If you are lucky, your child will not be on both the school team and the travel team of the same sport in a season, as that is a scheduling state so stressful that it has been known to cause mothers to develop trichotillomania. You can easily spot these poor women: They are the ones quietly plucking out their own eyebrows or eyelashes at red lights or in sports complex parking lots. They look pinched and backed up, because they have had to train their bowels to follow a certain schedule, as they have no time of their own to take a dump from seven A.M. until midnight on weekdays or at any time during the weekend, especially if they still have preschoolers at home.

This schedule reckoning takes a spreadsheet and enough wheedling and favor-trading with other carpooling moms to where the high-stakes détentes you manage to sustain are of the kind you might find at an international political summit. If you are like me, this herculean effort makes you cry at least once per season, or drink alone at night after everyone has gone to bed, or take Percocets left over from previous surgeries.

Then there is the ill-lighted, miscast pride that comes with knowing that you birthed a remarkable athlete. When other parents can't help but notice your child's extraordinary athletic ability, your ego swells as if they are complimenting you, and you can't seem to separate your child's personal accomplishments from your own. This is the shameful part of soccer momming. It is heady stuff that can weaken the soul. You see your child twist in space in an artful way, and watch them outrun or outthink a competitor, and even though the competitor is a ponytailed princess who sleeps with her own stuffed animal at night, your mind has reduced her to enemy status. Instead of seeing her as a person, you categorize her as an obstacle for your child, the star, to overcome, and what's more, you created that star. It came *out* of you. *You* did it. It's *yours* and there is a dirty aspect of ownership that comes with watching your child play sports, so when you think about it in the heat of the moment, the other child is a dangerous condottiere that you yourself must overpower. It's awful and thrilling at the same time, because it is the only bit of power you feel in your life. You are triumphing, by proxy, over a nine-year-old child. Bully for you. Kick the air and scream "Shoot it!" until your voice is hoarse and you will later need to cool down by overeating at the postgame fast-food restaurant after the victory you had nothing to do with.

If you are like me you cannot stop these thoughts and actions, even though you know you are a walking cliché, and it is something you swore you would never become. Like kicking an invisible ball on the sidelines like an idiot, this suburban movement is a part of something that has its own tide, a tide that moves in and out with the seasons, a tide you feel yourself drowning in on occasion, because after all, you were the tattooed, boot-shod rebel who swore she would never live in the suburbs and drive a minivan, and yet you have ended up rocking that minivan hard and living in the burbiest of burbs, which, frankly, bores you to tears, but is so, so safe and so good for the children. You are the woman who swore you would stick your kids in daycare the moment your maternity leave was over so you could go back to building your career, but that plan scorched up like a dried leaf the moment your first child was placed in your arms. You quit work "for a while," planning to go back when the child started school, but here it is ten years later and your second or third or fourth child has yet to start kindergarten and you have found yourself working pro bono as the chief operating officer of a very small, cluttered business called Your Family, which seems, at times, to have no purpose. Others might tell you to check your privilege for complaining about such a luxury, but it is more confusing and complicated than simple middle-class comfort. It is the battle between a loss of identity and its crooked bookend: the promise that women can have it all, the promise that we have choices, yet are looked down upon for choosing *this* path when we could have done "so much more."

Maybe, if you are at all like me, you struggle with job skills required for being a soccer mom, and must hide these struggles, because your natural skill set has slowly revealed itself to be the kind that prefers simplicity and order and quiet, and you know you are forgetful, and you know you will make mistakes because you are forcing yourself to do this hard job as best as you can when really, you would be better suited for a different job, a simpler job, say, perhaps as a painter (house or art), or a philosopher, or a clock repairwoman, or an artisanal baker of gluten-free masterpieces, or even cheesecake on a stick, which you sell at local farmer's markets. At times, especially during the middle of a given season, you may remember college, when you had the luxury to write short stories for fun and you wrote one about a married woman with kids who fakes her own death and uses a new identity to start over in the Pacific Northwest, a place that seems cool and woodsy and quiet, a far cry from standing in four inches of palm tree shade on the sidelines of a sports field, or your sour laundry room, or the inside of your sweat-soaked minivan.

You might even attempt to become the best soccer mom in all the land, wearing the bobbed hair helmet, keeping the minivan vacuumed, remembering which child wears which uniform, remembering to never again leave the middle defender on your daughter's team, who you are responsible for driving home Wednesday nights, at the field like you have done twice before, only you become easily overwhelmed by the responsibilities, often forgetting to bring the orange slices on your assigned game day. This deficit requires you to occasionally dump your kid on the field and race to the grocery store, buy oranges, race home and cut them up, and bag them and bring them back to the field, often missing the first quarter of the game. Or you forget to turn in the cookie dough or gift wrap fundraiser orders, or worse, you forget to sell the cookie dough or gift wrap at all.

Why do you suck so badly? If you are like me, it's because you either didn't read the job description of what parenting would be like before you signed up, or you were not willing to extrapolate "years of extreme sleep deprivation and constant chaos" from everything everyone has said since the beginning of time about parenting. It's as if you got drunk and joined the Marines on a lark and now want out, only there is no way out without going to prison.

Lest I appear to be one-sidedly bitter and negative, let me say this: Despite living your life on the sidelines, or setting up mission control from a seven-passenger vehicle shaped like a manatee, or listening to audiobooks through headphones to protect yourself from soccer mom colloquy, despite your bobbed helmet of hair reducing your sexual attractiveness by a factor of ten, despite worrying about your contribution to the collective cultural anxiety of women's achievements by staying home and devoting all of your energy to a few non-influential people who don't even thank you, and despite such an overall uncooperative reality, there is something golden about this time.

It is a season when your children are as beautiful as they have ever been, though you thought nothing could be as beautiful as their babyhood. The flushed, salty cheeks, the hair sticking to the sweat on their necks, their knobby knees, bandaged fingers, their giant protective equipment that seems to dwarf them at the beginning of the season, but which looks perfectly fitted by the last game. The effort they give forth that makes you weep at times. If you are like me, you have cried while watching the two teams shake hands after a particularly difficult game.

Your children are doing important work, even though it looks like they are playing games. They are building their bodies, learning how to move, learning how to listen, learning how to take a small desire such as "get the ball" or "stop the ball," and turn it into a hunger to make something bigger happen. They are learning how to lose graciously, one of the most valuable of life skills, and if they have good coaches, they learn about devotion: to team, to coach, to someone other than self, and this is healthy. It helps them grow up to be the kind of children who won't live in your basement after college.

This is a time when the children still need you to show them how to be. They won't always, and the assertion of this truth will be increasingly painful as time goes by, but for now, know that, even though they don't thank you and they leave their God-awful, wet, stinking shin guards on the cloth upholstery of the minivan time after time, they need you to orient them in society. You are training two or three or four little people to grow up and be better versions of yourself, and this is one way to leave your mark on the world, to time travel and leave part of yourself for future generations you won't live to experience. It's a marathon of slow growth.

You can see this growth transform them, sometimes from week to week. One day, you will see the coach introduce a skill and your child will fumble with it like a puppy, yet improve bit by bit, until one day during a game, when the pressure is on, you will see the child execute the thing perfectly, exactly the way she was taught. Later, you will see the quiet pride on the child's face when the coach praises her for it in front of the team.

If you are like me, the first time you realize that the effort you invest in making these activities happen is a finite thing, and that one day it will go away, it stops being a chore, and begins to be something precious, like oxygen. You watch them with a different eye while they repeat the same drills for weeks, running, jumping, getting knocked over, failing, laughing, weeping, building friendships, pushing their limits, and for a brief while, all things considered, there is no limit to the hope vested in these beautiful young people of yours. The ones who sit with quiet anxiety during breakfast before a game are the same ones who sing "John Jacob Jingleheimer Schmidt" at the top of their lungs in the back of the minivan after the game, and you see sublime work happening here—a slow burn of something transformative—and you think as you shove the balled-up, sweaty gear into the washing machine one more time, that like with all things parenting, it's not about you. It never was.

THE DRESS

Perhaps she is walking home, from work or from school, and she spies a ripped box filled with rolls of old plaster, half buried in a pile of garbage in a back alley. Maybe she picks it up and takes it home to her family's apartment. Maybe she is forced to work sewing cheap tracksuits after school and on weekends, or maybe she has quit school to do this because her family needs the money. Maybe she has moved from her village to the big city, signed a contract to work, and hates the work, yet she is unable to escape it. Maybe she is living in near slave conditions, or maybe she is just the daughter or granddaughter of a seamstress who has learned how to sew because that's what the women in her family have always done. Maybe she likes it.

My first daughter was born with a drive to achieve. If you forget the part where she exhausted me from the moment she was conceived because my body took to a tenant about as well as I would take to a tenant in my home now, she was an interesting challenge. Precocious, they said. She spoke her first word in the bathtub at four and a half months—"tu-tu," after I poked the floating plastic tub toy and said "turtle" sixteen times. She walked at eight months and two weeks, and though people might see this as a positive, it wasn't necessarily. Children who skip the crawling and move straight to walking miss critically important cross-lateral movment that engages both sides of the brain. Plus, they are wild and unsteady, flinging themselves through space and time like little drunkards without the muscular development in the upper body to save themselves when they fall. If memory serves, she sported a split lip for a good three months until she got the hang of staying upright.

She demanded books as a baby. Many of them per day. Since we didn't let her watch television until she was older, we read a lot. If I tried to get creative with the language in a book she knew by heart, she would correct me until I got it right. She spoke in full, complex sentences at around age one. By the time preschool started at two and a half, I was relieved to drop her off somewhere, even if it was only three days a week for three hours a pop. I was grateful for the silence, and when twelve o'clock rolled around, I wasn't always ready to pick her up.

By third grade she was in the "gifted program," which in Florida just meant extra homework, slightly more engaged teachers, and a better-behaved group of peers. She came home one day, dropped her Powerpuff Girls lunch box on the kitchen counter, and hissed through her teeth that she was going to get into a "top college." I was amused.

"What's a top college?" I asked her.

"A top college is one of the best colleges, which is exactly where I will be going. *The best.* Not like this stupid public school that doesn't even recognize that when someone has a different idea for doing something, it doesn't mean she should *get in trouble for it.* Sometimes different ideas are *better.* They don't understand me. I want to punch my teacher." She faced me with fists, her tongue pressing through the holes her missing teeth left behind.

"I've had that feeling before," I said, backing off slowly. "Can I help you?"

"No. I'm going to do all my homework now. *All of it.* And it's going to be perfect. I'll show them." She sat down at the kitchen table and slammed the cover of her math book open. "And you know what else? When I grow up, I'm going to leave this place. I'm going to move to Europe or Russia. I'm going to claim my rightful place as Russian royalty. I have Russian royal blood in me, I can feel it."

"Not one molecule of you is Russian," I said.

"Then forget Europe. Forget Russia. I'm going to move to France."

"France is in Europe, honey."

"Forget that, then. Paris."

"Paris is in France."

"See what I mean? They don't teach you anything at this stupid public school!"

This daughter seemed to learn best by debate, and by debate, I mean "fighting people with words until she made them cry." During mock trial in middle school, she made a boy, who knew he was acting a role, weep on the witness stand. I cried three times a week just dealing with her at home. This was a child on fire.

By high school, she had blood in her eyes. She took as many AP classes as she could, lettered in two sports, joined clubs I hadn't even heard of, clubs you couldn't have paid me to join if I had ever had the misfortune to relive high school. She ran for class president and crushed it. When it came time to apply to colleges, she did what she said she was going to do when she was still missing teeth and wearing her hair in Afro puffs—applied to eleven top schools, and got into ten of them. She chose the one that gave her the most funding—an alarmingly selective private liberal arts college in the northeast. The kind of school whose brochure made me break out in hives of incompetence. The kind of school where people wore ascots and didn't need safe spaces because they had drivers and summer houses. When she went away to school, everyone in the house was exhausted. We were a little bit relieved that she was gone. Our plain Florida town wasn't meant to hold her. Her future looked the kind of bright none of us had ever achieved: undergrad at a top school, then a top-ten law school, then perhaps a think tank or some policymaking down the road.

The only bump in the road, one we hadn't planned on, was the boy.

What if, so far away, she learned a running stitch by sewing two mismatched pieces of cotton together, then cutting off the tip of the knot, and reusing both the thread and the fabric to do it again and again, until the stitches looked as if a machine had made them? What if she learned this before she could read? What if this was play for her: producing straight stitches like a row of ducks following their mother, morphing into children playing tag in a zigzag stitch? Then graduating to a whip stitch, a high-risk visible stitch that gave her a small thrill when executed perfectly, the identicality, the cadence if you will, of each small stitch folding into the fabric in just the right place. One exactly like another, like tiny soldier spines. Almost hypnotizing. Then slip stitching spare zippers into slippery cuts of satin, just for the practice, and finally, when she was eight or nine, sitting down in front of the sewing machine she had never before been allowed to touch.

The summer before she went away to college, my daughter met a boy. He was a few years older, had already finished college and was well into law school, so calling him a boy might be a bit demeaning. He was a nice guy. Handsome. Earnest. He met my daughter for coffee one afternoon and they agreed to meet again.

The next few weeks were bumbling. The two of them acted like cute caricatures of people falling for each other. My daughter developed a skill of poring over outfit combinations for hours, then appearing from her bedroom as fresh as if she had just grabbed something from a pile and tossed it on. It looked effortless but the pre-date clothing angst I witnessed proved it was not. The two would watch television together, or, because they were poor, they would go on picnics and read. At night, they liked to take walks. When he came over to pick her up, I noticed he draped his arm over her shoulder like he would a fence post, and sometimes he would knead her neck with one hand, almost as if he were guiding her, or perhaps choking her. I filed this away.

When she went away to school in the fall, their distance caused more than a geographical rift. My daughter wanted to meet new friends, and go to social events, which made her boyfriend suspicious, and he grew afraid she was going to leave him. There would be bigger problems later, as there often are, but for now, the distance between them worried him, and stressed her out, to where she would call me nearly in tears before a Skype session.

"I know how you can fix this," I would say.

"How?"

"Break up with him. You're too young for a long-distance relationship. You're supposed to be having fun."

"I can't have fun. I love him."

"Well, if he loves you as much as you love him, he'll wait for you to finish college."

"I think he thinks I will meet someone else."

"I think that's kind of the purpose of college, isn't it?"

"I don't want to meet anyone else, Mom. I love *him*."

Maybe one night, after everyone is asleep, she folds her hair into a bun and molds the plaster around her nude form, pressing the white, cold, wet strips over and around her shoulders, under her armpits, across her breasts, her stomach, her hips, her upper legs, shaping the proof of herself, then after it dries hot and tight and itchy, she cuts it away, ripping the plaster from her young ribs like a first breath. She tapes it back together, and fills it, then covers it in cheap muslin stolen from a discard pile in the living room, pinning it carefully to her new self. She hangs the replica of her torso on an old IV pole, her pretend breasts the height of her real ones. She has made a dress form. She begins to sew her own designs.

There is something I've seen happen to men when extremely beautiful women are within their grasp. They can get paranoid. They can fear being dumped. They can lose whatever confidence attracted the women to them in the first place, and they can become possessive. I haven't experienced this personally, of course, but my daughters have. This young man was the kind of smitten that can only occur when the woman you are in love with is painfully lovely, extremely intelligent, and living in a college full of age-appropriate intellects fourteen hundred miles away. I think he was afraid of her getting away, so he bought a ring. It was exquisite. A perfect diamond solitaire in platinum. Then he did the old-fashioned thing: He asked my husband and me for her hand in marriage.

We said no.

In fact, I remember saying something like, "No! No! No! Please don't. At least not yet. My lord, she just turned nineteen a few weeks ago! Her college is ranked third in the nation. She's in a hard major. It's only three and a half more years until she graduates. If it's love it will wait." Knowing full well that this child of mine couldn't cook a meal, couldn't balance a checkbook, and was so wracked with anxiety over the strategic social steps required to date this boy that she couldn't communicate honestly with him, I was pretty sure that a *marriage* would push her over the edge. Note: She would be able to feed herself nicely within a year or two, and not only would she balance a checkbook by her sophomore year, she would be publishing economics essays, but that's simply an anecdote to illustrate that at nineteen, this person was not ready to be a wife. Marriage is hard enough without thwarting your academic and professional dreams.

He whisked her away during the first few days of her first semester break, just before Christmas—frantically, it seemed, as it involved a late-night pickup from the Orlando airport, and a drive, during bad weather and a cold snap, to St. Augustine, where both of his parents were waiting to watch him pop the question. There was a sparkling gelding pulling a carriage shaped vaguely like a pumpkin. And cameras. The ring gleamed like My Precious. It fit my daughter's finger as if it had been made for it, though people should never see a thing like this as *a sign*. Sometimes rings just fit right. The young man was handsome and full of promise. She couldn't communicate honestly with him, so she said yes. Of course.

So I spent Christmas explaining to our friends and relatives why I was *allowing* this child, who was over eighteen and didn't need my permission for anything, to get married and throw her future away. I spent a lot of time shrugging. There were no answers I could give without making us all look bad.

Despite her own quiet misgivings, my daughter spent the holidays floating six inches off the ground, leafing through bridal magazines, and extending her hand in the air above her head to admire her rock against the bright blue Florida sky. When you caught her unawares, she covered her mouth with her hand and giggled, and this child had no previous history of being a giggler.

Rushing a bad thing never makes it better. The two set a date; once again, against our desires. We had recently recovered from our oldest kid's college expenses, to which, I am sorry to say, we were unable to contribute as much as he deserved. This child, my stepson, was bright and athletic and did his fair share with athletic scholarships and hard work. His younger brother, equally as sharp and athletic, chose the military instead of college, but we still had two college-bound daughters, as well as another son to finance. I was in the middle of graduate school, so to say that we were in a position to pay for a wedding would be like saying we were in a position to take a hot air balloon tour through Europe and Asia. But love, even the idea of someone else's love, makes people do things they wouldn't ordinarily do. We said we would help, though by doing this, a part of me felt like I was kissing my daughter's future good-bye.

With my daughter away at school, and studying forty hours per week while also not knowing jack squat about vetting vendors or photographers or wedding locations, the planning fell to me. I didn't mind it, but if this wedding was going to be up to me, it would be modest. We decided that we would contribute three thousand dollars, and encouraged them to book a low-end venue on an off day. If they were truly in love, the wedding venue and all the trappings wouldn't matter. I reminded them of my grandparents, who had held their reception, which featured cookies and punch, in their church basement at eleven o'clock in the morning on a Wednesday. My grandmother had worn a two-piece skirt and jacket—her nicest—and my grandfather had worn a work suit. Then my grandfather went off to war, but that's not the point. The point is you don't have to spend a bunch of money on a dumb party when the marriage is what matters most. We could get a nice cake from the grocery store, and do something cheap with bales of hay and canning jars and baby's breath. We could do our own food with BBQ, vats of Southern mac-n-cheese, metal pans of salad and baked beans. The signature drink would be lemonade from a mix. My daughter could get a simple dress, perhaps a used one. Maybe a rental.

She starts with blouses, because she believes them to be simple. She learns the princess stitch, and fits the blouses to her shoulders and breasts perfectly, high-collared necks and perfectly fashioned wristbands in subtle colors, drawing attention to the fine bones in her hand, the angle of her jaw, in a way her mother does not like. She is beginning to set herself apart from others in this way, and she is told to stop. She sews tops and skirts for her mother's friends for extra cash. She works cheaply and stays busy, for the college entrance exam scores are skewed in favor of men, and she never performed well in school, anyway. When she has saved enough, she buys a bolt of bright white satin, half a bolt of silk, some stark white tulle as rough as sandpaper. She copies the dresses she sees in back issues of bridal magazines. She learns to control the fickle nature of charmeuse, the whine of georgette, the romantic longings of light cotton batiste, the serious weight of damask. At first she copies only the simplest dresses, fitting each to her own dress form. Each dress slips onto her perfectly and the possibilities dance in front of her eyes, though a marriage of her own will not likely happen. There simply aren't enough men in her town. If only she had some beads. And maybe a Web site . . .

A couple of days before she headed back to school, my daughter and I visited an upscale bridal shop. When we told the saleslady that my daughter was nineteen, she blinked, but held her tongue. My daughter unfolded a few photos of gowns she had ripped out of *Modern Bride* and handed them to the saleslady, who disappeared inside a row of tightly packed dresses covered in thick, groaning plastic, and came out nearly bowled over by the weight of several gowns draped over her shoulders. None of them had price tags. She disappeared with my daughter into a dressing room, while I sat outside and chewed a cuticle. When I had gotten married the first time, I bought an off-the-rack dress made of lace and plastic sequins. It looked like it was worth every bit of the ninety-nine dollars I paid for it. I bought used for my second marriage . . . a sleeveless bodice top and matching skirt of plain off-white satin that looked like a whole dress when put together. It was also under a hundred dollars. I'm the kind of person who buys a pair of shoes and has them re-soled when they wear out, so I couldn't see the point of wasting money on a dress I would never wear again.

"You ready, Mom?" the saleslady asked.

"Bring it on," I said. My daughter glided out covered in a creamy spillage of fabric . . . it was fitted, with a tight bodice, and a full skirt, there was some satin, and a lace overlay, and some sort of special lace see-through part on the top that hinted at a collar, but with skin underneath. That's about all I can say to describe it, other than the look on my daughter's face was more exquisite than the dress. I stood up.

"This is the one, Mom," she said.

"It's the first one you've tried on. It can't be *the one*. Can it?" I looked at the saleslady.

"It is," my daughter gushed.

"I *am* good," the saleslady said.

"What kind of dress is this?" I asked.

"It's a Pronovias."

"I don't know what that means. How much is it?"

"It's twenty-nine ninety-nine," the saleslady said.

"You're saying it's three thousand dollars?"

"It's worth every penny. You can't do better than Pronovias."

"I love it, Mom," my daughter said.

"I've paid less for cars I've owned, and I certainly drove them more than once. Sorry. I'm having a bit of sticker shock." I sat back down and fanned myself.

"Do you want me to get you a cup of water?"

Over the next hour, my daughter tried on several more gowns, each as stunning as the previous one, but her heart was set on the Pronovias.

"I've got to have that dress," she said. "It's like it was made for me."

"There were jumper cables pulling it tight in the back. It was clearly not made for you."

"I need it."

"Well, get a night job, because the cost of that dress is the budget for your entire wedding."

Later that week, I went online to see if I could track down a cheaper Pronovias source, perhaps a discount shop of slightly irregular dresses whose beading had come undone, or whose lace had sagged slightly, or perhaps one with a small smudge on the hem that would knock down the price by twenty-seven hundred dollars or so. An ad popped up that said, "Pronovias Dresses 70% off!!!" I clicked, and down the rabbit hole I went, into an online world of frantic brides-to-be who were looking to fit impossible budgets, and of Chinese dressmakers, happily copying custom gowns for a fraction of the price, and shipping them to privileged Americans looking for the ever-elusive deal.

First she must take pictures of her gowns. Her cousin was a good photographer. Then a Web presence in places where people don't know how to do anything for themselves anymore . . . like the UK, and America. If she could get a few international clients, and they told their other rich friends, her business could take off. She would have more money for materials, she could hire other workers to sew. In fact, other dressmakers were using the original gowns as representations of their own work. Perhaps she could do that . . .

Dear WeddingGown96,
I am looking to have a wedding gown made for my daughter. Can you copy designs from photographs?
Gratefully,

Dawn Davies

Dear Mr. Davies Dawn,
Yes. I make all wedding dresses any type. Handmade. Please upload photos of dress you would like. And photo of your daughter please. Then click on link here to see how to send measurements. Send all measurements and photos to me and I will make dress for you. I will give you price when I see dress.
Gratefully,
Joan
WeddingGown96

Dear Joan,
Thank you so much for taking this project on. The dress is a Pronovias from the 2013 collection. Attached are three photos of it. Also attached are a few photos of my daughter,

as well as her measurements, as requested. I am looking for-
ward to getting your quote. She really likes this dress.

Yours truly,
Dawn

Dear Davies Dawn,
I will make dress for you for $168 USD. Shipping $20 USD.
Please see attached link for how to pay. Also, please choose
your satin color from the list in another attached link. I will
make dress custom and ship to you. You have found the right
dressmaker to make your dreams come true, but please be
patient. Special things take time.

Yours truly,
Joan
WeddingGown96

Dear Joan,
Thank you very much. Are you sure you can make this dress
exactly like the one in the photo for $168 USD? Same materi-
als, same cut? Same everything?

Dawn

Dear Mr. Dawn,
Yes. Dress will be exactly the same. We have three generation
dressmaker in my family. I will start as soon as payment is
made and your daughter will have beautiful dress for her
beautiful day.

Thank you,
Joan
WeddingGown96

I began to wonder about Joan, often late at night, when scrolling obsessively through Pinterest for cheap wedding ideas. First, I suspected her given name wasn't Joan, because, well, she was Chinese, and the Chinese I knew seemed to choose American names when dealing with Americans. This made me sad, although I recognized that if I were in China, I would be thrilled to choose a Chinese name to replace my American one. The Chinese people I knew also seemed to pick odd, vaguely Catholic names from older generations, as if they watched television shows from the 1960s and 1970s: Maryann, Fiona, Margaret; Bobby, Nick, Walt. It's as if they suspected a communication breakdown because we can't handle pronouncing foreign names, or we demand that things feel comfortably American in order to hand over our money. Mostly, I wondered about my Americanness: wanting a $3,000 gown for $168, demanding something handmade by someone whom I wasn't convinced was free from working in a sweatshop. Was there even a Joan?

I found a wedding forum thread for women who had, foolishly or not, taken a gamble on Chinese knockoff gowns. They each posted their original dress inspiration, shared the names of the Chinese companies that were making their custom gowns, waited a few months for the dresses to arrive, then took pictures of everything, from the packaging, to the package partially open during mid-reveal, to the white or off-white of the gown bursting from the package like a canister of ready-bake biscuits. Then came the unfolding of the gown and the selfies of the bride-to-be wearing her new creation. Sometimes there was a hit—a well-made gown of decent material that, when you squinted, somewhat resembled the original gown enough to wear it with only minor alterations, but most of them were misses. Cockeyed, acid-trip misses with mismatched satin colors, cheap glued-on beading, badly sewn, poorly sized monstrosities that the women, in a sort of unwritten rule, had to declare that they wouldn't be caught dead in, although it had been worth a try.

I realized that these were more than women who simply wanted a deal. These were women who were willing to gamble and lose. They liked the idea of the unknown and weren't afraid to be disappointed for the chance that they ended up sticking it to the wedding industry man by getting a $2,000 gown for $150. The smart ones built in time to find another dress if the Chinese one came out badly, but a few were forced to scramble and buy something last minute and—horror of horrors—off the rack. I realized I was one of those women who liked the gamble. I wanted to play the game. I envisioned Joan poring over the Pronovias gown late into the night, using her savant-like dressmaking skills to re-create a live gown from a photograph and some measurements. Despite seeing some of the other Chinese knockoffs, I hoped my daughter's dress would be perfect. I knew this could be done—my grandmother had been a seamstress and could study a dress in a shop window, then go home and make it from memory with patterns she cut out of brown paper bags.

I imagined Joan taking her lunch break, perhaps sitting outside of her shop in an alley, talking to other shopkeepers, a bowl of noodles and meat balanced on her knees, her straight black hair cut neatly to her chin in the type of simple bob that caused swells of jealousy in me when I saw one on the street. I wondered what kind of personality she had to have to pore over a seam for two hours until she got it right, to sew satin button loop closures by hand, pairing them with round, satin buttons spaced a quarter of an inch apart, all the way from the sacrum to the neck. Did she listen to the radio, or perhaps watch television? Did she work with other seamstresses or tailors? Was she committed to her craft, or was dressmaking a fallback? I grew to believe that Joan was a college-age girl like my own daughter, a quiet spirit with patience and a domestic side, one who loved the romance of weddings, one for whom US$168 represented a tidy sum of money. I became deeply interested in the creation process, and loved that I was communicating with someone across the world. I would compose an e-mail at night to someone so far away, and wake up, with a little thrill, to a return e-mail from Chinese Joan, the magical seamstress, with a price quote, or an update, or a photograph. This dress became *my* precious, and also a symbol of my ability to do one final thing for my daughter to make her happy before she grew up and got married. I wanted this dress to be perfect with all my heart for those reasons, and also because I didn't want to have to tell anyone I had bought a Chinese knockoff.

> Dear Joan,
> I'm not trying to rush you or anything, but I was wondering if you have any pictures of the dress in whatever stage of completion it is in. I like seeing the process. Would you mind sending me a photo or two?
>
> > All best,
> > Dawn

> Dear Dawn,
> Don't worry. Your dress is almost finish. Here are some photos of it. You can see fine satin we use. It will be ready in a few weeks.
>
> > All best,
> > Joan
> > WeddingGown96

Dear Joan,

Thank you for your kind attention. The dress looks very nice, although it looks like it is a very bright white satin, and not the off-white we selected. The color we selected was more like a candlelight white, or ecru. Can you confirm that you are indeed using off-white-colored satin? And the lace at the neckline doesn't look as small as the lace on the Pronovias gown. In fact, it looks like a large-pattern lace all over the chest, which is nothing like the Pronovias gown.

Thank you,
Dawn

Dear Dawn,

Don't worry. The lace is fine. I changed it. The satin is off-white. It's just photograph lighting that make it look white. Please be patient.

Joan
WeddingGown96

Meanwhile, the summer after freshman year, my daughter signed with a modeling agency in Miami and decided to take her fall sophomore semester off from school to figure out how to make her educational dreams match her impending marriage reality. One option would be to model for a while, because not everyone gets that opportunity, then finish up at a state school in the armpit of a town where she and her husband would be living after he finished law school, though neither of us liked that idea.

"Remember how much you hated the meaninglessness of public school? How it made you nuts?" I said.

"Yeah."

"That's exactly what it's going to be like at Sunshine State U. This school is basically a community college with 'state' in the name. When all is said and done, you will have not escaped a Florida government education and you will have not escaped Florida. In fact, I predict you will never leave Florida if you choose this path." My daughter started to cry.

While she was deciding what to do, she dieted down to stick size to please the modeling industry, she went on casting calls, and she argued with her fiancé about the merits of an elite liberal arts education. She lived at home with us and saw her fiancé in the evenings and on weekends. A few weeks after I plunked down a nonrefundable $1,500 to hold their wedding venue, they broke up. My husband and I cheered silently for a few days until they got back together. My daughter became disgusted with the modeling industry and went back to school in the spring, taking a double load so she could make up the lost time of her missing semester. She took econometrics and two honors seminars, in addition to a regular course load, practically killing herself to catch back up to her class. Still the dress had not arrived.

Dear Joan,
It is now February and it has been nearly three months since I have ordered the dress. I am wondering if everything is okay. Has it been lost in shipping, perhaps?

Worried,
Dawn

Dear Davies Dawn,
Like I say, special things take time. We had Chinese New Year and holiday time in our village. I ordered different lace since

you were not happy with the lace. Dress will be shipping soon.

> *Joan*
> *WeddingGown96*

Davies Dawn,
Your dress has shipped on 28/2. I hope you find it satisfactory and that your daughter has the wedding of her dreams.

> *All best,*
> *Joan*
> *WeddingGown96*

I came home one afternoon in late March to find a large paper-wrapped throw pillow on our front porch. My heart started to pound. I took it inside to the kitchen counter, where I turned it over and over, marveling at the Chinese writing, and odd international stamps, the old-fashioned paper wrapping that made it look like it was from another era. I snipped it open carefully, using a bikini incision in the lower half of the top section. A scramble of yellow plastic erupted forth like a spill of abdominal fat. This I cut through gently, pushing it aside to find a smoother, shiny, almost fibrous section of plastic wrap underneath that was tougher and tighter. I needed to go more carefully now. Underneath this shiny layer was another protective layer wrapped crosswise, this one red and ball-like. I snipped through this one more precisely still, and saw my first sign of skinlike satin . . . white and clean amidst the yellow and red and brown wrapping. I pulled the final layer of wrapping away and lifted the gown out like a baby. It unfolded reluctantly, stiffly, as if it had held its position a long time. I held it at arm's length and let the skirt fall to the floor. I looked carefully, and my hopes fell. The dress was nothing like the Pronovias gown my daughter had tried on. It was ice-cold white, and the lace around the neckline and covering the bodice was the kind of lace I saw dressing the kitchen windows of the old Polish and Italian Catholic ladies in my grandmother's alley in Scranton, Pennsylvania—thick, squirrelly, curtain-looking stuff. The waist was too high, the satin cheap, and in the back there was a zipper, a finely sewn one at least, where a trail of buttons should have been. The workmanship was lovely, the stitches fine and neat, the lining done beautifully, the bodice had a structured shape to it. However, this ugly baby was no Pronovias copy, not even a bastard son. This was a distant cousin, if at all.

When my second daughter got home from class, I made her try on the dress so we could send pictures to her sister. She did so reluctantly, since she thought her sister getting married at nineteen was about as smart as playing live Frogger across the highway at night. She also didn't trust the fiancé.

"I've met horses I trusted more, and I've known some nasty horses," she said as she slid into the dress. "She's going to wear this? This thing is wretched. I feel like a turd in a candy wrapper." She held her elbows out as if her armpits had a rash.

"Here. Stand better. Like this. Smile. No, never mind. Don't. Just stand there."

The sneer pulling at her upper lip was not able to be disguised by the pose. We texted the photos to the bride-to-be. *Call us when you get this,* we said. Two minutes later the phone rang. We put her on speaker.

"What the fuck is this? Is this from a Halloween store?" she asked. "Why is she posing like that? Was something biting her?"

"I ordered it online. It didn't work out."

"You bought a Chinese knockoff, didn't you?"

"How'd you know?"

"Because it's exactly the kind of thing that would attract you, Mom. I'm not at all surprised."

"Neither am I," said her sister.

"Don't worry," I said. "We still have time to get something legit."

"Yeah, about that . . . we might not be needing it."

"You found another dress?" we said together.

"No, but things aren't looking good on the wedding front."

"Well, okay, but could you at least make up your mind before I spend any more money?"

"I'll pay you back, Mom. Every penny. At this point, I think it would be worth it to just cut our losses."

She called me on the phone right before finals. She was sobbing, which was nothing new, because she'd called me sobbing during every finals week since she left for school, the kind of sobbing where she sounded like she had just fallen off a seesaw or gotten hit in the solar plexus with a football and had knocked the breath out of herself: shallows gasps of air and a gibberish with no Germanic language base. But this time was different. This time she could talk. And she was mad.

"Mom, I think it's over. He wants me to transfer to Sunshine State U. Get a respiratory therapy or teaching degree or some other fuck-all degree people get from Sunshine State. An economics degree from there is a joke, do you hear me? A joke!"

"I hear you."

"I can kiss any sort of meaningful internship good-bye if I go to Sunshine State."

"I believe you."

"He says our marriage should be worth the sacrifice, but I don't see him offering to move up here and practice law until I graduate."

"Nope. He's not. Baby, what do you want to do?"

"I want to stay here. I started here. I want to finish here. I want an education from a *top school*. I want doors to be open for me that couldn't be opened in other ways. It's what I have to do, Mom. I've worked for this my whole life. I'll never be happy if I don't get it."

"I agree," I said.

They broke up for good during finals. My daughter made herself sick crying for a few weeks. The following summer she interned as a researcher at a hedge fund in Boston, and the summer after that, won a fellowship to a think tank in D.C. She moved to Paris after graduation, like she swore she would so many years before.

I bought a plastic protector for the gown, zipped it up, and draped it over the deep freezer in our garage, where it sat for a year. Every once in a while, I unzipped it a few inches to see the white-hot bullet my daughter dodged. Yep, it still looked like frilly, cheap queso blanco on a stick. Eventually I sold it on Craigslist for fifty bucks. I used the pictures of my second daughter wearing the dress, disguising her identity by putting an enlarged emoji over the sneer on her face.

I met the new bride-to-be in a Hooters parking lot in Pembroke Pines, Florida. She looked low-rent, possibly hungover, too sallow of skin to look good in such a frosty white. Her mascara was smeared and it was only eleven in the morning, and she had pockmarks on her face and cigarette-brown teeth. She handed me fifty dollars in cash, asked no questions, and shoved the dress into the backseat of her car, draping it over the baby seat. She didn't wave good-bye. Because I'm me and I can't stop, I have imagined this woman's wedding day several times: someone with a stringy weave and tattoos zipping this new bride into her shock-white monstrosity while she sucked in what was left of her baby weight, then walking down the aisle in an unloved dress, which was perhaps lovingly made, perhaps haphazardly so, then squeezed into a tiny package, and shipped across the world, to be opened by a heartsick mother of the bride who wanted the best for her young daughter, even if the best ended up being a broken engagement, and for a while, a broken heart.

She wakes up to fifteen new e-mails. Eleven from America and three from Britain. She will be busy this season. There will be satin to order, organza to size and slice, new designs to copy, and impossible promises to make. She begins.

Dear Gilbert Rebecca,
Yes, I can make dress exactly like original. Please upload pictures of the dress you want and pictures of you. You have found the right dressmaker. I make perfect dress, but please be patient. Special things take time.

Yours truly,
Joan
WeddingGown96

KING OF THE WORLD

You are being romanced by William Wallace, the real one, not the blue-faced, thick-fingered Mel Gibson version, while in real life you lie sleeping next to your snoring husband. That kilt, those thick, dirty thighs, all that bushy chest hair, the crust of Scottish sweat dried over older layers of Scottish sweat, smelling of bog moss and political passion. He grabs you by the hair and stretches your neck taut and you wake up at civil dawn, the boulders of the Highlands disappearing into Ikea curtains and coordinated wall art from Marshalls HomeGoods. Your seven-year-old is standing at the side of your bed, with paths of tears coursing down her cheeks and a mutilated hamster in her soft, cupped hands.

"You left my bedroom door open again," she says.

Damn that stinking cairn terrier. He bided his time until you were all asleep, didn't he, waiting for a still night, driven nearly mad by the daily smell of the cedar bedding in the dark, or the little turds of buried poo, or the hamster snatch he could smell from as far away as the laundry room he was locked in while the girls played with the fuzzy hors d'oeuvre. He waited until the Labrador was asleep so he could enjoy the carnage alone, after watching the girls' half-cracked bedroom door that you left open when you went in to check on them in the middle of the night, waiting until the nearly oppressive pre-sunrise hours when the birds were still dreaming on their perches, while he knew you were all deep into your REM, to slink along the walls of the living room, and slip into the bedroom, climb up on the hope chest, leap onto the dresser, and knock the Habitrail to the ground, releasing the hamster to run for its life before he made a sport of it. The cairn didn't have the decency to consume the animal, but left it with neck bent and broken in a tiny patch of dark blood, eyes dull and empty, for your daughters to find.

"This is the worst day ever," this daughter says to you through her tears, through her deep sorrow, while you sit up and take the hamster from her cupped hands, wrapping it in the bottom of your nightie. That is the first hamster the cairn gets to. There will be four more.

Rocky weighed in at fifteen pounds. All work, no play. He hated fetch, he hated chasing or being chased, he hated tug-of-war and disdained any kind of toy unless it was stuffed with peanut butter for him to eat. He regularly patrolled the perimeter of our property, keeping out stray lizards, flying birds, crooked crabs, canal ducks, neighborhood cats, and other creatures, real or imagined. His greatest foes were the fish that leaped for their lives in the canal, tempting him to jump in after them with loud smacks of their fat white bellies against the water, though he would never voluntarily go into water of any sort. He would stand at the seawall and retch at the fish with all his might, his back legs pointing out rigidly behind him, his anus winking in and out with each bark, afraid to take a false step lest he splash into the brackish water and melt like grubby sugar. Yet, when we threw the double kayak down, he would beg to go with us for a ride. We would lift him over the seawall and into the boat, where he would position himself at the pointed bow, legs locked, standing in silence and leading with his nose—the king of the world.

At dark he would snap through the dog door, called to midnight sentry duty by the whispers of tree frogs, the sniffling of possums and raccoons on the other side of the fence no one dared cross. He would bark at the glinting stars in the night sky that perhaps, to him, were the eyes of his foes, foes that never blinked or barked back.

Rocky had no time for pampering. He ossified like a carcass when you picked him up, he shuddered when you brushed him, and he had no interest in a cuddle on the lap. His most powerful love language was a flick of table scraps. Rarely, after a long day of work in the yard, he would come to me when I was lying on the floor, push his snout into my armpit, and fall asleep there, his body sticking out awkwardly from mine. When I petted him, he woke up annoyed. We appreciated him, though—in fact, when we brought him home as a pup, I recall the girls saying, with shining eyes, their hearts full of love, "We love him. This is the best day ever!" We did love him, but he stank to high heaven, no matter the bath schedule, and killed almost all of our other pets.

We were a pet-friendly family. My daughters, especially, were drawn to small animals, and I, who liked all things biological, and didn't have as much pet opportunity as I would have liked as a child, rarely said no to their pleas to bring in a new family member.

We started with hamsters. Rocky killed all of them, no matter what protective system we devised. Like a highly trained hit man, he could wait as long as necessary until he marked a chink in the armor, a small break in routine that would give him an opportunity to strike. After the death of the second hamster, a soft blackish teddy bear with a gentle spirit, my younger daughter stopped crying when she found their bodies, and took it as a matter of course that there are no guarantees in life, especially when you take the kind of risks we forced upon those hamsters each time we brought another one home.

Most of the deaths were my fault. I am extremely forgetful, and even when I followed a system, such as locking the dog in the laundry room before taking out the hamster cage to clean it, or closing the door to the bedroom the hamster was in, I would neglect a small step, popping back in to get something and then not latching the bedroom door all the way closed, or not shutting the door to the laundry room all the way when we put the dog in. I could do everything right for a year and a half, long enough for the dog to appear to have forgotten that a rodent was in residence, and the moment I assumed he had released his desire to kill or I slipped up on the safety protocol, he would strike with sure-footed confidence, without batting an eye, as if all time were lost to him and it is what he was born to do.

Somehow, despite the hamster carnage, my older daughter became bent on getting a pet rat. I wasn't keen on it. The only people I knew with pet rats were the kind of people who wore pewter, Anglophilic jewelry and long black trench coats. They frequented Renaissance festivals, watched *Doctor Who,* and worked at RadioShack. They often looked like rats themselves, and what's worse, they were also the kind of people to keep a lot of cats, or a lot of ferrets, which I noticed they dressed up on occasion like little jesters for Internet photos. I did not want to align ourselves with this division of folk. My daughter, however, had an early interest in psychology. In eighth grade she declared that she wanted to write some sort of thesis on the domesticated rat. She presented me with a study that demonstrated how rats laughed when tickled, and likely, swayed by her precocious drive to write a thesis in the eighth grade—for like all mothers, I labored under the misapprehension that my children were exceptional—I broke down and said yes. There was a thesis at stake, after all (one that would never be written, but that's another matter).

Posy was darling, for a rat. We locked my daughter's bedroom door and allowed the thing to run free for much of the day. She loved chicken bones, and when presented with one, would scurry behind the night table to gobble it in secret. She bit holes in all of my daughter's pockets, stored treasures around the room in private piles, lunged at a pair of socked feet as if it were an enemy, and was occasionally slightly aggressive toward fingers, which my daughter thought was cute, though I found it terrifying. Rocky had smelled the rat but had never laid eyes on her. We had a strict closed-door policy to my daughter's room, only partly because of the dog. My husband also hated everything about the rat.

"It's a destructive, disease-riddled pest," he said.

"This is a clean rat," I told him. "She washes herself all the time."

"There are no clean rats. You want proof, Google 'rat king.' I don't want to ever see this thing, or hear about it. Do not ask me to touch it or feed it or take care of it in any way. It seems you have forgotten my one pet request."

"Don't keep any pet that shits in the house?"

"Oh, you remember."

"Of course I do. You still love me?"

"I'm trying to."

"You are the best husband ever," I said, and flashed him a boob.

"We're getting there," he said. I flashed him two boobs.

"Now you're talking." I left to go look up "rat king," and was subsequently horrified enough to purchase a gallon of hand sanitizer, which I then kept outside of my daughter's bedroom.

Once, when the kids were away for the weekend, Posy took a fall from between the bed and the night table and broke her front leg.

I called thirteen veterinarians before I found one who would cast a rat's leg. I lined a shoebox with a soft hand towel and drove the rat to another county, where I paid 165 dollars for an X-ray and a tiny splint job that I could have done at home. That evening, I gave Posy a drop of baby Tylenol, and her very own chicken wing, which she ate quickly at once. Then she sat at the back of her cage like a princess, her broken leg, wrapped in hot pink splint wrap, resting on the scepter of leftover chicken bone, which she licked from top to bottom, then shredded for the marrow. I called my daughter and told her the rat was resting comfortably.

"This is what I get for leaving you alone with my rat," she said.

"I just took your rat to an orthopedic surgeon."

"Pet her on the tail. She likes it. It will make her feel better."

"I can't even look at her tail," I said. Her tail was fleshy and ringed and pocked with sparse hairs and looking at it reminded me of a rat king. I couldn't.

"Mom. She's injured. She needs it."

"All right. I'll do it, but if she bites me, she's sleeping outside." I reached out to Posy's tail and she lunged for my fingers. I screamed.

"Posy is the best rat ever, isn't she, Mom?" I could hear my daughter's mean streak crackle through the phone.

We made it past a year. One Saturday morning, we took Posy's cage outside to clean it. When we cleaned her cage, we would lock Rocky in the laundry room, and put the top wire part of the cage over Posy in a patch of grass. She liked digging in the dirt to bite juicy roots and grubs.

"She needs bricks on her cage, Mom," my daughter said. "We have to weigh it down or she will get out."

"We're almost done. It'll only be a minute," I said. While we were hosing out the bottom of the cage, I got a phone call. The girls went inside to get a drink, and when we weren't looking, Posy dug herself out and took a stroll across the back deck. At the most inopportune moment, someone had forgotten Rocky and opened the door to the laundry room, and within a few seconds, he shot through the dog door and shook the rat to death, before we had time to register it. My daughter saw the whole thing.

"You're the worst mom ever," she sobbed later, as she cleaned up runes of tiny chicken bones that Posy had laid out behind her night table. "I told you we needed to put the bricks on her cage." She had been right.

Later that night, my husband said, "Thank God for Rocky."

"No more rats," I said. "In fact, and I'll say this once only: I was wrong. I don't care how cute Posy was, I can't get the image of 'rat king' out of my mind. When you hear 'rat king,' you think it's going to be one big, pimpilicious, mac daddy rat. It's not that at all."

"I told you," he said. I flashed him two boobs.

"You are the best wife ever."

After watching twenty-two YouTube videos on the proper care and feeding of parakeets, you find a used cage on Craigslist, buy it when the children are at school, bring it home, and scrub it in the front yard using a bucket of bleach water and a sponge. It is hot and you are wearing a tank top and cutoffs and no one else is around, so you spray yourself with the hose, then look down at your chest and think: *I've still got it.* Or maybe not. A male neighbor pulls out of his driveway and drives past and you wave and watch his eyes to see if he notices your wet T-shirt. He doesn't. You've been married so long that nobody will ever notice you again, you think. Sure, men will still open doors for you, but it's not because you are delicious; it's because no matter what pants you wear, the shape of your ass turns them into mom jeans, and opening the door has become a social obligation, a thing younger men do for their elders.

You run the sponge back and forth over the metal bars of the cage with no inkling that this cage will soon make you crazy, that you will hate keeping birds locked up in it the same way you hated seeing other animals in their cages, but you do not know this now. You think of your daughters, and how this birdcage, and the parakeets you plan to keep in it, might act as a recovery gift, aimed to repair the trust they have lost in you, but then you consider that you might just be bored. You have been home with these children for fourteen years, after all, and the routine is mind-sucking: shoving stinking aggregations of stiff, sticky laundry into the washing machine's pie hole, monitoring homework like a Nazi, constantly decluttering kitchen counters and bathroom counters and floors and cars, battling closets stuffed with sports gear, and planning menus that include a variety of nutritious, yet affordable foods when you don't even like to cook and you never once had an interest in elementary education, and the best part of pre-marriage life included such minimalist living that everything you owned could be packed into one midsized car. Admit it: Part of the reason you are so open to getting new pets is because you need something different to do or you will scream.

The cairn is outside with you, traumatizing the lizards that live in the bushes, pouncing on them and ripping off their tails with his teeth. He is as immersed in this as a teenage boy is in a video game. When you call his name, he startles. Runs over to you. Sniffs the birdcage and begins to guard it stiffly, hunching over in the same manner he uses when he attempts to guard a new bag of dog food you bring into the house.

"Go play," you tell him, but he doesn't. You have to shove him with your foot before he goes back to the lizards. You walk over to the bushes and begin to pull a few weeds, and he suddenly growls once and pounces into a pile of brush a foot from your hand. He plucks out a snake, and shakes it quickly at the head, two, three, four times, and flings it several feet away, then runs to check if it is moving. It is not. You hate snakes.

"You are the best dog ever," you say to him, and you reach over to pet him, but he is adrenalized from the kill, shaking, not interested in anything you have to say. He goes back to work in the bushes, checking every three minutes—like a serial killer revisiting the scene of the crime—the dead state of the snake, which remains so.

The first two parakeets were Felvis and Pretzel. They were dark blue and white and bright-eyed and innocently trusting. They liked to sit on the girls' fingers and cock their little heads in academic concentration while my daughters taught them phrases such as "Pretty bird" and "Here, kitty kitty." I thought it would be smart to hang the cage high on a ceiling hook in the dining room, several feet above Rocky's peak vertical jump. While I cooked or while the girls were doing homework at the table, the poor parakeets would climb up and down the sides of the cage and cry, like the incarcerated monkeys at the zoo I had recently seen that had made me so sad. I hate to see a thing in a cage, so I took them out as often as possible.

"No one is watching them when we do homework, Mom," the girls said.

"*I'm* watching them."

"No, you're not. You're cooking. Just put them in their cage until we can give them our full attention. It's not safe."

"I hate the thought of them being locked up," I said.

Rocky ate Pretzel first. I had put him on my shoulder one afternoon while I cleaned the mirrors and windows. I'm not exactly sure how it went down, because it happened so fast, but it involved the dog coming from behind, barking once quickly until I jumped and the bird fell off my shoulder. Because his wings were clipped, Pretzel's frantic flapping did him no good and Rocky inhaled him like a line of cocaine. My younger daughter, who had named Pretzel, picked up his little body and handed it to me. She looked grim.

"Are you okay?" I asked her.

"Put it this way, I'm going to make a good vet, because I'm already used to animals dying in my arms. Rocky sucks, and, I think, so does your pet sense."

After that, I was not allowed to take the birds out when I was home alone. One day, while the girls were cleaning the cage, and I was watching Felvis, I let him fly to the curtain rod, then had a sudden urge to take the Browns to the Super Bowl, if you know what I mean, and I had been waiting for this event all day long. *I'll be quick,* I thought. *Rocky is in the backyard, Felvis is way up high. I've got the one moment this is going to take.* I was on the toilet for the execution, but the girls witnessed the event.

"I hate Rocky," my older daughter said.

"I still love him," the younger one said, "but I never will trust him. This is the worst pet family ever."

We replaced Felvis with Otto, a darling green parakeet. We put the cage high up on a bookshelf, and hung him outside on the patio during the day, so he could listen to the wild, rogue birds taunt him from high branches in the neighbor's yard. The new house rule was that I was not allowed to handle Otto, or clean his cage, or make any decisions about his care, no matter who was home. Otto made it six months before Rocky got him. One day, when the kids were at school, I felt so sorry for the little bird sitting locked up in his cage that I broke the rules again. I took him out, only once, because he had looked so forlorn dinging the cheap little bell on his stupid little mirror. I put him on my shoulder while I did laundry and he was a happy thing. The pet store had clipped his wings when we bought him, and his feathers were beginning to grow back. We had seen Otto fly short trips from our shoulders to picture frames hanging on the wall, but on the day he died, Otto attempted a transcontinental flight from the living room to the big, lighted wall of windows in the back room that may have looked like real Outside to a bird, with the trees swaying behind the clear glass. Otto's clipped flight feathers were about as useful for sustained lift as the waxed wings of Icarus, and he dropped, inches per half second, until he found himself two feet off the ground, when Rocky lunged from nowhere and snapped him out of the air. I hadn't heard the dog come back into the house.

Why did we continue to bring animals into our home with a high-prey-drive dog? Why did I continue to break the rules? Why would I do that to the animals, let alone the children? The simple answer is: I am a fool. As an idealist, I always carry hope that a given situation will change for the better and that people and well-trained animals, especially me, will contribute to that change, although I am an idiot to have thought that an animal could curb its instincts.

It seems that in this case, neither Rocky nor I was able to improve. Each time I thought it wouldn't happen *this time,* that we had it under control *finally,* that we thought we knew all the ways in which this devious dog could achieve a creative kill, he would find a new way to get to them. He was a dog—how many ways were there? I mean, he had a dog brain, for Pete's sake. We were humans. We could see patterns. This higher-order ability should trump dog instinct, but it never did, because Rocky had no pattern, only infinite patience for the right moment, and a gifted dark art of knowing when we let our guard down.

Only one daughter was interested in replacing Otto, so we got a sky-blue-and-white baby and called her Claudia. We scrubbed the cage clean and the girls moved it, this time to a high dresser in my daughter's bedroom, where I was not allowed to even look at the bird. Claudia made it long enough for both girls to become devoted to her, and one day, when they were out, I thought I would do them a favor and give the cage a quick cleaning. It would be better for Claudia, I thought. If she was going to live in a prison, it would be better to live in a prison that was not dotted with turds. I set the cage on top of the high breakfast bar, pulled out the poop tray on the bottom, washed it, then set it out in the sun to dry. Sun has antiseptic properties. I then went to lie down for a few minutes and enjoy my menstrual cramps, which had come upon me suddenly.

While I was lying down, Claudia climbed to the bottom of her cage and slipped through the gap where the tray slid in, and Rocky, who must have gone crazy from seeing the bird bouldering around the outside of her cage, vaulted up, knocked over the cage, and destroyed the bird. I had nothing to say when my daughter got home from school. There was nothing to say. After that we got fish, which, it seemed, I could also kill without effort, but Rocky had no interest in them.

You are sitting alone on the back patio reading *Lust for Life* by Irving Stone while the kids are at school, as you have vowed, for no reason, to only read books published in the 1930s and 1940s until you have finished all that you can locate. You have also taken up knitting and furniture painting, and tropical gardening, and feng shui, and you have decided to let your hair grow very long, so you can re-create Victorian updos in a tacit protest of the other soccer moms' bleached, hacked bobs shingling up the backs of their necks. You want to be prettier than the other soccer moms, you think. You want to set yourself apart somehow, and you do, because it is too hot for your kind of hair to be worn long, and you sweat and frizz under it all day long and mostly look homeless.

Beside you is the cairn, who has come up panting from digging a hole and licking the dirt inside it, because he had located a scent trail of the worm belly that dragged across the same dirt the previous night. The worm belly is as easy for him to smell as the hamster snatch, and even though there are no more animals to tantalize him inside the house, he stays plenty busy protecting the yard from interlopers. You reach down to pet him on the top of the head and he feels sticky, even though he was bathed and brushed, against his will, two days before. An unwelcome iguana jumps from the neighbor's passiflora vine onto the avocado tree that leans over onto your property, and the cairn leaps vertically in a paroxysm of excitement, lands, then scrabbles his feet on the wood of the deck, grunting hard, trying to dig his claws into the wood the way spinning rubber grabs asphalt, smoke erupting from his back paws, powering up to launch himself off the deck wall and three and a half feet down into the backyard. The iguana bolts and leaps into the canal, the dog roaring at it from the seawall. In the distance a phone rings. You sigh. There are mounds of laundry coming to life in the garage. A rotten zucchini liquefying in the fridge. You still haven't planned dinner and you have all of this book to finish. Something needs to change, you think, but you can't see how it ever will.

One fall, right after Thanksgiving a few years after we were finished with the hamsters, and the rats, and the birds and the fish, the eccentric old lady at the top of the street stood on a stool in her kitchen to reach a high shelf, and fell, hitting her head hard on the way down. It was a day before anyone noticed her absence; she was not out front flagging down neighbors for rides to the supermarket or the doctor's, or complaining about unseen barometric molestations of the plants on her front stoop. On the second day the neighbors began to try and peek through her windows, which were always covered by heavy blinds. By the time we broke the door in, she was in a coma, her head stuck to the linoleum by thick, dark, congealed blood, her fingertips resting on a can of soup, the stool upended and tangled in her feet. After the ambulance took her away, we milled about in her living room and kitchen under the pretense of putting things in order and locating her relatives, but we took advantage of the unfettered access to her life to look around and have a good gossip.

We had never been inside her house and were surprised that, instead of the hoarded piles of newspapers that we had imagined, her home was a tidy 1967 time capsule that smelled of toilet bowl cleaner and mothballs. An empty amber ashtray sat on top of an old console television set, and above it hung a dark, velvety clown. A bedroom dressed in pale pink chenille hosted a collection of tiny dancers, figurines, embroidered pillows, paintings, a small jewelry box, a ghosted hint at a previous life with a daughter. When we opened the box, a ballerina popped up and began to dance. I wondered where this daughter was now, and thought of my neighbor left alone for so many years with nothing but a few relics of childhood to dust on Saturdays. Off the kitchen, a small, bright green lovebird sat in a cage in the middle of the dining table, hopping from perch to wall, screaming for our attention.

"I found an address book," someone said. "I'll see if I can get ahold of her family."

"Should we clean up the blood?"

"No, leave it. There will probably be some sort of investigation."

"What are we going to do with the bird?" someone else said.

"We'll take it for a couple of days," I said without thinking.

"At least until she gets better." The dog was older, the kids were older. It would be fine for a few days, I thought.

"I don't think she's going to get better," someone said. I hooked my finger into the ring at the top of the birdcage roof and we walked home, the bird, stunned quiet by the sunshine, blinking in the corner of its cage. I would be careful, I thought, and besides, this would be only for a few days.

Lovebirds are busy, squat, feathery fireplugs of mischief, and this one didn't look back when I took him home. I set him up high on the kitchen bar. He popped from perch to perch to floor to food bowl, hung upside down from his roof, looked around brightly, and shrieked at me every time I walked past his cage. Rocky loitered conspicuously around the kitchen like it was a methadone clinic and he was looking for a fix. He stood unnaturally still, somewhat secretively so, hunch-walking slowly around where the birdcage sat, a single-focused predatory stare in his eye.

"I'm watching you," I told the dog. He didn't break his gaze at the bird.

"Okay, get out," I said, and put him on the back deck. His tight little body was stiff, and once outside, he turned and ogled the bird through the window until the girls got home from school.

It didn't feel right to name a bird that wasn't ours, so we ended up calling him Birdy Bird, a noncommittal nickname that I called all birds. The girls loved him. They locked Rocky in the laundry room and took the bird out to play several times per day. He crawled up and down their backs, hid inside the collars of their shirts, played in their hair, and sobbed for them when they walked past his cage and he was locked in it. He sat on their shoulders when they did homework. He squawked incessantly, a sharp caw that was so bracing that it caused me to see stars out of the corners of my eyes, but the goofy spirit in which he cried out was possible to appreciate. The girls would take him into a bedroom, close the door, and play Red Rover with him.

"Red Rover, Red Rover, send Birdy Bird over," they said, and with a tiny flick of the finger on which he perched, he would take off and fly to the other daughter's finger. Back and forth he would go until it was time for his bath in the sink. He would slide around the bottom curve of the porcelain and play in the thin stream of water they turned on from the tap before they put him in his cage for the night and let the dog back in.

"This lovebird is the best bird ever," one daughter said.

"He is," the other one agreed.

We heard our neighbor died on the day we brought home the Christmas tree. The girls jumped up and down and clapped their hands.

"Wow," I said.

"We're sorry she's dead," they said. "But can we keep the bird?"

"I don't know. I'm worried about Rocky."

"We'll use the system," they said. "We'll lock him up when we want to take the bird out. It'll be fine."

"We say that every time," I said.

"It'll be different," they said.

"We say that, too."

"It will be this time if you promise to stay out of it," they said. "We're not the ones who screw it up. Please can we, Mommy? Did we mention how particularly youthful and lovely you are looking lately?"

"Don't come crying to me when he kills it," I said, though I was well aware that the weak link in the system was me.

The bird loved the Christmas tree. Every evening, the girls would put Rocky outside to occupy himself with his patrol and then they would let the bird out in the living room. He would fly a few laps around the room, then land on the lower half of the tree. There he preened the branches, then hiked to the top of the angel, stood on her arm, opened his throat, and sang like a toad. Occasionally, he would rappel down to a feathered bird ornament and make a pass at it, clicking his beak into the reflective glass chest, and stealing the glued-on tail feathers, which he would fling at us. Occasionally, when we walked through the room, he would fly at our heads, grabbing our hair with his feet the way a jet landing on an aircraft carrier hooks the arresting gear to keep from toppling into the ocean. These were happy times.

Rocky killed the bird on Christmas Eve. I don't know what to say other than this: A melee of people came in through the front door, which startled the bird away from his perch in the Christmas tree, forcing him to fly directly into the mouth of a very surprised Rocky. The dog, whom we hadn't known was indoors, had come in from a stint outside and was minding his business for once, certainly not expecting to be given this rare gift. He hadn't even had to hunt, which may have been a little anticlimactic, but no matter: He ate the bird whole.

On Christmas morning we watched Rocky squatting out back under the avocado tree, straining to crap out the bird's skull and beak. It would take him two days to complete the project and would leave him with hemorrhoids.

"This dog is the worst dog ever," my younger daughter said.

"I hate to say it, but it serves him right," I said, trying, as always, to see the humor in unfortunate situations. My older daughter side-eyed me.

"I can't believe you said that," she said. "What were you thinking allowing that lovebird into the house with our kind of history? You are the worst pet owner ever."

Years later, when the kids have all moved away and your husband is out of town and you are lonely, you take the cairn for a walk. When you pass your old neighbor's house, you think of the pink chenille ballerina bedroom, and the sense of emptiness the leaving of a daughter can produce. The old dog has slowed down some in his senior years, but still likes to stroll up to the park twice a day for a sniff and a poo, and he still guards the yard with a single-minded focus, as if his life or yours depends on it. The yard remains free of intruders. While walking back, you notice he lags behind, a strained look on his face. At home, his wheezing, which you have never before heard, fills the room. Perhaps he ate something in the yard, you think, some old bones, or a stick. He is gross like that. Sometimes you have had to hinge open his jaws and hook things out of his throat with a crooked finger to keep him from choking. You look in his mouth and see nothing, so you call your husband.

"It's Sunday. What do we do?" you ask, knowing that you can't afford to pay for unnecessary vet bills. "Should I watch him?"

"He's a tough little bugger, but I'd say no, not with that wheezing. Let's take him in."

"It's going to cost extra with the after-hours fees," you say.

"I don't care."

While the vet listens to his heart and lungs, the cairn shoves his nose into your armpit, and allows you to pet him on the back. The dog does not want to be there on a Sunday any more than you do.

"He sounds perfect," the vet says. "His vitals are great."

"Yeah? Good."

"I'm going to take a quick X-ray to make sure we are covering our bases." The vet tucks the cairn under his arm like a football and carries him to the back part of the clinic.

He comes back ten minutes later without the dog, wearing an uh-oh on his face. He shows you the X-rays of the dog's lungs, which are so stippled with cancer that they look like marble. It is nothing he has ever seen before, he says, and he doesn't know how the dog is even upright. It is more of a marvel that the sudden wheezing had been his first symptom, and that his lungs sounded as clear as a puppy's through the stethoscope. There is only one thing to do, so you do it.

The cairn goes out like an old soldier fifteen minutes later, stoic, no lingering, no complaints, dignity intact as he slides softly into your arms for the first time in his life, dreaming of white bellies that he can bite, fields of shaded fern under which lizards writhe and replicate endlessly, the undersides of waxed wings flashing bright in the sky, mile-long borders of soft grasses to defend, and winking stars in the tarnished bowl of night sky that finally bark back. It seems impossible that he is lying so still on the metal table. You pet him all over, under his arms, his belly, between the pads of his feet, exploring his little body as if for the first time, and for the first time, he doesn't resist.

I called my daughters to tell them the news that Rocky had died. I chose the second daughter first, the one whom I thought would take it the hardest, the one who had bathed him, and walked him, and brushed him, and fed him and attempted to teach him tricks, the one who knew his nature and didn't hold a grudge against him for killing most of her other pets. This daughter was away at college, in the middle of studying for finals, but I was sure she would not want me to withhold that kind of information. During the conversation, she was factual, concerned, and sad, but there were no tears. Those had dried up with the death of the second hamster. She waited patiently at the other end of the phone for me to stop crying.

"Are you okay?" she asked.

"Yes. It happened so suddenly. I didn't even have time to take him home and give him a steak or something."

"He probably wouldn't have enjoyed it if he was that sick."

"I mean, it was such a hard thing to do."

"I'm sure it was," she said.

A few minutes later, I called my other daughter, who was walking from her dorm at a different college to an off-campus store. It was a busy road and I could hear a roar in the phone.

"Are you safe?"

"I'm fine," she said. "It's just the traffic. It sounds worse than it is."

"I've got some bad news."

"Shit. Okay. What?"

And I told her the version of the story I thought she'd want to hear, the no-nonsense, factual version, because that's how she likes to hear news, and because after all, I was the soft-shelled woman weeping all over myself because of a dead dog, trying to get my act together, and stating the facts helped me to speak without my voice wobbling. When I finished, I heard a truck blast past her. Then I heard her sniffle. Then I realized she was crying and my heart broke in the kind of way that can only happen when you are listening to one of your children weep at the other end of a very long phone line.

"You're crying," I said.

"What do you expect? He was a good dog." She said something else but I missed it because a car drove past.

"What?"

"I said, he was a terrible dog, too, Mom. He was terrible and good at the same time."

"He was," I said.

We hung up and I sat alone on the back deck, and a quick glimpse of an empty pink chenille bedroom crossed my mind. I missed my daughters and the life I lived when they were mine, and I missed my dog with his protective, slightly obsessive yard barking, his hyper-vigilance, his electric energy. The silence made my head hurt.

I looked around at the backyard, which had been Rocky's world. In the canal, a fish leaped and smacked the water. Two birds initiated the mango tree, flailing up and down on a lower branch with no concern, and along the fence line, I heard a rustle and saw a glint of wily green, a flat, dispassionate eye, and the flick of a crested tail. An iguana hovered a cautious foot across the fence, looking to the left and to the right before he stepped onto our land, the borders breached, the king nowhere to be seen.

MOTHERS OF SPARTA

It is close to midnight on a Friday night and my husband and I are driving up and down a stretch of highway outside the Jacksonville, Florida, airport, cross-eyed with fatigue, looking for a motel. We are so tired that we have had trouble choosing one from the long list of lower-end motels that the tiny demon called Siri, who lives inside my cell phone, is listing for us in her impassive, slightly condescending voice: Days Inn, Ramada Inn, Holiday Inn Express. We are so tired that the choice is confusing. This one costs ten dollars more, but it has a free breakfast buffet, which would be a good deal for the three of us who will be eating in the morning. This one has a pull-out couch. This one my husband had once stayed at and he reported a particularly fine sleep. This one has a gym, which we will not have time to use. Unlike my husband, who wants a nice experience, I like to stay at the cheapest motel possible, even if someone had been murdered in the bed mere nights before, even if we catch lice (which we have done), even if pimps and hos flow through the place like a stream of bloody water, all night long. In fact, I am two steps away from suggesting we sleep in the car when we pull into the parking lot of the one motel Siri hasn't yet belittled.

In the backseat, my lanky sixteen-year-old son lies across duffle bags full of his clothing and Ikea bags full of his shoes and other gear, listening to his iPod. He is looking forward to seeing the motel room, because he likes aspects of the hospitality industry, specifi-cally: vacationing. He is relaxed and unfettered, despite the immi-nent changes in his life.

We are in the process of moving him several hundred miles away from our home state of Florida for the school year, to live with my mother so he can get the kind of specialized education we can-not offer him where we live. It seems odd to me that we are driving this boy, who is beginning to resemble a man in stature—he is tall with beard hairs and a deep voice—to leave him somewhere far away from us to live, before I have finished parenting him, simply because I can't get a handle on what he needs and provide it for him.

I have previously been a stereotypically fierce mother, a warrior who doesn't quit on her children, one who will not allow the machine of life to toss them about while she still has breath left in her body, *a mother who doesn't leave her job to others.* I am full of devotion, like most mothers are. I once shoved a man in the library because he laid hands on one of my children for wearing flip-flops that were too loud. I have also been the kind of mother who has correctly second-guessed doctors. When my son was a baby and was ill with an un-categorizable kind of rubbery diarrhea, the doctor told me it was the flu. This didn't sit right with me, so I begged them to test him for salmonella when everyone in the doctor's office was saying, "What eight-month-old gets salmonella?" In order to shut me up, they ran the test and he had salmonella.

I have been the kind of mother who arranged my personal and career aspirations around the needs of my children, because I knew I had one shot to do this parenting thing right. I understood that I needed quantity over quality because important, yet nearly invisible stuff happens when you aren't trying to construct it. There are divine connections made during the mushrooming minutiae of slog that is impossible to ignore when you spend all your time with young people, the loop of events that make you want to quit life the umpteenth time you step on a Lego in the dark or they barf and don't make it to the toilet and the puke splashes into the cracks of the baseboards. The recurring ear infections are laborious, as are the waterworks and snot and constant explanations and negotiations. But when you look back on all of it: the bone-wearying ingemination, the cumulative hours spent putting away their Tupperware drum sets, and homemade Gak, stained-glass tissue paper art that leaves dried, colored gluey paper all over the windows, and tub toys that pee cold leftover bathwater onto the clean, dry socks you just changed into, and the hours watching reruns of *Full House,* and the endless hamster wheel of the bedtime process where you fight to stay awake during encore readings of *Stellaluna,* and the hours driving them places in the car, those mundane traffic-jammed hours where they accidentally initiate quiet, critically important character-building discussions that you might have missed if you had even been talking on your cell phone. Those hours are gifts given to those who pay attention. Until now, I have been the kind of mother who starts the job and finishes it right, despite the tolls I must pay along the way. So it seems odd—not wrong, necessarily, but odd—that I am driving my son away from me to live somewhere else. It seems odd that I am about to send my son away for his own good.

SPARTA

Mothers of Sparta conceived their sons in the fine-silted dirt of the banks of the Eurotas, the same place where they scrubbed the stains from their clothing, scoured their cooking pots with sand, the same place where they would lie in the brackish, cool pebbly wet and birth the future defenders of their nation, smooth, soft waves of river water cooling the roil in their bellies. Mothers of Sparta had a duty to bear warriors, leaders, controlled savages, thieves with fleet feet and stealthy hearts, devotees of the city-state, above all else. In every culture, women desire to raise useful, self-sufficient children, but in Sparta, giving over their offspring to the state was a calling.

Although this is disputed by some historians, they say that when a Spartan boy was born, soldiers, or members of the Gerousia, a council of elders, would come to the family's home to examine the baby. The mother would hand him, warm and soft and pliant, to the men, who would uncover him in the cool air, go over his small body with their calloused hands, their sharp eyes, and assess whether the baby was healthy enough to be allowed to live, and maybe, even at that early age, his war-worthiness. They would look for weak eyes, crooked limbs, clefted lips, curved feet, or perhaps even a weak will or a weak mind; a baby who cried too much could be trouble, a baby who didn't respond enough to stimuli might be stupid. They say that if the baby did not pass the test, he was thrown into a pit called the Apothetae, near Mt. Taygetus, where he would either die from the fall, or from exposure, or be eaten by animals. Imagine the sense of duty a Spartan mother must have felt to willingly open her arms and release her infant from her breast, allow the state to manhandle him, with his eyes still milky, his dusky or bright skin, his curly or straight soft baby hair, his nose that looked like his father's, his fingerprint of a smell, still warm from the womb, to be condemned to death without understanding, a death without having a life. Imagine being the person who tossed that baby into the pit and walked away.

THE BEGINNING

My son—my final child—has autism and a form of frontal lobe brain damage that causes serious behavior problems that are not within his control. This damage may or may not be related to the autism. It may be a result of the focal seizures he has, or his focal seizures may be a result of his brain damage. Who knows? What I know is that my son didn't take the breast at birth and he didn't cry. I imagined, even on that day, marble statues of men with cold stone beards and togas, coming to take my son away, throwing him in the Apothetae for the weasels to pick at his remains, wondering how much of this was my imagination and how much of it was labor fatigue. Two hours after delivery, my son choked, turned purple, and stopped breathing. My parents, who were visiting my hospital room, witnessed the event and my mother went tearing out into the hallway, screaming for help. A nurse snatched my son from my arms and took him upstairs to the NICU, and I heard nothing about him for the next nine hours. I was not allowed to visit, but instead, encouraged to sleep. I could not. At four A.M. a doctor slipped into my room and told me that my son had a cleft palate, a split in the muscle of his soft palate that had been difficult for them to identify, partly, I think, because they didn't look. I mean, all you needed to do was open the kid's mouth and it was there. My four-year-old could see it without a flashlight. The doctor said my son had been choking on the mucus leaking down from his nose. They wanted to keep him in the NICU for a few days to monitor him and do some tests.

The next day, I went home without him. I don't know how well they watched him. Who knows what nurse was on the phone while my son was turning purple before his monitors beeped and cued her in? Who knows how well people do their jobs when no one is watching them? Who knows how many cyanotic episodes he had, how many times his brain was without oxygen in those first few days? This is me still looking for an original excuse for the whole of it, something I have done for the past sixteen years.

THE WALLS OF SPARTA

Because a mother's influence was seen to be weakening to boys, the state took them away to live in group dormitories at the age of seven. They began their military education by learning to fight each other, find their own food or go without, and endure beatings by older boys in order to strengthen their abilities. This helped to develop the warrior code that would allow them to become good soldiers of the state, successful members of Spartan society, "the walls of Sparta."

The boys lived in groups under the tutelage of an older soldier, and were trained to forswear their families in favor of loyalty to their warrior community. Who knows how much blood was shed during training alone, or if any boys fondly remembered the softer lives of their early youth? Records show that these boys were trained to kill without sound, to turn on each other, in fact, ratting out those who weren't toeing the line. There's the legend of the Spartan boy who stayed silent and immobile of face while the fox chewed out his innards. If that's true, that takes a special kind of discipline that you might not have gotten from a weaker baby, had he been allowed to live.

A BRIEF HISTORY

Because of his cleft palate, my son could not breastfeed or create a suction to take a bottle. Within a week of birth he was classified as "failure to thrive" and began dropping weight quickly, ounces per day. We used special Haberman feeders that cost thirty-five dollars each, to drip liquid into his open mouth, as if he were a stray kitten being fed with a milk-soaked hankie. He could manage two ounces of milk per feeding before becoming exhausted and falling asleep, but he needed much more than that to maintain his weight. I would wake him every two hours to feed him his two ounces, which would take him two hours to drink, after which point he had spent all the calories he took in trying to eat and it would be time to feed him again. He began life at eight pounds, thirteen ounces, and when we intervened with special high-calorie formula a few weeks later, he was down to under six pounds, despite the round-the-clock feedings. My then-husband was out of town for a six-week stint of work, and I was essentially alone with this baby, and my daughters, who were two and four. If it weren't for my mother, who shared night feedings with me, I believe I would have gone insane from sleep deprivation.

By the time of his surgery at nine months, my son could not sit up on his own. Doctors said it was because cleft palate kids fall behind developmentally, but only for a short while. They said he would catch up within a year after his palate repair. They said not to worry, but to continue the regimen of interventions they prescribed: speech therapy, occupational therapy, physical therapy for the coordination of the left and right sides of his body, which didn't move in sync.

At age nineteen months, my son developed an inguinal hernia that needed to be repaired. During a pre-op visit, the resident noticed that I had not given him his fifteen-month-old immunizations. This was true, I had told them. I had been avoiding the doctor's office because every time I spoke to them, they badgered me about immunizations, and my son had been ill nearly every eight weeks since he was born. A small, instinctive voice inside me had told me to postpone the shots until his immune system was stronger, and I listened. I was divorced by then, and Medicaid was paying for the surgery, so what the doctors did, what I expect they do for poor mothers all over the place, was bully me into giving my son the immunizations.

"We're not going to do this surgery unless you give him his shots," the doctor said.

"I'm not going to do that until he gets better," I said.

"He's not going to get any better when he's dead from a strangulated testicle or a dead bowel," he said, which scared me. After all, I was just a welfare mom. What did I know? I agreed to the immunizations so he could have the surgery. Eight hours after he received the immunizations, my son developed a fever of 105.5 and executed a series of terrific febrile seizures. We spent the night in the ER, where the nurse nonchalantly breezed in and out of our room and told me he would be fine, and that *this happened all the time.* That was the day something changed in his eyes, although if this inclines one to think I am an anti-vaxxer, I'm not. My kids have been appropriately vaccinated, although vaccine injury theory has made me scratch my head from time to time. Don't condemn me. Wondering is what people do when there are no answers.

By the time my son was three, he had experienced multiple pneumonias, some requiring hospitalization, multiple ear infections, multiple emergency room visits for fevers, and three surgeries, two requiring general anesthesia. Research now suggests that general anesthesia may impair brain development in young children, another point I revisit when trying to come up with the answers that don't exist.

By the age of four, he had still not caught up like the doctors had promised. He could only speak in echolalic phrases, repeating, like a bird, things people said to him, and asking possessive questions: That your car? That your cake? That your toy? He did not play with the toys he pointed to, nor did he play with other children. He had been kicked out of two preschool playgroups for biting. By the age of five, when he started kindergarten, I asked the school to test him for autism. They told me there was no way that, with his glowing eye contact and big smile, which worked to confound all sorts of professionals, he had autism. When I insisted that they test him, they reluctantly agreed.

Yep, he had it.

SPARTA

Beginning around age twelve, Spartan boys would be given only one item of clothing per year—a purplish red cloak known as a *phoini-kis* that I presume was not warm at all. Exposure to the elements helped to toughen them up. They slept in beds made out of reeds that they pulled by hand from the Eurotas River. By eighteen, scarred, strong-jawed Spartan boys became reserve members of the army and were well on their way to being full citizens, with the right to marry, own land, and fight for the glory of their nation. Though this is disputed, Spartan mothers were said to have told their sons on the eve of their first battle, "Either come home with your shield or on it." I can imagine that these new soldiers, with blood in their eyes, didn't look back when they left.

NOW

We move my son into his new bedroom at my mother's house. While I unpack his bag, he sits in a chair in the bedroom and talks about technology. He is unaware that I am working while he sits, even after I ask him to help me unpack. He waxes eloquent about iPods, iPads, Android phones, cell phone chargers, and types of applications available through both Android and iOS operating systems. He talks about technology and his desire to own it, play with it, and explore it, nearly constantly, without the ability to see that it bores the pants off everybody else. He talked about it the day I came home after a serious hospital stay without asking me how I was, he talked about it through a migraine headache I once had, he talked about it immediately after getting in trouble for using technology inappropriately. He talks about it constantly, even though he is under strict restriction from its use. He will talk about it five minutes after being reminded of why he is no longer allowed to use technology unsupervised. He never stops talking about it. He asks, "Do you think I can get a smartphone so I can keep in touch with you when we are apart?" "I'm not sure," I say, which is what I say when I don't know what to say.

NEURODIVERSITY AND THE PUBLIC SCHOOLS

By the time my son was eleven, we had removed him from six elementary schools for a variety of reasons, some of which were related to bullying, and some of which were due to the school's inability to come up with any sort of "resources" that would work for him. Now, I hail from Florida and I love my state, but here is what I tell people who have the misfortune of educating a special-needs child here: Move away as soon as possible. There are any number of states ranked higher in special education funding than Florida. Just pick one and go to it.

In the spring of his kindergarten year, my son was barely verbal. He could not grip a crayon. He could not recognize letters. Auditory processing tests showed that his processing was so poor that he understood 20 percent of what was said. He had a diagnosis and an education plan in place, but no one seemed to notice how much help he needed, because he was handsome, he smiled and looked you in the eye, and he didn't drool or spin or flap his hands.

The school held a field day, though Lord knows why they don't do these things in December when the weather is a little less dangerous. By spring, Florida can produce temperatures over ninety degrees with a heat index of over one hundred. The school had asked parents to pack bottled water and sunscreen and towels for their kids to sit on during this field day. Before they went outside that morning, the teacher told her class to get these things out of their cubbies. My son could not process this information and the teacher assumed his act of noncompliance was belligerence, so she let him go outside without them, and my son sat in the dirt all afternoon without his towel, without any water, and without sunscreen. When I picked him up, he was sunburned and limp, with red ant bites all over his legs.

"What the hell happened to him?" I asked her.

"This is what he gets when he doesn't listen. Your son is very disrespectful," she said. "I hope he learned his lesson."

"He has autism, you idiot. He needs help," I said, and that's when another teacher had to step between us. This is a small example of how badly the schools responded to our special educational needs, and it is also an example of a person who could not execute the most basic actions of self-preservation, and who still needs help to survive, both socially and physically, every day.

Third grade was when my son first confessed that he wanted to kill himself. The kids were mean at his new public school, a borderline inner-city school that had the good fortune of hosting the "autism cluster" that did him no good whatsoever, because wherever he turned, a teacher would accuse him of not trying hard enough, or a student would kick him in the backs of the knees to make him fall down, or trip him in the cafeteria, or blow spitballs in his hair, or call him "faggot." We left that school two days after his suicidal confession, using a scholarship to attend a private special-needs school that cost $24,000 per year.

THE PASS AT THERMOPYLAE

In 480 B.C., Spartan King Leonidas led a small number of Spartans and Greeks, reportedly under fifteen hundred in number, to hold off over four hundred thousand Persians at the pass of Thermopylae. It was supposedly a remarkable battle. Leonidas was told by the Delphic Oracle that either Sparta would be destroyed or he would lose his own life. Leonidas was so devoted to Sparta that he chose the latter, and the three hundred Spartans and some nine hundred Greeks inflicted high casualties on the enormous Persian forces before finally being encircled and losing their lives. This battle fascinates me. The force of desire versus the force of numbers, the betrayal, the last stand. I often think about that pass in that moment, the holding back of the troops pressing down on them, the bloody, rocky, scrubby earth beneath their feet, the battle screams, the rage they must have felt against their impending defeat.

CURRICULUM VITAE

My son was slow academically. He read no social cues, which left him with a large, invisible "Kick Me" sign on his back that every other kid in school could see. He didn't understand the schoolwork, and seemed to have a virulent lack of motivation to do anything that was important to his future. We could not stir him to do a single act he didn't want to do, and we tried rewards, punishments, incentive charts, even bribes. He didn't care for the reward. Punishments were something to sit through until they were over. When we asked him why he didn't want to do the most basic of things he said, "Because I don't feel like it."

By this time, right before the hormones hit, my son had overcome his physical infirmities. He barely got colds, had never had strep or a puking flu. He was also pleasant and compliant. He had learned to smile brightly to disguise his confusion. He never talked back to authority figures, and he was friendly and extremely handsome. Adults loved to talk to him. He came across, and still does, as more capable than he is, which sets him up for disappointing people. As a result, perhaps as an act of self-preservation, he developed a prodigious ability to lie through his teeth about everything: what he did, what he said, what he understood, what he felt or thought. Once he figured out this skill, he used it regularly, even when he didn't need to lie at all.

When my son was nine, he watched a neighbor punch in her garage door code, then a few days later, when he thought the neighbor wasn't home, used the code to let himself into their house. He stood in their kitchen, without any kind of plan, when the neighbor walked in on him and shrieked in surprise before marching him home to us.

When he was ten he started masturbating in public. In school, in our family pool, in the living room of our home, in front of other children, on the summer camp bus when his sisters were present. When we asked why he continued to do this when he clearly knew it was wrong, he told us he did it "because he felt like it."

At eleven, we discovered that he had killed his friend's hamster while over at the friend's house, by squeezing it to death. When we confronted him, he admitted to having killed several other animals, mostly neighborhood children's pet hamsters or rabbits, and twice, baby chicks at the feed store, quietly, when no one was paying attention, and he had also hurt our family dogs by squeezing their noses until they screamed. When we asked why he did this, he said, "Because I felt like it."

Immediately after this confession, he declared he wanted to kill himself. We had him admitted to the children's psychiatric ward that night, where he stayed for five days. On his first night there, against my suggestion—for I had a keen understanding of this child's impressive sensitivity to any sort of medication—they put him on a cocktail of psych meds that triggered hallucinations and frightening manic episodes as soon as the drugs soaked into his brain cells, right about the time he was released from the hospital and sent home to us. On his first night home, he said he still wanted to kill himself and he felt like doing it with a knife, so we locked up all the knives, and also our shoelaces, medicines, forks, rolling pins, kebab skewers, scarves, toothpicks, bug killer, and sports equipment, and I stayed up in the living room, expecting to intercept him at three A.M. on the hunt for a knife or a skewer to help him end it all. When I asked him why he wanted to kill himself, he said, "Because I feel like it."

The next morning, he talked about how he thought he could fly if he could get to the top of a tall enough building, and when I announced that I had misplaced my keys, he disappeared into my bedroom and flung all of my clothes out of the drawers and closet and onto the floor, looking for them. He also said he heard voices. I called the doctor simply to say, "I told you so." Within two days of being off the meds, the mania and hallucinations disappeared. This was the same week that both of my daughters voiced concern for their own safety and each one independently mentioned that she couldn't wait to graduate and get the hell out of our house.

My son was released from the psychiatric hospital with a label of conduct disorder, a strange diagnosis for a child who never raised his voice or talked back, but it was given, the attending psychiatrist had said, because he could not legally diagnose my son as a sociopath until he was over the age of eighteen. He also told us to brace ourselves for a lifetime of violence, drugs, theft, and prison, and that there was nothing that could be done with "these kinds of people." Sociopaths are damaged in the brain, he told us. No amount of therapy can make them feel anything but a continued drive to have their own needs met.

When my son was fifteen we discovered a history of child pornography he had looked up on the Internet. A few years before we had come to the absurd place of being able to laugh about the experiences we had gone through with this child. We would say things like, "Well, he's broken into someone's house, but at least he didn't start any fires." When he grew attracted to fire, we would say, "At least he's not killing animals." When we discovered he had killed animals, we joked a horrific joke. We said, "At least he's not into kiddie porn." Somewhere during the discovery of the child pornography, something inside us died. We found we were unable to be shocked by anything. We can now talk about little kids being tied up. We can talk about a toddler getting a rim job. We have seen clips from videos of three-year-old boys being anally penetrated by fat, hairy, fifty-year-old men. We can talk about Japanese anime child porn, and the legality and morality of it. We know the Supreme Court's stance on it. We know what kinds of people have gotten what kinds of prison sentences at what ages, for making child porn, for trafficking it, for downloading it. We can talk about murder of and cruelty to small mammals, because our son had told us how their eyes popped out of their heads when he squeezed them, and how the warm weight of them in his hands after their deaths made him feel: powerful. We have felt the frosty, cold horror, anger, resentment, and fear of two teenage daughters who slept with their doors locked, stopped bringing friends home, and left for college as soon as they could. We know what it is like to live under self-designed house arrest, tag-teaming our parenting, or bringing our son with us wherever we go, because the lines between his autism and his supposed sociopathy have blurred so we don't know which is causing what. If we leave him alone in the house, he might find his way to the neighbor's house and kill their cat, though he hasn't displayed an interest in that for several years now, or molest their young son, which he says he would never do, but come on. We've seen what he is attracted to and we have seen how he has such poor impulse control that he can't leave a gallon of lemonade alone in the refrigerator. He will drink the whole gallon in an hour and a half if left alone to do it, going back to the fridge over and over when no one is looking and pouring himself one small, surreptitious glass at a time until it is gone. He cannot stop himself.

We put passwords on our computers and cell phones, and only allowed him to use the computer while we sat with him. When I noticed he was taking extended naps during the day, we found he had stolen our Wi-Fi password and used it to connect his game system to the Internet and looked at child porn in the middle of the night. We took the system away. He then looked up child porn while at his other grandparents' house, using their computer. When we squashed that, he stole his sister's old iPod touch, connected to Wi-Fi with it, and used it to watch porn. We had a fear of the feds busting down our door and arresting my husband, or worse, my son's grandfather. One day when at the public library, I left my son alone for two minutes while I went to the bathroom, and I found him in the children's section, looking at cartoons of naked kids in a potty training book.

And still, because he didn't choose to be this way, he requires compassion. He is a boy. He is a boy with autism. He is a boy with autism and focal seizures and brain damage. He is a boy whom I love. He is a boy for whom I have depleted myself, a boy who may or may not become dangerous, a boy who, had he been born in Sparta, would not have made the cut.

A DISCLAIMER

Here is the disclaimer I manage, out of compulsion, to slip into conversations I have with therapists, doctors, and attorneys. Lest you are wondering, because everyone does, though no one asks me directly, neither of my two daughters nor my two older stepsons have ever been in trouble with the law, with the exception of a rare traffic ticket. All are gainfully employed or in college full-time, socially accepted and acceptable, and are unusually contented, productive people, though my daughters are jaded from living with their troubled brother. There is not likely any social or emotional reason for my son to exhibit the behaviors he has. Like one doctor told us, "Sometimes you just get an unlucky roll of the dice."

HOW CAN YOU LOVE A SOCIOPATH?

You do because he is yours and has always been. You do because you know he is more than the sum of his dangerous behaviors. You do because you know you didn't raise him tied to a pole out in the backyard, or beat him, or tease him. You love him because when he says, "Because I felt like it," he may have reached his depth of ability to articulate a complex emotional situation. You love him because whatever accident that tossed his brain happened to him as much as it did to you. None of this is his fault. You've seen the big, bright white hyperintensities on his MRI. You held him while he seized after his shots. You've seen the IQ test results, which are a stubble of points away from classifying him "intellectually disabled."

A SOCIOPATH'S PURPOSE IN LIFE

We all need to know our life's purpose. As a woman with many choices and a jack-of-all-trades attitude, I struggled for years to find mine. As a mother, I have nudged my children toward ways of thinking that would help them know themselves. As a member of a modern society, I am expected to support aborting Down syndrome babies, hell, even perfectly normal babies, yet rail against the institutionalization of mentally deficient citizens, because *that would be wrong* and because *institutions are inhumane,* though people don't seem to realize that prisons have replaced mental institutions for many who would have once benefited from structured, medically managed living. As a mother of a special-needs child, I must figure out for my son what his purpose is, then help him do it, so he doesn't end up in an institution. I suppose the question here, after I spend forty hours writing this paragraph, requiring respite from the concept itself, getting up from the computer and pacing through the house, eating cold meat straight from the refrigerator, my dogs hopeful on my heels, is: What is a sociopath's purpose? What is this child's purpose? How can I direct him toward a purpose when he has no desire for anything other than feeding his desires? I want to know his purpose, and just as important, I want to know how we are to keep on living like this, raising what could be a ticking time bomb, a kind, pleasant ticking time bomb.

WHERE IS GOD IN ALL OF THIS?

I've read the Bible. I've read the apologetics. I've talked to pastors, all of whom had healthy children. I've read the spiritual warfare theory. I've read the saints. I've read the rabbis. I've read the philosophers. Where is God in all of this? I have no idea whatsoever. It's a problem.

REGISTERING FOR SCHOOL

On the first day at his new school, my son walks into the guidance office, shakes hands with the guidance counselor, and calls her ma'am. He wears black, fashionable glasses that make him look studious and clever. She asks him about his academic interests and he says he wants to go into medicine, so the guidance counselor, based on my son's looks and countenance, begins to enroll him in college prep classes. I stop her. Tell her obtusely, without hurting my son's feelings or embarrassing him, that we are thinking of *para*-medicine, perhaps patient transport, or certified nursing assistant, or phlebotomy, and that we have a specialized educational plan that we must follow, and she should probably take a look, here, right here, at the paper I slide across her desk. I point to his latest neuropsych evaluation, which reveals a processing speed score that, if it were a stand-alone IQ, would be a 54. "Oh," she says. "Let's take a look at some other options, then." Part of my worry is illuminated by the fact that my son can snow anybody, at first sight, into thinking he is neuro-typical. He shakes hands like a man, locks eyes, says please and thank you like a Norman Rockwell painting come to life.

THE FACTS

No one has any advice. We have consulted neurologists, neuropsy-chologists, psychiatrists, behavioral therapists, autism specialists, and experts in sociopathy, conduct disorder, and organic brain dysfunc-tion. I have written letters to sexual deviance experts at universi-ties. I have reached out to minor-attracted therapy groups and pedophile programs, and no one has told us anything of value, out-side of certain medications that might put a damper on his sex drive, some of the same medications that caused him to hallucinate and go manic when he was younger. After our first bout of neuro-psychological testing when my son was thirteen, the psychologist felt so sorry for us that he didn't charge us the second half of the two-thousand-dollar fee. He told us we were going to need every penny we had for inpatient treatment, and perhaps lawyers to keep our son out of jail when he started breaking the law. When we asked about residential treatment, we were told that he hasn't broken the law so he doesn't belong in a state-funded institution, and thera-peutic boarding schools, a temporary beacon at best, can cost up to $90,000 per year. Basically, we were told, home is the safest place for him.

Here are some of the things I think about: What might I be doing wrong in his life that could make him snap? What lifestyle system could I design that would keep him from turning toward children for his sexual release? What can I do that I have not already done?

BETTER LIVING THROUGH MODERN MEDICINE

A mere hundred years ago, my son's first pneumonia might have killed him. His cleft palate would have been unable to be repaired, leaving a hole into his nose that left his ears vulnerable to infection, which might have killed him. Many people in my family might not have made it to adulthood without modern medicine, myself included. Medical advances have put a stop to a natural form of eugenics, that of letting diseases cull weak children before they had a chance to grow up. Now, thanks to science, children who once would have died young will live for years, sometimes requiring group homes and government funding, either in the form of Medicaid, disability payments, and Social Security, or "support" in the form of incarceration for the rest of their lives, though the funding is never enough to stop the constant financial and emotional drain severely damaged children create. Also, there is often no place to live until they commit a crime or require hospitalization. After discovering what my son is capable of, after watching his own early sickness and recoveries from illness and surgeries, after his struggle through therapies, social failure, and educational failure, after learning of his frightening deviant inclinations, is it wrong to have thought, however briefly, if it would have been better to have the marbled men in togas come and take him away? We're not only talking about my son here; we're talking about the potential damage of innocent children, the kind of damage that can't be undone.

A QUICK NOTE

Both my son's history and the promise of his future are exhausting. Since he has been born, I have not slept well. I have developed three autoimmune diseases. The level of stress we live under is almost too much to bear at times. I find that even while writing this essay, I can only write for twenty or thirty minutes before becoming stupefyingly drained, as if I myself had staved off the Persians at Thermopylae pass. I must nap every few pages. Even writing this is a battle. Yet, I love him with a two-fisted grip. A fierce love.

IF I HAD BEEN A SPARTAN MOTHER

If I had been a Spartan mother I would have physically trained for motherhood in order to produce the finest, strongest of sons. I would have run holes in my sandals, I would have thrown a javelin many meters past the target and into the woods, I would have spun a discus to the farthest clearing. I would have squatted, over and over, with rocks on my shoulders to strengthen my hips and legs. If I had been a Spartan mother, my husband would have come home from battle to find me on the riverbank, washing my cooking pots, and he would have taken me on his shield, his beard scratching my face, his sweat smell grinding into my pores. I would have prayed to Zeus to conceive a fine son who would go into battle for Sparta.

My son would have wrestled the dogs in my yard until it was time to send him away, on the land I purchased with my own money and operated while my husband was at war. I would have ignored him when he cried. I would have prepared him for his hard life by spanking him when he was disobedient, and he would have learned to mind me. He would have obeyed, for in obedience there is both honor and the greatest freedom.

I would have willingly given my son to the state, knowing that the action of letting go is what would shape him into the most supreme of warriors. In his teenage years, I would have seen him with his mentor, high on a hill, his thick hair blowing in the wind, his purple *phoinikis* cloaking his strong, muscular legs. I would have seen a set in his jaw there against the horizon line that foreshadowed the resolve it would take for him to kill to protect Sparta, or to die for her. There on the hill, I would see a foreshadowing of the man he would become and I would ache for him, yet I would be nearly vicious in my pride. I would turn my back on him, then walk into the woods by the river and howl the howl of a wolf, part anguish, part ferocity, part joy.

The unpoetic reality of this foray is that in Sparta, the council would have examined my newborn and deemed him unfit, would have pulled him from my arms and prepared to take him. I would have heard the words "Mt. Taygetus" murmured under a dirty cloak, from under a filthy beard, and I might have begged, "Please, I understand. I have not done my duty. I have not borne a strong son. Let me kiss him good-bye," and I might have reached for my soft, sweet-smelling child, my weak son, with his blue skin and his crooked neck. I might have snatched him and run, as I was trained to run, faster than the dogs could track me. I might have. Who knows if I would have abandoned my state for my son?

Knowing what I now know about what his future holds, what his life will be like, the struggles he has already had, the alienation and sadness . . . would I have allowed him to be taken from me and laid out on the cold rocks for the eagles to pluck out his eyes and feed his flesh to their young? Would I have kissed him good-bye for the sake of society? Knowing what I know about child sexual abuse, about criminal pedophilia, about the unlikelihood of my son's brain ever being different, I have to think of things honestly. Knowing what I know now, I might have said yes.

Are some people better off dead? Unless you are at a college party and have done the kind of drinking that allows you to shout philosophical debates over a booming sound system, this is hard to talk about. For a mother, it is a near-criminal thought, yet, I understand the desperate, empty apothetae some parents find themselves near when they try to imagine a humane end to their child's severe suffering, or in rare cases like ours, an assurance that the child they created and raised will not hurt anyone. We have to remember that Sparta didn't mercy-kill for the sake of the child. Sparta mercy-killed for a stronger, better, safer Sparta.

A SPECIAL KIND OF CLUB

In March of 2014, Michigan mother Kelli Stapleton attempted to take the life of her fourteen-year-old daughter, Issy. Issy, who is strong and heavy, has a degree of autism that compels her to violently attack her caregivers, teachers, siblings, and parents. Issy had hospitalized her mother twice with her violent acts, and had recently been rejected from several treatment programs that would have offered hope to her family. Issy's family was constantly fighting insurance companies and school systems to find an educational situation that would accept their child, a treatment facility that wouldn't boot them out. Near the time when the murder/suicide attempt occurred, Issy's mother was being forced to bring her daughter home from a facility that had once offered them their only hope. Kelli Stapleton, with a mother's understanding of how little things were likely to change for Issy, was facing a future of physical danger for herself and her other children, violence, and the kind of hopeless unrest brain damage can bring to an entire family. I imagine that, without any sort of societal resources, without any hope of help from an expert, because there are no experts in this instance, Kelli Stapleton was at the end of her rope. I do not feel as horrified as many people seem to be by the murder/suicide attempt. I understand why she did it quite clearly, and from one exclusive club member to another, I have sympathy for her situation and will not call her a monster.

Anyone who condemns Kelli Stapleton should remember that the woman tried to kill herself, too. She wasn't simply attempting to murder her daughter. She saw no future for her daughter, and as a mother, would rather die than watch her daughter face no future, and as a mother, could not die and leave the uncertain future of her difficult daughter to someone else. Some would see it as a mercy killing, a flinging of the child into the apothetae, because she saw no way for this child to positively impact anyone in the world.

People who do not have children with autism, brain damage, or other severe conditions do not understand what families of these children, not to mention the children themselves, go through. I know what it can lead you to do, how it can depersonalize your thinking to where you feel like you can't go on and both you and your child would be better off dead.

I understand the Spartans for wanting to eliminate weakness. I understand people who believe in this; it is tempting and easier than doing what we do. Sometimes I can understand this easy way out, but I love my son with a weakness and a fierceness at the same time. I want to reject that doctor's bleak prediction of his future. I want to reject that he is headed for prison. I want to reject that he is attracted to death, dismemberment, autopsy videos, and sex with young boys. I try, day after day, to find the right way to do things, thinking that if we find the right way, we can keep him from breaking the law. This, of course, assumes that we have not yet discovered the "right" way, and also that there is a right way. Perhaps there isn't one, though when I say we've tried everything, I believe myself.

Recently we saw a new doctor who suggests that my son's executive functioning ability, the part of his brain that gives him self-control, may develop to a point where he could be functional somewhere in his late twenties. If this is true, we would only have to figure out how to keep him and others safe until then. Will he kill or hurt another animal? Not sure. It's been some years since he's done it. He claims he is finished with it. Would he harm a child? There is no telling. He is driven by a sexual desire for young children, and he has damage in the area of his brain that controls even the most basic impulses, so I would have to assume, for the sake of the children, that yes, he could, given any sort of chance. To be on the safe side, we keep a line-of-sight contact with him at all times, steer him toward work that will not allow him access to children, and are trying hard to develop a sense of routine in his life that makes him so comfortable that he will not wish to step outside of it.

THE HAPPY SOCIOPATH

Sociopaths are not all evil. Some of them, friendly, harmless, parasitic ones, are stilled by simply giving them the things that make them comfortable: good food, an easy job, and pleasant recreational activities. And at this point, I am sending my son to live with someone who loves him differently than I do right now, me with my heavy, burdened, and sometimes hopeless expectation that nothing I do will change him, nothing in my power can ever make him be whole in the mind, can ever give him a conscience. I have sent him to someone with a fresh heart who still has faith that good will come of him. Meanwhile, I catch my breath from sixteen years of nearly daily anguish. I recharge my batteries and get ready for when it is my turn again. Our son will likely live with us for the rest of our lives. Who knows what will happen after we are dead?

NOW

A month after the move, my husband and I are home, rattling around in an empty house, not sure what to do with ourselves. It is the first time in our blended marriage that we have been without children, and we find ourselves doing things that we wouldn't do if the kids were home, like cooking meals without any pants on. My husband has taken to calling the bubbly La Croix water I drink "La Crotch," and I head off on bike rides whenever I feel like it, or start supper at eight P.M. We sleep and sleep and sleep. We are processing, my husband says, what it is like to not have the constant worry surrounding us, although in the back of our minds, we still have constant worry.

We left my mother's house after having locked her electronics up tight with parental controls, porn-blocking software, and a plan for changing her passwords weekly. We have located a good psychiatrist and a therapist who understands autism, and my mother, who doesn't take any crap, is hounding my son about his schoolwork the same way she once hounded me. He is never left unsupervised during waking hours. The school he attends has a superb special education program that might give him a chance at employment someday, and the kids in the school are nice. He says he no longer feels like killing himself at all. This has to be a step up from where we've been, and it will have to do for now.

My son was thrilled when we got him a smartphone so he could communicate with us while we are apart. He knows that we locked it the hell down with all sorts of parental control software, which we manage from our computer. He doesn't appear to know how to bypass the software. It shuts off at nine P.M., and he is not allowed to take the phone upstairs to his room. We can see every keystroke he makes, and so far, with the exception of some typical skanky teenage song lyric stuff, he has been behaving. In fact, it has given him something to be excited about. He uses his phone to take pictures of homework assignments on the whiteboards at school. We use it to stay in touch many times per day. He knows that if any porn shows up, we are selling it. We have found that technology, the one desire he values more than his other desires, the mouthpiece of his most unsettling deviance, may be the thing that trumps his deviance. If he wants the phone more than he wants the porn, we may be out of the woods.

We Skyped the other day. He looked relaxed and content. I mentioned how we had taken his sister to the airport to go away to college and without acknowledging that, he said, "Oh, by the way, I learned something amazing at school today. Did you know that the Samsung Galaxy S5 is actually better than the Samsung Galaxy S5 Active?"

"That's good to know," I say. He then tells me that my mother is taking him to a movie with a neighborhood kid he met at school, and he would need to put his phone on silent when he was in the theater, and that the family next door to his new friend has a very cute little baby. We agree to touch base before bed and I hang up feeling, however cautiously, like my son is in the right place, that I have made the right choice to send him away for now, but that we are still a long way from okay. I dial my mother's number to give her the heads up on the baby. Like Thermopylae, there may not be any hope, but that doesn't mean you can stop fighting.

*   *   *

Within a few months of having the phone, my son figured out how to bypass his parental control software, looked up child pornography every chance he could, and lied to my mother about all manner of things, to the point where my mother could no longer handle caring for him. We took away his smartphone and I moved to South Carolina to help him get through school while my husband stayed home in Florida. After he began sexually grooming an eleven-year-old boy through texts on his old clamshell phone, my son dodged a bullet when the boy's parents declined to press charges.

A few months later, my son accessed child pornography on his school computer and was suspended, and also, while on school property, accused a family member of sexually abusing him. The police were called to the school, and after a few hours of intense questioning, they believed my son when he admitted that he made it up to hurt the family member. We moved back to Florida. A few months later, he installed a Tor browser on his new school's computer and downloaded child pornography. The police said they didn't have enough evidence to charge him, since the browser did not keep a record of the illegal images, and he was given the minimum punishment—a two-day in-school suspension. The attorney we consulted said that home is the safest place for him, since no one can watch him the way we do. I unenrolled him from public school and we are home-schooling him senior year.

FOUR ANIMALS

Screw this.

—*DAWN S. DAVIES, ON GETTING UP IN THE
MORNING, UNABLE TO OPEN EYES*

In the beginning of April, after having watched the bats exploding from the bat house at dusk, skyward slices of half-moon climbs and angular dives, she dreams she is a bat, and in the morning, wakes up so. Black skin wings warm and fluttering, sharp elbows easing out of bed, throwing herself around in dark space, barely controlled, one small screech away from disaster. She must trust the physics of sound for her orientation, the longitudinal waves, the percussive smack of vibrations against the dimensional mysteries that surround her, but secretly she trusts nothing, *because she can't see,* and it's not like she's been a bat her whole life, used to avoiding disaster in the grille of a car, or the trunk of a tree, or the flight path of a sharp-clawed hawk. No, she has relied on her eyesight—myopic, yet constant—and now the eyes aren't working right. The bat folds her wings and walks upright, smashes a toe into the vacuum cleaner, misses the doorway, fumbles around in the bathroom for the toilet paper. Gobbledang, dawndangit. Cusses. Every morning the eyes are sealed shut. Perhaps she used superglue accidentally, instead of the magical night drops the doctor has given her, the concoction that is supposed to allow her to awaken in the morning as a woman, not a bat.

At least it's not lupus.

—DOCTOR #4

In the summer of 2014 I was diagnosed with Sjogren's syndrome, though I believe I have unwittingly participated in Sjogren's-related suffering for several years. Not that big of a deal, according to many of my doctors. It's not the worst autoimmune disease you can have. I mean, at least it's not lupus. Sjogren's is an autoimmune disease that causes a person's white blood cells to attack the moisture-producing glands in the body. It can attack the lachry-mal glands, which causes a loss of tear production that works to degenerate the entire workings of the eyelids and eyeball. Some days I can't open my eyes but a sliver. When I can there is a dry, stiff film over them that makes it hard to see clearly, and I have to keep blinking. I often can't keep my eyes open in restaurants or movie theaters or malls or grocery stores or other places that push air through big HVAC systems, or anyplace there is bright light. In these venues, I must wear special sunglasses with foam seals around them, so the air and light won't get to my eyeballs. Before I got these glasses, which cost three hundred dollars, I walked around with my head tilted slightly back and my eyes nearly shut, my hand on my husband's arm. Eye drops, which I use as frequently as a pothead, didn't help.

Sjogren's can also cause neuromuscular pain, which, for me, feels like random, small stabbings throughout the body, and a generalized fibromyalgic aching, and pain in the joints that makes it feel like I have arthritis, though I seem to have no diagnostic proof of arthritis. It can cause inflammation of the parotid glands above the jaw, and the salivary glands under the jaw, which dries up saliva, causing tooth decay, tooth loss, and mouth sores and infections. After Doctor #4 said, "At least it's not lupus," I found a Sjogren's forum where many of the members reported use of full dentures in their forties. I immediately pronounced Doctor #4 a "glib bastard." Yet in a sense he is right. Sjogren's isn't *that bad,* in that it is not likely to kill you, only make you suffer.

Sjogren's also affects the throat, causing a painful hoarseness that comes and goes, with laryngeal pain that splits up into the ears. I have profound tinnitus and a progressive hearing loss that may be Sjogren's-related. Everything feels hot. Hot eyes. Hot throat, hot skin. Hot mouth. I have not yet mentioned the unconquerable overall exhaustion that leads you from the sink back to the bed, to the refrigerator back to the bed. To the laundry machine and back to the bed. Out to the grocery store and back to the bed. Gone are the days of P90X, fifteen-mile bike rides, and hoisting the free weights like a Russian power lifter.

Internally, Sjogren's can cause a reduction of mucous gland production in the digestive tract, and eventually affect internal organs, which I hope will never happen to me. It can also cause neurological problems, such as neuropathy in the hands and face and legs, which I already enjoy. I periodically reach down and wipe the nonexistent ants from my toes, or have to check to see if there is an ice cube melting in my socks, or fiberglass in the bottom of my feet. Having Sjogren's syndrome also increases your risk of developing lymphoma, a type of cancer, something I want no part of, no way, nohow.

Basically, Sjogren's dries you up like a ninety-year-old lady and makes you as tired as an old hound. Skin? Like a paper towel. Throat?

A dog chew. Lady bits? Barren enough to make sex a desert. Nose? Painful burning on inhalation. Eyes? Like rocks in a dirt hole.

Nope.

—DAWN S. DAVIES, ON ATTEMPTING A SUN
SALUTATION IN JUNE 2014

Some mornings, when she is in the middle of an autoimmune flare, for that's what autoimmune disease does—it flares like a forest fire—she wakes and can't straighten her knees or flex her feet. She folds inward, circular, insular, like a burnt fiddlehead fern, or an old, toughmeat goat, eyes slit sideways behind sandpaper lids, hands fisted into hard hooves with brittle tendons that will not soften in the sun. She hobbles out to the back patio and does yoga in the heat, hoping it will help. Her back is a crook. She attempts downward dog, and when she presses into the V shape, she bleats, "Owwwwwww." *A goat's body does not bend into a V.* She goes inside and lies down on her bed of straw. She picks a piece and chews it. She presses her lips open and closed. Meeeeeehhh. It's hell getting old, she says, though she is still several years away from fifty, and the women in her family live into their nineties. She closes her eyes and dreams of younger days in the sun, when she leaped over high hills and butted people in the head. Meeeeehhhh.

Stop looking things up on the Internet.

—HUSBAND, ON HEARING THE
SJOGREN'S THEORY

One morning before I was diagnosed, I woke up with my tongue stuck to the roof of my mouth, my eyes stuck shut, my voice a ghost of its former self. I rolled over for my phone and Googled my symptoms. Got a hit. I felt my way out to where my husband was and croaked, "I don't mean to be a hypochondriac or anything, but I think I have Sjogren's syndrome."

So I go to my primary care doctor and say, "I think I have Sjogren's syndrome."

"You think you have what, sweetie?"

"Sjogren's syndrome. It's an autoimmune disease. They say you are more likely to get it if you already have an autoimmune disease, which I have." I explain my symptoms.

"I know how autoimmune disease works, and I'll tell you what. You don't have another autoimmune disease. It's probably just the beginning of menopause combined with some seasonal allergies. Your throat looked awfully red. Probably some postnasal drip."

"But I'm not in menopause," I say.

"Well, you're getting awfully close."

"I'm forty-five. My mother was in her mid-fifties."

"Everybody's different, hon."

"But there's nothing in my nose to drip."

"I'm still going to prescribe an antihistamine to dry you up. You'll start feeling better in a couple of days."

I leave the office feeling stupid. I take the antihistamines, which, indeed, dry me up so vigorously that I cannot open my eyes for two days and my sinuses begin to crack and bleed. My throat becomes so dry that I don't speak without pain for the better part of three months, the symbolism of that not being wasted on me. My larynx is terribly affected by Sjogren's. It is inflamed. It is hoarse. It hurts to push air through it. It hurts to eat. The pain makes me use a heat pack and an ice pack, which I switch back and forth because neither one works.

I used to talk too much around people who knew me; I always thought about myself and talked about myself and put myself first as a child above all else. It was always about me and I let everyone know it. Me me me. My ideas, my what-ifs, my lava of dreams and desires frothing forth from my mouth as if I had a disease that made me vomit words. Even when I was doing it, I knew I was doing it and couldn't stop. I could hear the tone in my parents' voice that said they were just marking time through a conversation until I would shut up. I know my husband's mmn-hmm. And my ex-husband's. When I was little my mother told me she would pay me if I could make it from the grocery store to home, about a three-mile distance, without speaking, and I never earned a dime. I couldn't do it.

Now I don't speak unless I have to. I gesture wildly. I use my eyebrows. I text my children, who are sitting in the same room with me. Sometimes they answer me out loud, but sometimes they text me back.

I saw a werewolf drinking a piña colada at Trader Vic's.
                                                —WARREN ZEVON

At social gatherings she becomes a changeling, a long-legged werewolf, skittish and resentful of the people eating and drinking and living it up as if they own their own time. There is no smile. Wolves don't smile. There is a baring of the teeth. She circles the outside of the room, sniffing the smell of the food she cannot eat because she is suddenly allergic to most of it. In the corner, someone approaches and offers a piña colada, as if she is trapped in a gully and the drink is a hunk of meat with a tranquilizer in it. She says no, but inside she snarls it. *Don't you know I can't have that?* The wolf cannot tolerate alcohol. One glass of alcohol does something inside of her that jump-starts an arrhythmia in her heart, a series of premature ventricular contractions that last for several hours. She was admitted to the hospital once after half a glass of champagne. A piece of chocolate or cup of coffee might trigger a dysautonomia that makes it impossible for her to walk upright before one P.M. for several weeks. She lopes around the house, head low, sometimes on all fours, to keep from fainting. For the most part, the wolf stops going out. It's far too tiring. She lies in her corner, tail curled around her hot body. Licks her nose. Sleeps.

It's not Jeffie. It's Jeffrey.

—*JEFFREY*

Why do I have Sjogren's? Perhaps the payback fairy finally found me, the one who has been hot on my trail since I teased that poor boy Jeffrey on the school bus in elementary school, even though I knew he would be unable to defend himself, with his stiff, rectangular smile that masked his pain, his confused eyes, his soft, white underbelly, his divorced parents. *Does your mother call you Jeffie, Jeffie? Does your father?* I said the word "Jeffie" in a condescending baby voice, which is probably when the payback fairy, the one who floats quietly inside the hoodies of bullied children, got my name and put me on the list. I've moved around a lot but still—she's a fairy and fairies clearly have otherworldly advantages of all sorts, spells, et cetera. Perhaps she finally caught up. Perhaps the payback fairy used Google Earth to locate my house, and eased like smoke through the window air-conditioner unit, and cast a spell, boo-ya, bitches!, that I never again be allowed to open my eyes without scratching my corneas, drying up my lachrymal ducts with a smitely kind of spite, requisitioning all my tears as payment to Jeffrey, who was running around Hoboken, or Duluth or Akron, in a lifelong deficit, having depleted his own supply of tears in the fifth grade on account of being bullied by a girl. He had been an unmanly, sensitive boy who cried, which is probably why I teased him in the first place.

Perhaps the payback fairy has taken back all my tears and given them to everyone I ever made cry, a friend or two, relatives, my children, a few choice boyfriends whose hearts I wounded. Perhaps I owed them their tears back. Each morning I feel my way to the kitchen sink, where I have a washcloth ready. I run hot water over the washcloth, then feel my way over to the couch and lie down, pressing the washcloth to my eyes. I lie there until the washcloth cools. Then I do it all again. A few minutes later, I peel my right eye open, feel a sharp pain across the surface of it, as if several pieces of sand have been set there, like little tiny diamonds, in the night. The action of my lid against my cornea scratches my cornea and my right eye slams shut like a safe. Sometime later, my left eye opens partially, though I cannot will it to stay open, and I walk around cocked in the head, wearing my goggle glasses so the air won't touch my eyeballs and dry them out further. I use whatever drops they give me. I cannot see. The bat wings unfold and I use them to pat my way through the house, touching simple landmarks: the bar stool, the refrigerator, the coffee table in the living room, squinting through the eyelashes of one eye. This goes on for months. Payback fairy done got me good.

Fuck a knuckle, look! There's nothing coming out. Not one tear!
—*DAWN S. DAVIES, POINTING AT EYES DURING THE DEATH*
SCENE IN TERMS OF ENDEARMENT

I first realized something was wrong on the day I drove away from a weekend of visiting my daughter in college, when, welled up with emotion at the sight of her waving good-bye, this long-limbed beauty of my soul, this baby with her chin wobbling and her brave face on, I felt my eyes stinging, and my nose pinched up in that familiar burn that comes right before weeping . . . only no tears came. There I was, my face screwed up, my own chin wobbling like a hobbyhorse, a small sob choked in my throat, and I had nothing to show for it. It was like puffs of smoke coming from my eyes. There is something about the crying process that gets stunted when no actual tears release, so I stopped trying. Cleared my throat. Drove home and started looking things up on the Internet. A season later, after seeing a general practitioner, an ENT, a rheumatologist, an ophthalmologist, an optometrist, a neurologist, another special kind of neurologist—this one a sadist who tested my muscles with needles and jolts of electricity—and an infectious disease special-ist, I am the proud owner of another autoimmune disease. My Sjo-gren's is "mild," they tell me, so it is up to me to decide if I want to take the dangerous immunosuppressants or TNF inhibitors they commonly prescribe, the ones whose television commercials read like death threats, with lists of side effects such as low platelets, liver damage, holes in the intestines, bloody urine, hair loss, severe infec-tions, and certain forms of cancer including, once again, lymphoma. I don't want to take these drugs, so my treatment includes a strict anti-inflammatory diet recommended by my rheumatologist, and management of my symptoms. "It shouldn't be too bad," say all my doctors, who are male. "You'll be fine. A lot of women have this." They say this with the same panache that some men tell women that semen is a fantastic facial skin rejuvenator. As usual, I feel dismissed.

> *She can go take a flying fuck at a rolling donut. She can go take a flying fuck at the moon.*
> —DAWN S. DAVIES, AFTER LISTENING TO A CHURCH LADY
> SAY THERE IS NOTHING PRAYER CAN'T HEAL

After one doctor tells me I need to improve my vitamin D levels naturally, I buy a blue bikini, my first bikini in years, the same color bikini I wore in junior year of high school, and start sunbathing for ten minutes per side on the days that I remember to do it. A friend tells me to soak in seawater whenever possible, because the water is filled with magnesium, which when absorbed transdermally, may reduce some of the pain I am in. So I go to the beach on a hot spring day.

It's crowded. I pick a place that is not too close, nor too far away from others, and spread out my towel. I start on my stomach first, checking my watch for the ten-minute mark. I'm tired so I lie there quietly, sand in my fists, listening to the muffled sounds of voices over the lower growl of the waves. I peel open one eye and see a ring-tailed lemur walk carefully, on tiptoe, across the hot sand. I do a double take. The lemur is sporting a rhinestone harness in an odd place on its body, low and under the arms, and the harness is attached to a leash, which is attached to a woman who has a gaggle of fascinated children following her. One child, barely a preschooler, a pink boy with a fifties side part and fat cheeks, young enough to still have dimples in his knees, crawls behind the lemur with his hand out, trying to catch a feel of his tail, until his mother snatches him away. I put my head back down.

The steady growl of the waves is comforting. I taste salt in the air like tears. Around me are families and friends adjusting bathing suits, flipping themselves like hamburgers, spreading out towels, digging into mesh bags, snacking, reading, napping, wiping sand off bottoms, running back and forth to the waves, moving umbrellas, a collective consciousness of beach culture, with a din of all the noise they make floating thinly somewhere above the sound of the waves, in the way that sound travels funny at the seashore.

My back is hot. It is almost time to turn over. The roar of the ocean is growing louder. I look and there is nothing. It recedes to a normal roar. A man with a phlegmy throat says, somewhere near the back of my head, "I don't let it worry me. I don't worry about much these days." On my eye side, a pucker-tight father has just arrived with his little girl and is already chastising her for getting sand on her shorts. I close my eyes again. Cover my face. Listen. My salivary glands shoot pains in my neck, traveling up to some inside part of my ears, and I wonder about lymphoma, or another kind of cancer that would cause this kind of pain. I'd like to cry but that's not happening.

The waves sound closer than they should. Anticipating the tide, I peek out, and see a garden-variety wave pull away from the shore. I go back to thinking I am fine. Then I hear it again. Below me, toward the shoreline, I see families being nipped in the ankles by the waves, snatching up their toddlers and blankets and beach chairs, and moving back some yards. I figure I still have a few minutes so I drift off, thinking of the fire in my throat, the grit in my eyes, the uncertainty of autoimmune disease when you are in a flare and you think things will never be better than they are right now, when your joints hurt and you can't stay awake, or concentrate, or swallow food, or blink with ease, and your feet and legs burn, and you can't stand up without your autonomic nervous system shooting you the bird and causing your blood pressure to plummet. You think, when you are in a flare, in the middle of another cyclical low-grade fever, that you might die, or at least be better off dead, because you can't see well, and you can't hear well, and you can't even swallow. That if this is what you thought life in your forties would be like, back when you wore your first blue bikini and your future was like a constellation in the sky, sparkly and hopeful, and not quite real, then you might have done some things differently. If your forties are like this, what's going to happen in your fifties? Sixties? Will there be a fifties or sixties? Sometimes you're not sure you want there to be.

The roar of the sea becomes larger once again, but you can't fool me four times. Twice, yes, three times, usually, but not four. I grew up on the beach. I know how long it takes for a tide to come in. I don't open my eyes.

Then I feel the first small lick at my feet, like a tease, like a cool balm on my angry, neuropathic feet and legs. I think it is my nerves playing tricks on me. I ignore it. Then the wave is up and back, then it hits my crotch, and I realize the tide is in much faster than I anticipated, so I roll over and sit up, and I see that the sea is not messing around. That it is coming in now like a quiet storm, all business, and it is quickly up to my neck, so I stand up, and the people who were down at the shoreline are floating in the water, past me, as it fills up the land, picking up plastic things, coolers and buckets and balls and umbrellas. I stand up. I am tall, but it pulls me off my toes and sets me alight in its swell of salt. The weight lifts off my joints and I feel a relief.

All around me people scream and reach for each other. The uptight father has grabbed ahold of his little girl and a Styrofoam cooler, and they float past. To my left swims the lemur, his tail dark and wet. I reach for him but miss and he bobs away with the sun hats, and bottles of sunscreen, and colored umbrellas.

My face is hit by the salt water, and it feels like all of the tears that I have wanted to cry for months but have not been able to. It fills my eyes, washing my corneas with saline, and I feel an instant relief. I press my face into the water, and open them. My eyes, for the first time in months, are moist, salinated. My lips feel supple. The roar of the water has masked the ringing in my ears. I no longer think about my body, my dried-up state. I am carried up with the flow of the water, with hundreds of others, past the rows of cars, past the preserved sea oats, past the parking lots and restaurants, past the intracoastal line. We float over the bridge, brushing over million-dollar properties.

This sea is a sea of my tears, I decide. All the tears I have cried, and all the ones I deserved to cry but have been unable to. The tears I have cried over autism, and my inability, despite everyone's inclusive mentality, to celebrate the neurodiversity that is my son, the tears I have refused to cry because I will never see him catch a football, or go to college, or have a family, or balance his checkbook, the tears I have wept because his future is so uncertain.

A mother and her three children pass me, linking arms in a chain. "Swim," the mother yells, and her children, none looking at another, split off and obey like synchronized dancers, with fine, well-practiced strokes. I reach out to them but a wave swells and splits them away, and I realize there are only eight people in the world I can touch without permission and that my universe is very small and these are my tears coming back to haunt me. These are the tears I cried when my first husband and I divorced, turning our children into a statistic, products of a broken home, ferried back and forth between houses, skinny, forlorn, knock-kneed things wearing backpacks at the airport during holidays. These are the tears I cried, and the tears I absorbed, for making their footing unsure in this world. My tears for my parents' own divorce, and the prophecy I seemed to have fulfilled as an oversensitive child who grew into an oversensitive adult. These are the tears for my losses, my compensations, the difficulty of the rebuild, over and over, the rebuilding of many broken things: my hearing, my eyesight, chronic pain, exhaustion, kidney stents and stones, hospitalizations and surgeries and heart monitors and tilt table tests. My stamina, my thyroid, my memory. My trust.

Below me, some feet down, I see the white roof of the tourist trap that sells shell mobiles and shell ashtrays, stiff flip-flops and cheap beach towels made in China. *This isn't right,* I think. I've been so pain avoidant that I have been very, very careful. I don't get too close to people, lest I hose them in some way. I don't make big commitments.

I eat right. If it comes out of a box I won't eat it. I'm telling you, I only eat real foods from the earth, fruits and non-inflammatory vegetables, and meats. I don't drink alcohol or coffee. I exercise. I keep my weight down. I follow a doctor-advised inflammatory protocol all the time. I take thyroid medication to replace the hormones that my previously attacked thyroid can no longer produce on its own. I take magnesium. I juice. *I eat kale.* I eat so much stinkin' kale I might as well smoke it like crack, or have it shot straight into my blood. Why does my body still attack itself? Why do I have auto-immune disease?

You are so ridiculous, I think, and then I realize it: I'm the pay-back fairy. I'm doing this to myself. I always attack myself. When there is a problem, I assume it is my fault, by default. When there is an argument, I assume I am the one in the wrong. I have called myself names: "idiot," "fool," "stupid," "dumbass." Knowing this, my husband will sometimes jokingly blame me for something ridiculous that no one would think could be my fault, and I will end up apologizing for it, even though logic tells me it is ridiculous as well. I have hated myself. I have hated my height, my face, my crooked nose, my voice. I have apologized for my dreams, my goals, my son, for the extra space I take up as a six-foot woman, for the audacious hope of wanting to be a writer and not a middle school teacher or a sales rep, for being so anxious and weak. In my mind, things are always my fault. I always blame me, as you can see. I'm even blaming myself for this. Why, then, am I surprised that my body is attacking itself, too?

I stay afloat by doing an eggbeater kick, a water polo technique I once learned, though I never played water polo. My lower legs circle around hard underwater, and I kick something. Up surfaces the little fat boy who was so fascinated by the lemur. When he pops up, he gasps for air as if he is sucking back his soul. I grab him and push his face above water while kicking with my feet to stay afloat, and his added weight begins to press my body down. I crane my neck for his mother, for anyone in his party, but there is only a sea of heads being washed away. A small toy raft floats by, and I right it and shove the little boy into it before being hit by a wave. When I surface, the raft is several feet away, Americana Moses wailing westward. I look around and it's just me.

It's time to forgive myself, I think, but I don't know how to do it. I use my arms to stay afloat now. I use everything I've got. I am tired. I am so tired I don't think I can swim this current much longer, but my eyes are finally free of grit and for once, nothing hurts. All the tears I've cried are being given back to me as a measure of my grief. I need something to grab on to. I need a lifeline, but everywhere I look is the salt-filled sea. "I forgive you," I say out loud, to everyone and everything. To myself. This is when I feel it begin. My legs begin to weld, my body thickens and waves me afloat in the water and it feels right. I move without effort now, shoot like a jet stream just under the surface, then up again, leaping in an arc above the blue for a gasp of breath before plunging under again. Just before my arms are absorbed, I feel down the sides of my body to the smooth, slick scales and spiny fins. The refracted light reflecting off my tail is a dull silver that mesmerizes me. I plunge down and skim the rocks, breathing freely. There is no dry or wet here, there is just the need to keep moving, and I shoot away into the water that has no name. My eyes no longer need to blink. My doggoned heat is cooled and I swim, not away after all, but toward.

ACKNOWLEDGMENTS

In order of operations: Much gratitude to my parents, DBD and VMW, for raising me right; to my sister, DDM, whose devotion is priceless; to my stepsons, M and M, steadfast men whom I'm proud to call family; to my daughters, S and A, whose strength and grace and humor are unparalleled; to G, my brave son who has agreed to let his story be told in hopes that it will change future discourse; and to my husband, T, my steady, with whom I can do all the things.

Thank you to Julie Marie Wade, the merriest person I know, who gently guided early versions of this manuscript; to John Dufresne, who inspired and motivated me to improve my work; to Vernon Dickson for providing astute and much-needed mentorship; to dear friend Doc Suds, aka PC, for being my literary sounding board; to my friend MO for opening a door; to my splendid agent, Ellen Levine, the cleverest of Weebles; to editor Caroline Bleeke for her razor-sharp eye; and to my captain, Amy Einhorn, a brilliant and fearless editor who worked this book with me like she was riding a dragon.

I often use music to fuel my writing. When writing this book,

I listened to plenty of Jaco Pastorius, Pablo Casals, Dire Straits, Aretha Franklin, Jack White, Tom Petty, Gaither Vocal Band, Rush, Yes, Nelly, Steve Morse, Afro Celt Sound System, Adrian Legg, Peter Gabriel, Curtis Mayfield, Patty Griffin, Tim McGraw, Trick Daddy, and Earl Scruggs. I often play one song on repeat for days or weeks. I found myself listening to "Some Things Are Better Left Unsaid" by Hall and Oates several times per week for much of the three years it took to complete this book, as its lyrics are a musical warning for the memoirist.